DANIEL X
ALIEN HUNTER

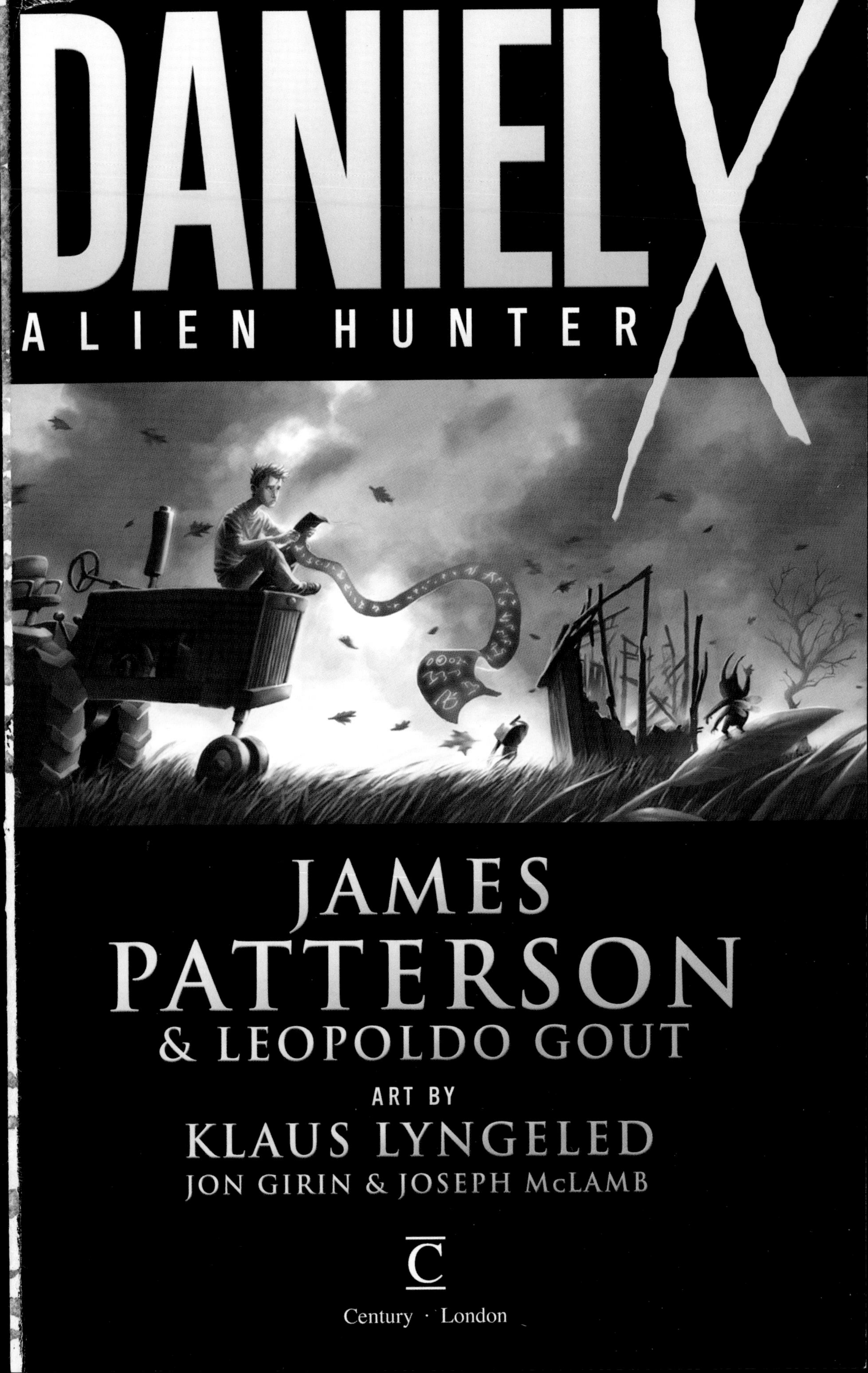

JAMES
PATTERSON
& LEOPOLDO GOUT

ART BY
KLAUS LYNGELED
JON GIRIN & JOSEPH McLAMB

Century · London

Published by Century 2008

2 4 6 8 10 9 7 5 3 1

First published in Great Britain in 2008 by
Century
Random House, 20 Vauxhall Bridge Road,
London SW1V 2SA

WWW.RANDOMHOUSE.CO.UK

Addresses for companies within The Random House Group Limited can be found at:
WWW.RANDOMHOUSE.CO.UK

The Random House Group Limited Reg. No. 954009

A CIP catalogue record for this book
is available from the British Library

HB ISBN 9781846053146
TPB ISBN 9781846055294

The Random House Group Limited supports The Forest Stewardship
Council (FSC), the leading international forest certification organisation. All
our titles that are printed on Greenpeace approved FSC certified paper carry the
FSC logo. Our paper procurement policy can be found at
WWW.RBOOKS.CO.UK/ENVIRONMENT

Printed and bound in Slovenia by
MKT Print, Ljubljana

CHAPTER 1

KEEPER OF THE LIST

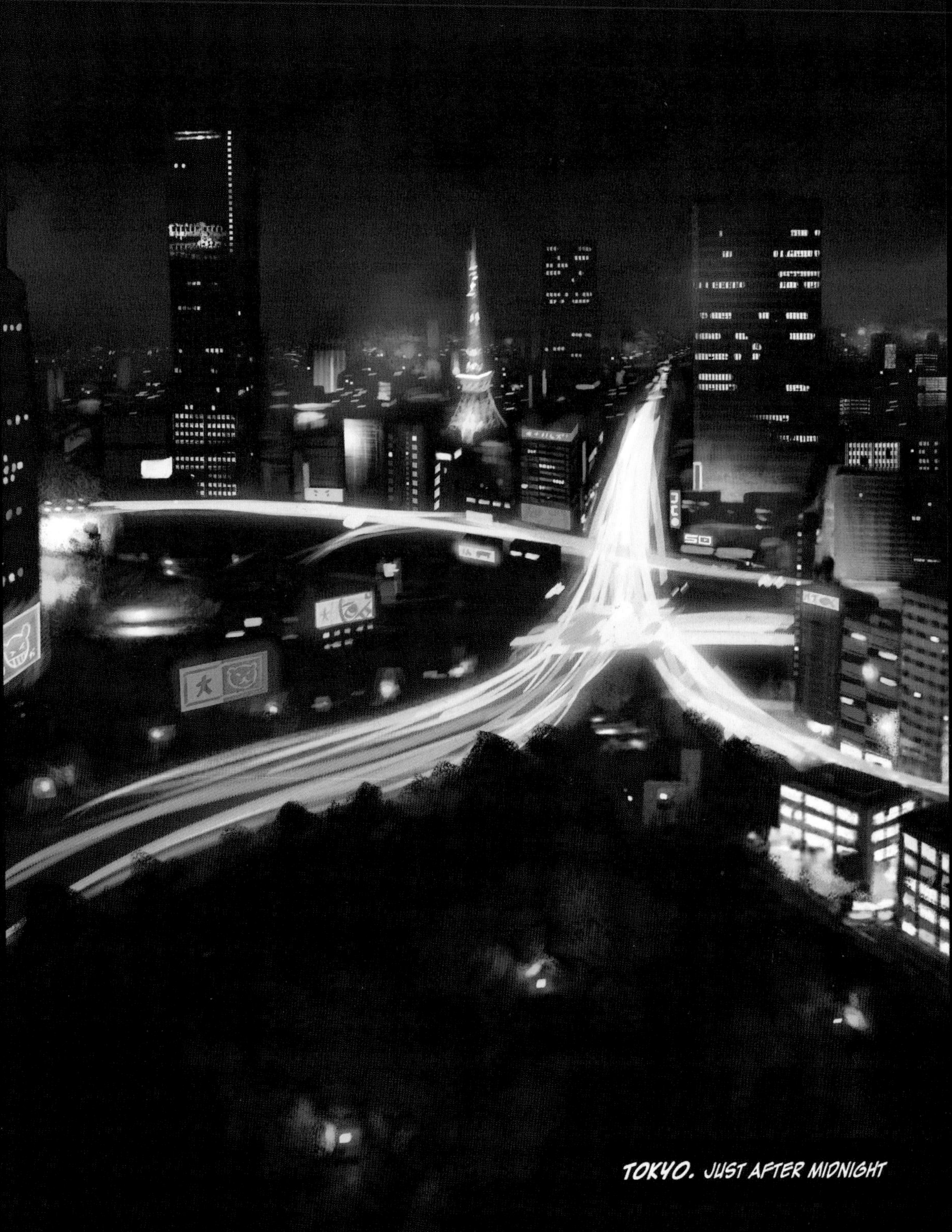
TOKYO. JUST AFTER MIDNIGHT

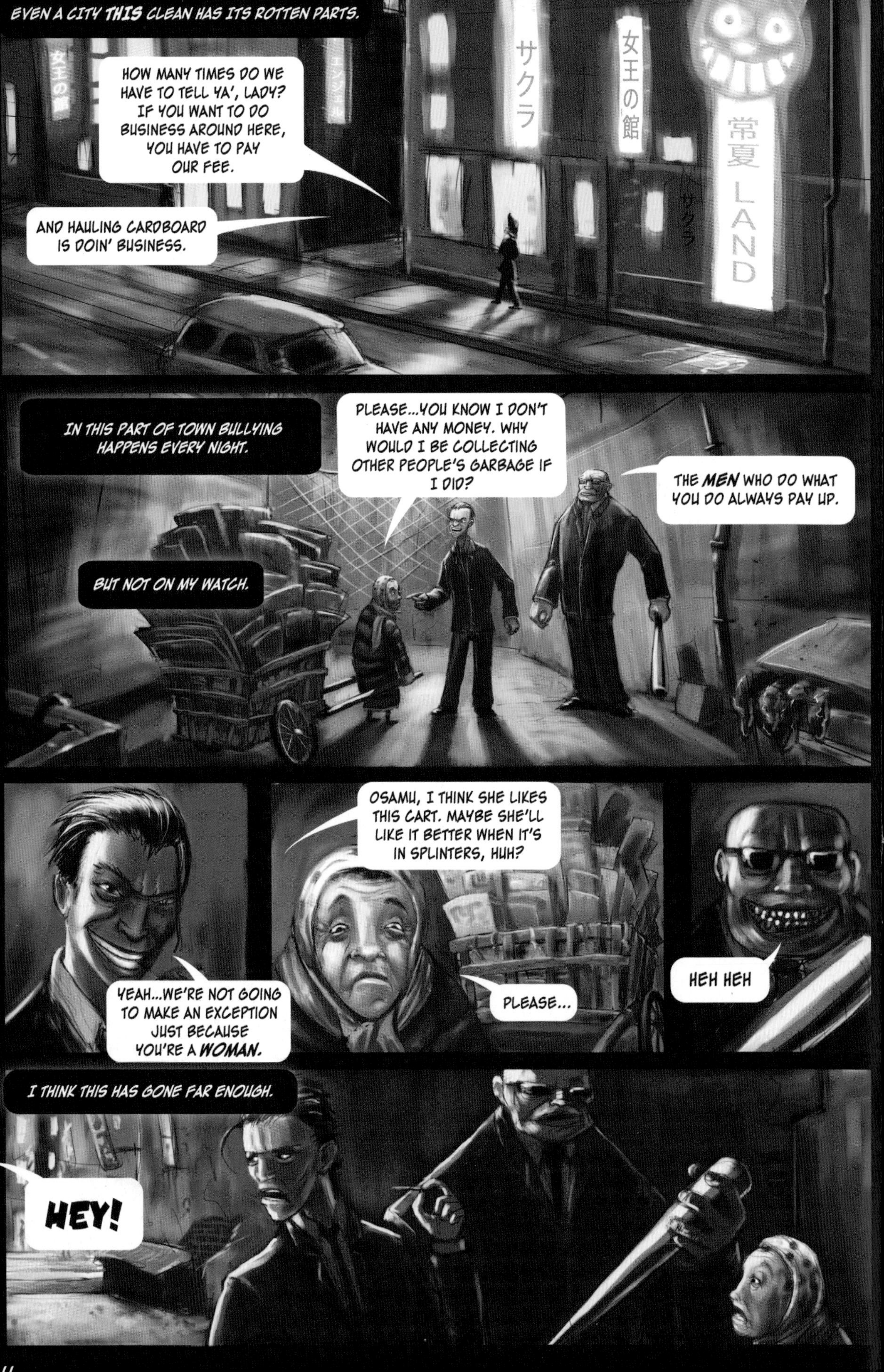
EVEN A CITY THIS CLEAN HAS ITS ROTTEN PARTS.
女王の館
エンジェル
HOW MANY TIMES DO WE HAVE TO TELL YA', LADY? IF YOU WANT TO DO BUSINESS AROUND HERE, YOU HAVE TO PAY OUR FEE.
AND HAULING CARDBOARD IS DOIN' BUSINESS.
サクラ
女王の館
常夏 LAND
サクラ
IN THIS PART OF TOWN BULLYING HAPPENS EVERY NIGHT.
PLEASE...YOU KNOW I DON'T HAVE ANY MONEY. WHY WOULD I BE COLLECTING OTHER PEOPLE'S GARBAGE IF I DID?
THE MEN WHO DO WHAT YOU DO ALWAYS PAY UP.
BUT NOT ON MY WATCH.
YEAH...WE'RE NOT GOING TO MAKE AN EXCEPTION JUST BECAUSE YOU'RE A WOMAN.
OSAMU, I THINK SHE LIKES THIS CART. MAYBE SHE'LL LIKE IT BETTER WHEN IT'S IN SPLINTERS, HUH?
PLEASE...
HEH HEH
I THINK THIS HAS GONE FAR ENOUGH.
HEY!

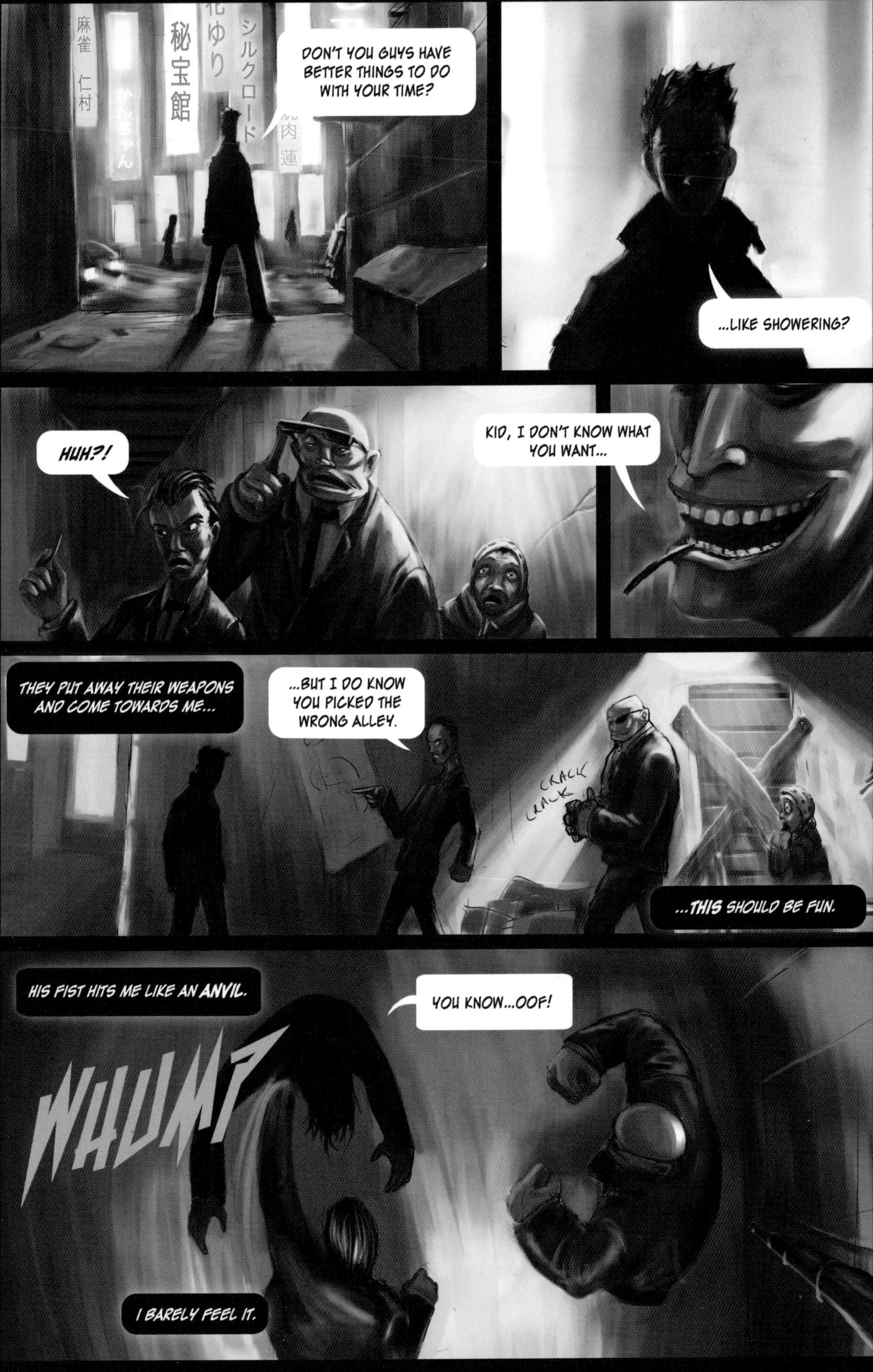
麻雀
仁村
秘宝館
シルクロード
DON'T YOU GUYS HAVE BETTER THINGS TO DO WITH YOUR TIME?
...LIKE SHOWERING?
HUH?!
KID, I DON'T KNOW WHAT YOU WANT...
THEY PUT AWAY THEIR WEAPONS AND COME TOWARDS ME...
...BUT I DO KNOW YOU PICKED THE WRONG ALLEY.
CRACK CRACK
...THIS SHOULD BE FUN.
HIS FIST HITS ME LIKE AN ANVIL.
YOU KNOW...OOF!
WHUMP
I BARELY FEEL IT.

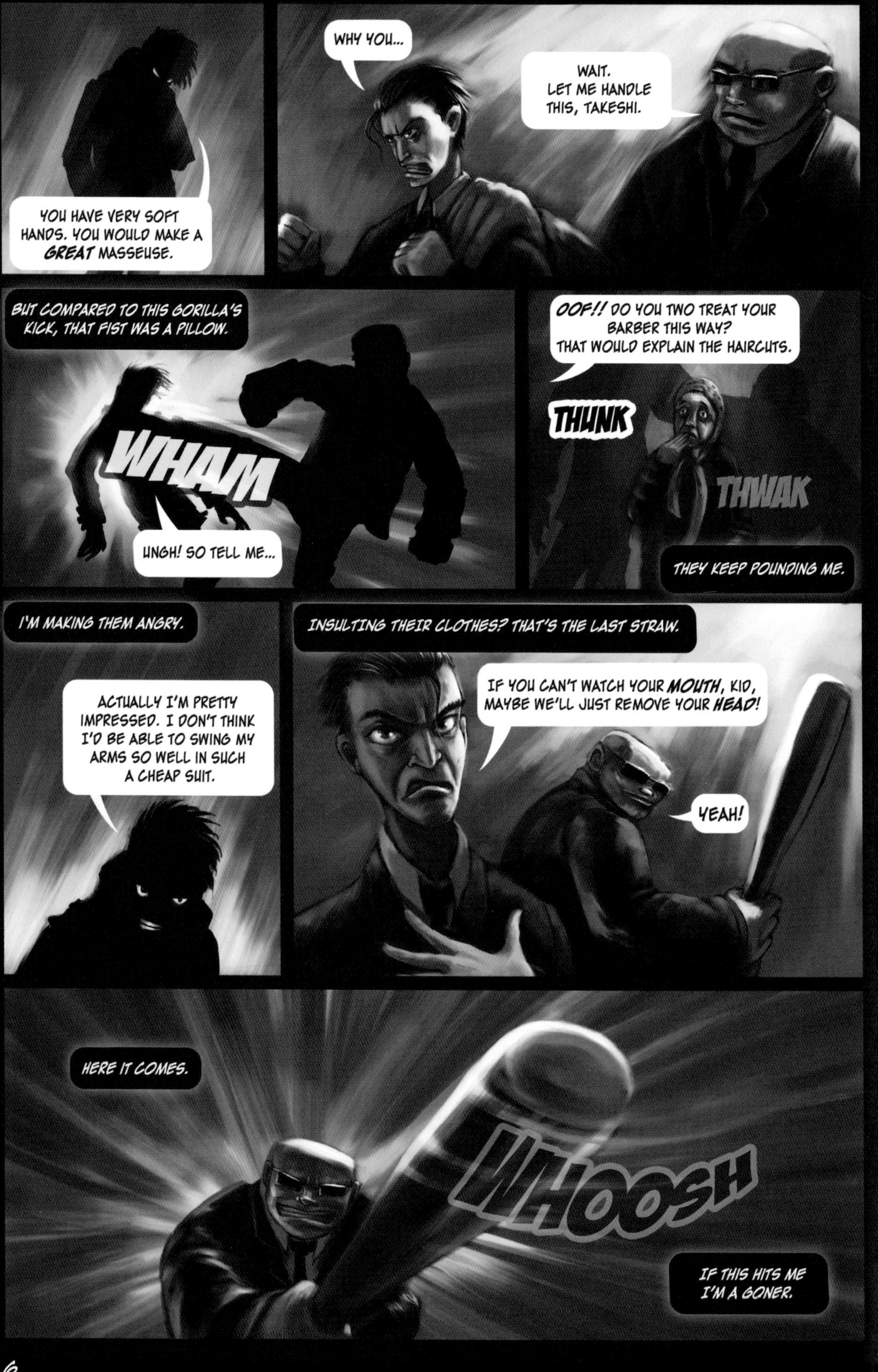
YOU HAVE VERY SOFT HANDS. YOU WOULD MAKE A GREAT MASSEUSE.
WHY YOU...
WAIT. LET ME HANDLE THIS, TAKESHI.
BUT COMPARED TO THIS GORILLA'S KICK, THAT FIST WAS A PILLOW.
WHAM
UNGH! SO TELL ME...
OOF!! DO YOU TWO TREAT YOUR BARBER THIS WAY? THAT WOULD EXPLAIN THE HAIRCUTS.
THUNK
THWAK
THEY KEEP POUNDING ME.
I'M MAKING THEM ANGRY.
ACTUALLY I'M PRETTY IMPRESSED. I DON'T THINK I'D BE ABLE TO SWING MY ARMS SO WELL IN SUCH A CHEAP SUIT.
INSULTING THEIR CLOTHES? THAT'S THE LAST STRAW.
IF YOU CAN'T WATCH YOUR MOUTH, KID, MAYBE WE'LL JUST REMOVE YOUR HEAD!
YEAH!
HERE IT COMES.
WHOOSH
IF THIS HITS ME I'M A GONER.

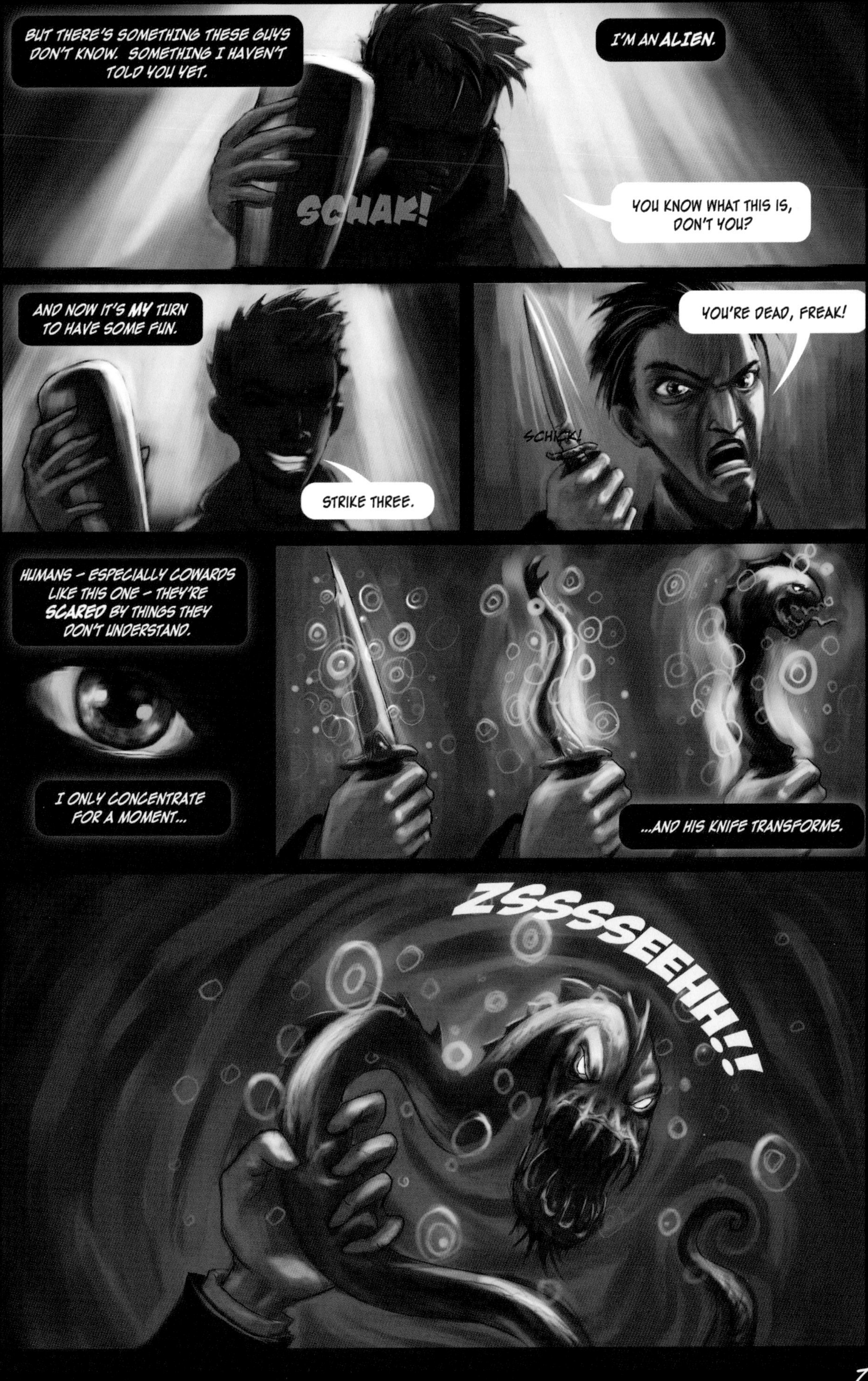

BUT THERE'S SOMETHING THESE GUYS DON'T KNOW. SOMETHING I HAVEN'T TOLD YOU YET.
I'M AN ALIEN.
SCHAK!
YOU KNOW WHAT THIS IS, DON'T YOU?
AND NOW IT'S MY TURN TO HAVE SOME FUN.
STRIKE THREE.
YOU'RE DEAD, FREAK!
HUMANS - ESPECIALLY COWARDS LIKE THIS ONE - THEY'RE SCARED BY THINGS THEY DON'T UNDERSTAND.
I ONLY CONCENTRATE FOR A MOMENT...
...AND HIS KNIFE TRANSFORMS.
ZSSSSEEHH!!

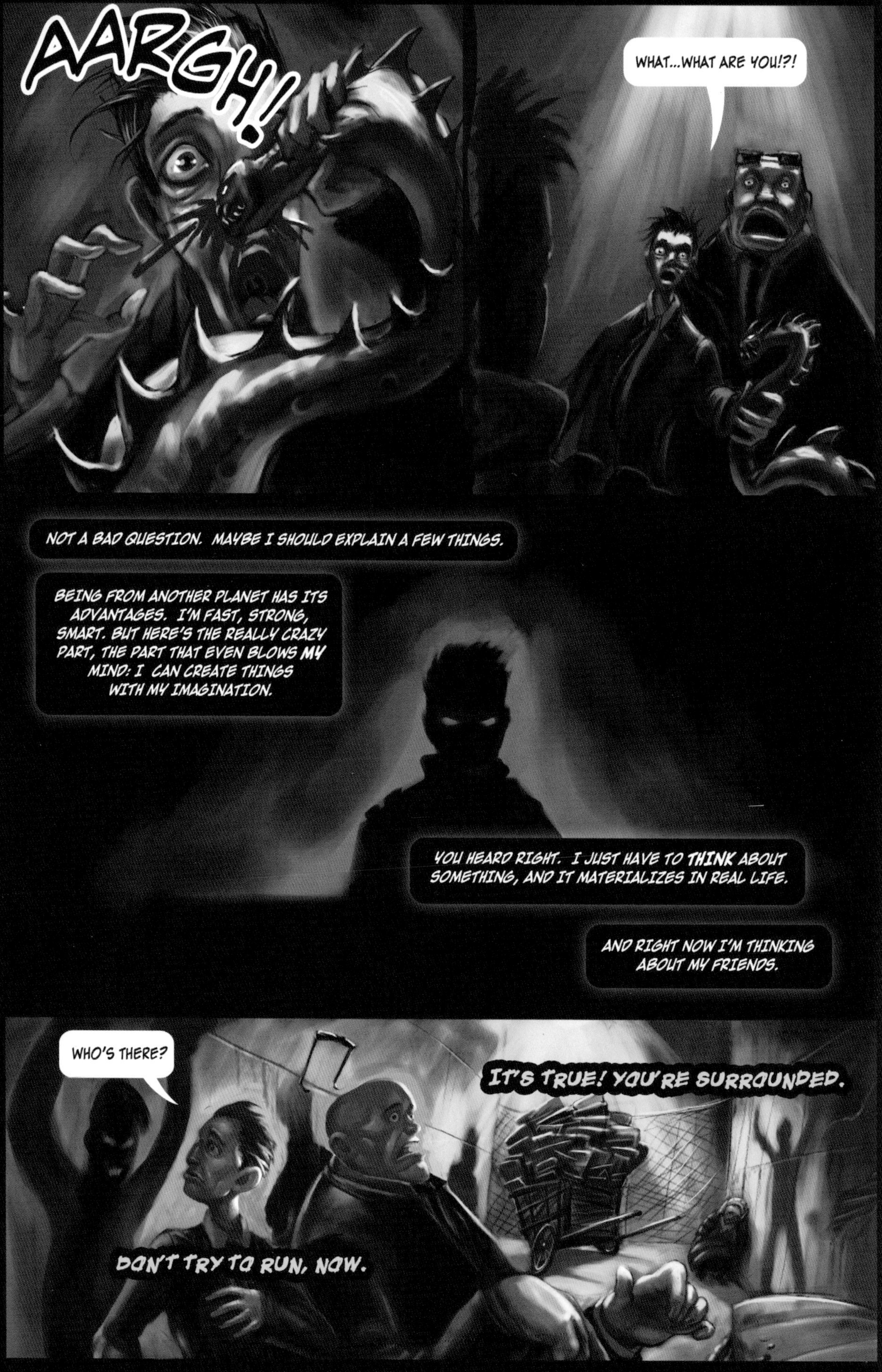
AARGH!
WHAT...WHAT ARE YOU!?!
NOT A BAD QUESTION. MAYBE I SHOULD EXPLAIN A FEW THINGS.
BEING FROM ANOTHER PLANET HAS ITS ADVANTAGES. I'M FAST, STRONG, SMART. BUT HERE'S THE REALLY CRAZY PART, THE PART THAT EVEN BLOWS MY MIND: I CAN CREATE THINGS WITH MY IMAGINATION.
YOU HEARD RIGHT. I JUST HAVE TO THINK ABOUT SOMETHING, AND IT MATERIALIZES IN REAL LIFE.
AND RIGHT NOW I'M THINKING ABOUT MY FRIENDS.
WHO'S THERE?
IT'S TRUE! YOU'RE SURROUNDED.
DON'T TRY TO RUN, NOW.

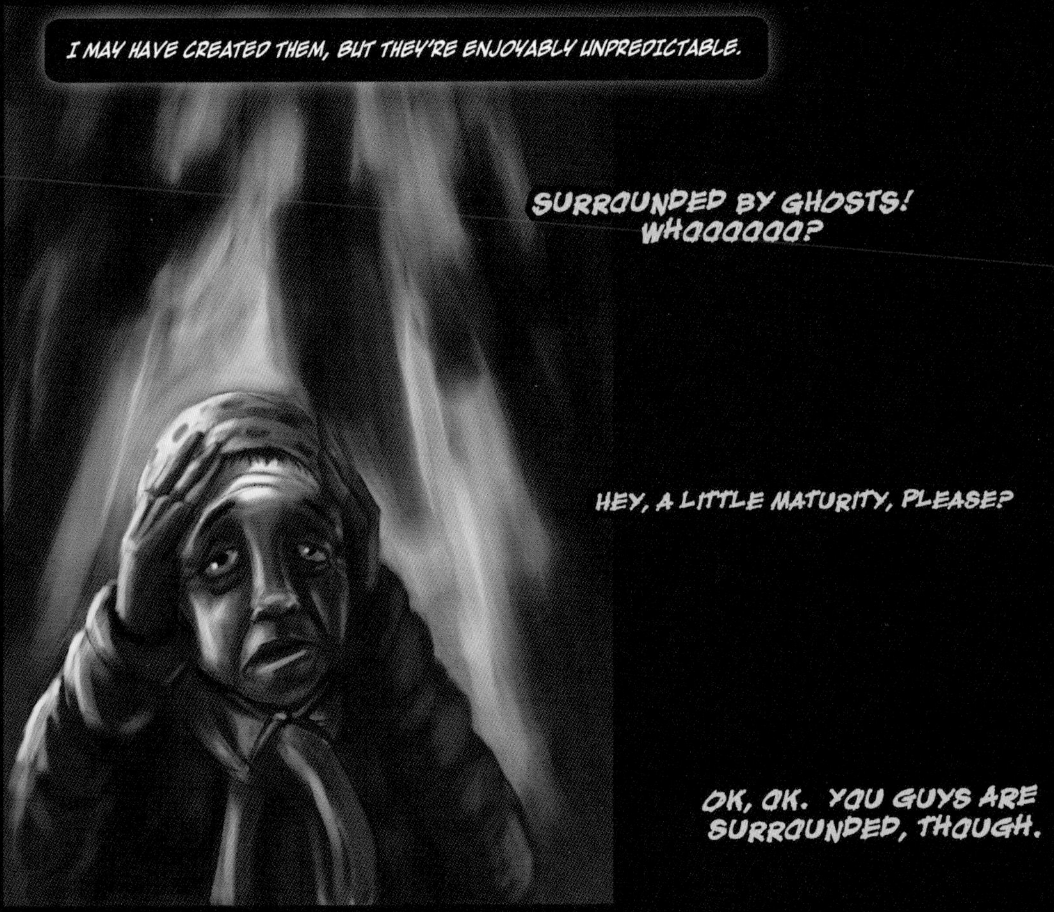
I MAY HAVE CREATED THEM, BUT THEY'RE ENJOYABLY UNPREDICTABLE.
SURROUNDED BY GHOSTS! WHOOOOOO?
HEY, A LITTLE MATURITY, PLEASE?
OK, OK. YOU GUYS ARE SURROUNDED, THOUGH.

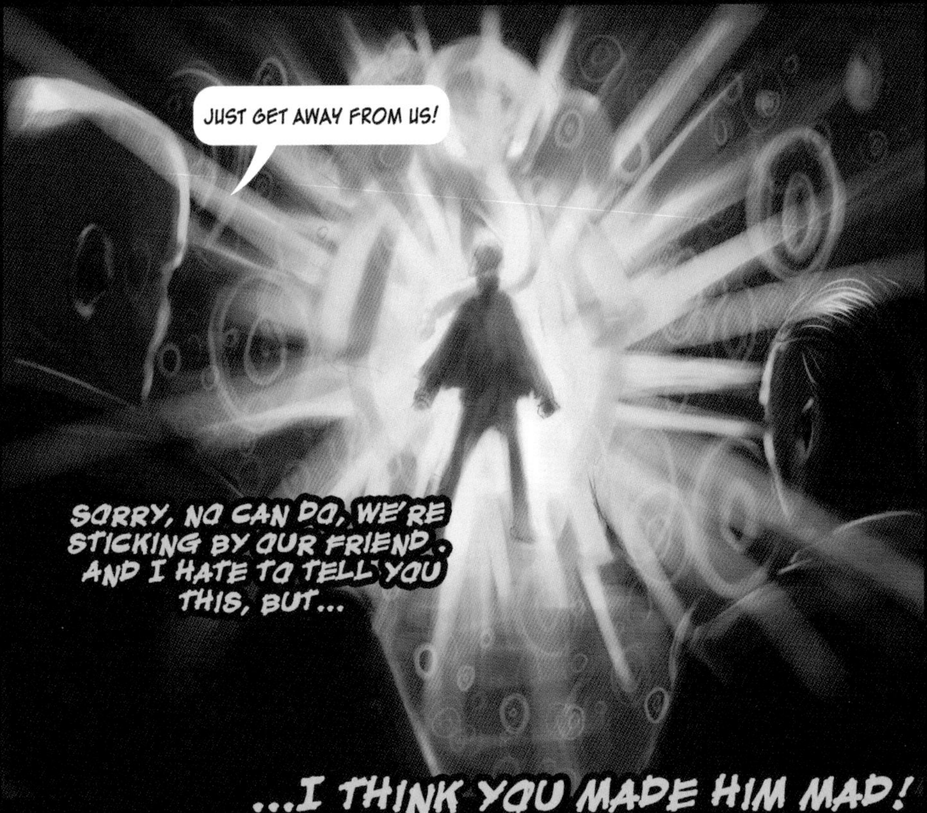
JUST GET AWAY FROM US!
SORRY, NO CAN DO, WE'RE STICKING BY OUR FRIEND. AND I HATE TO TELL YOU THIS, BUT...
...I THINK YOU MADE HIM MAD!

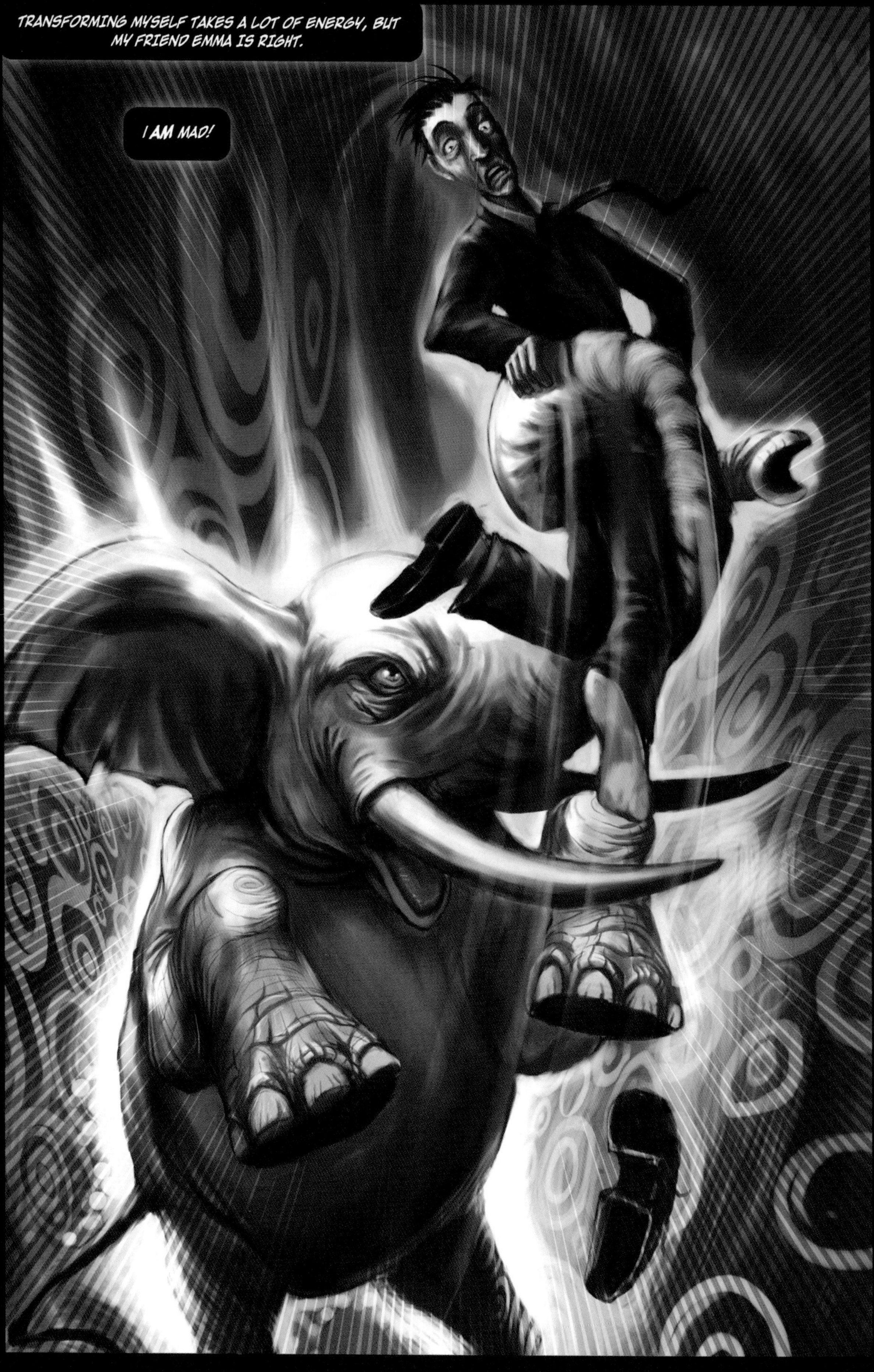
TRANSFORMING MYSELF TAKES A LOT OF ENERGY, BUT MY FRIEND EMMA IS RIGHT.
I AM MAD!

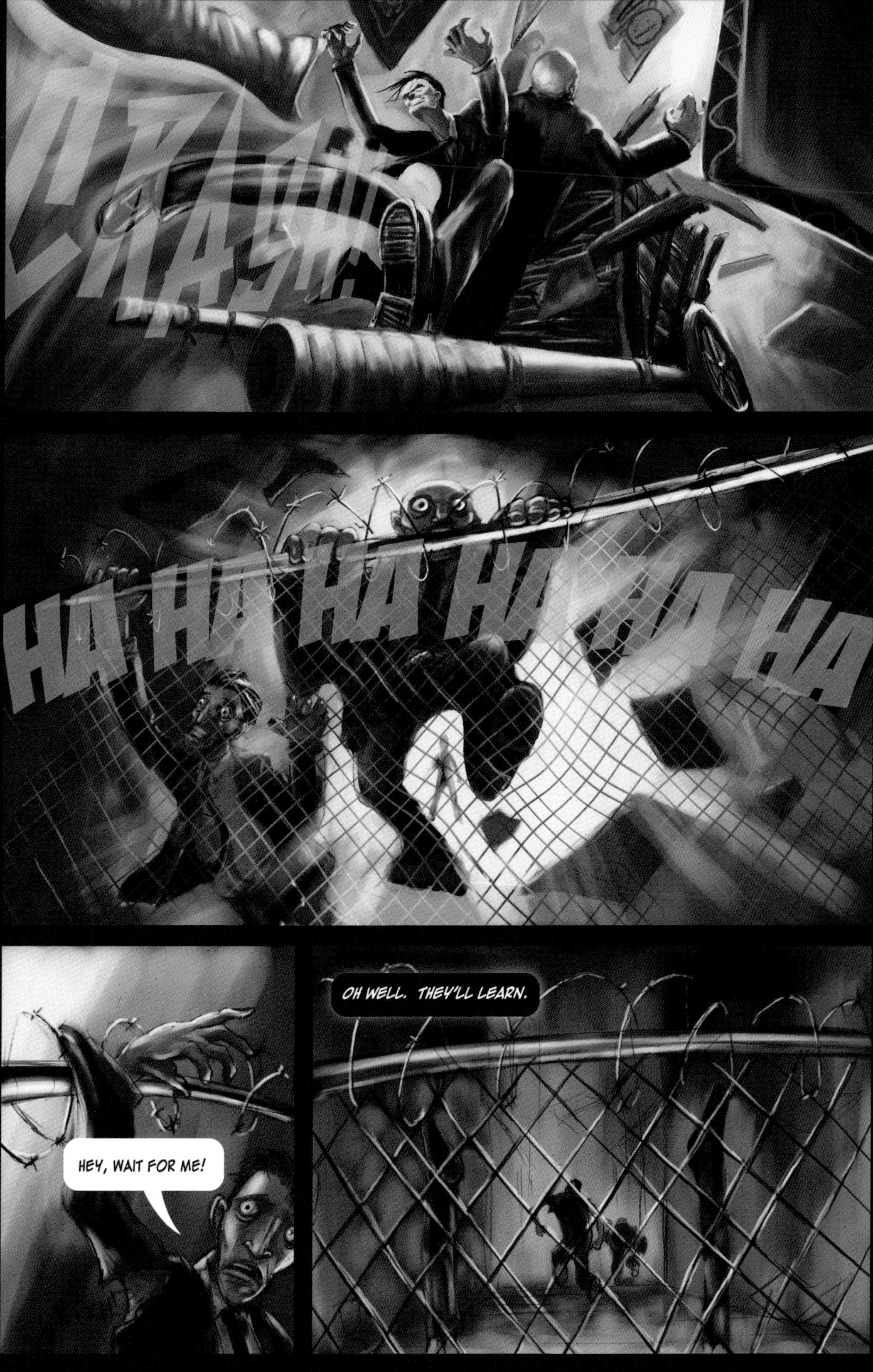
CRASH!
HA HA HA HA HA HA
HEY, WAIT FOR ME!
OH WELL. THEY'LL LEARN.

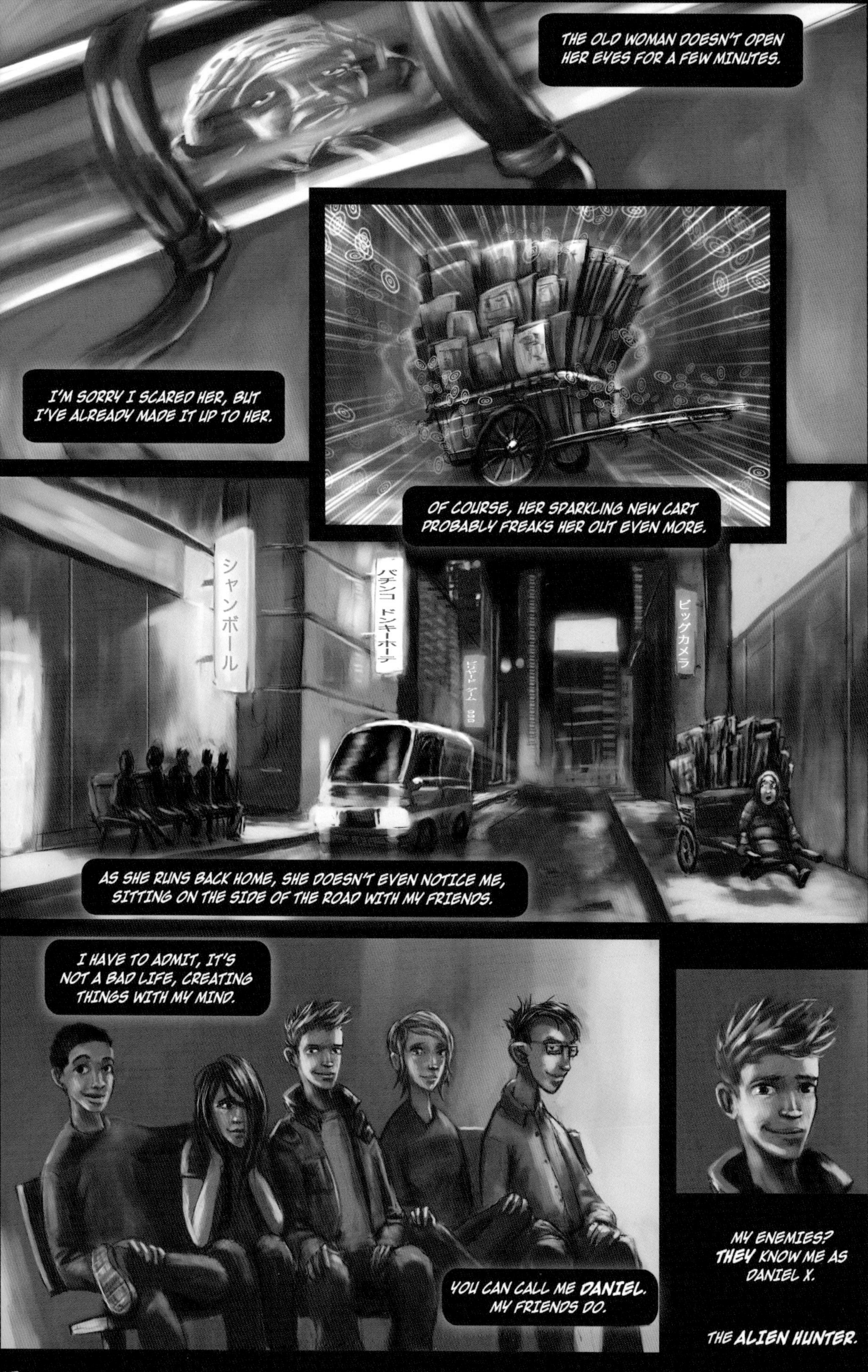
THE OLD WOMAN DOESN'T OPEN HER EYES FOR A FEW MINUTES.
I'M SORRY I SCARED HER, BUT I'VE ALREADY MADE IT UP TO HER.
OF COURSE, HER SPARKLING NEW CART PROBABLY FREAKS HER OUT EVEN MORE.
シャンボール
パチンコ
ドンキーホーテ
ビッグカメラ
AS SHE RUNS BACK HOME, SHE DOESN'T EVEN NOTICE ME, SITTING ON THE SIDE OF THE ROAD WITH MY FRIENDS.
I HAVE TO ADMIT, IT'S NOT A BAD LIFE, CREATING THINGS WITH MY MIND.
YOU CAN CALL ME **DANIEL**. MY FRIENDS DO.
MY ENEMIES? **THEY** KNOW ME AS DANIEL X.
THE **ALIEN HUNTER**.

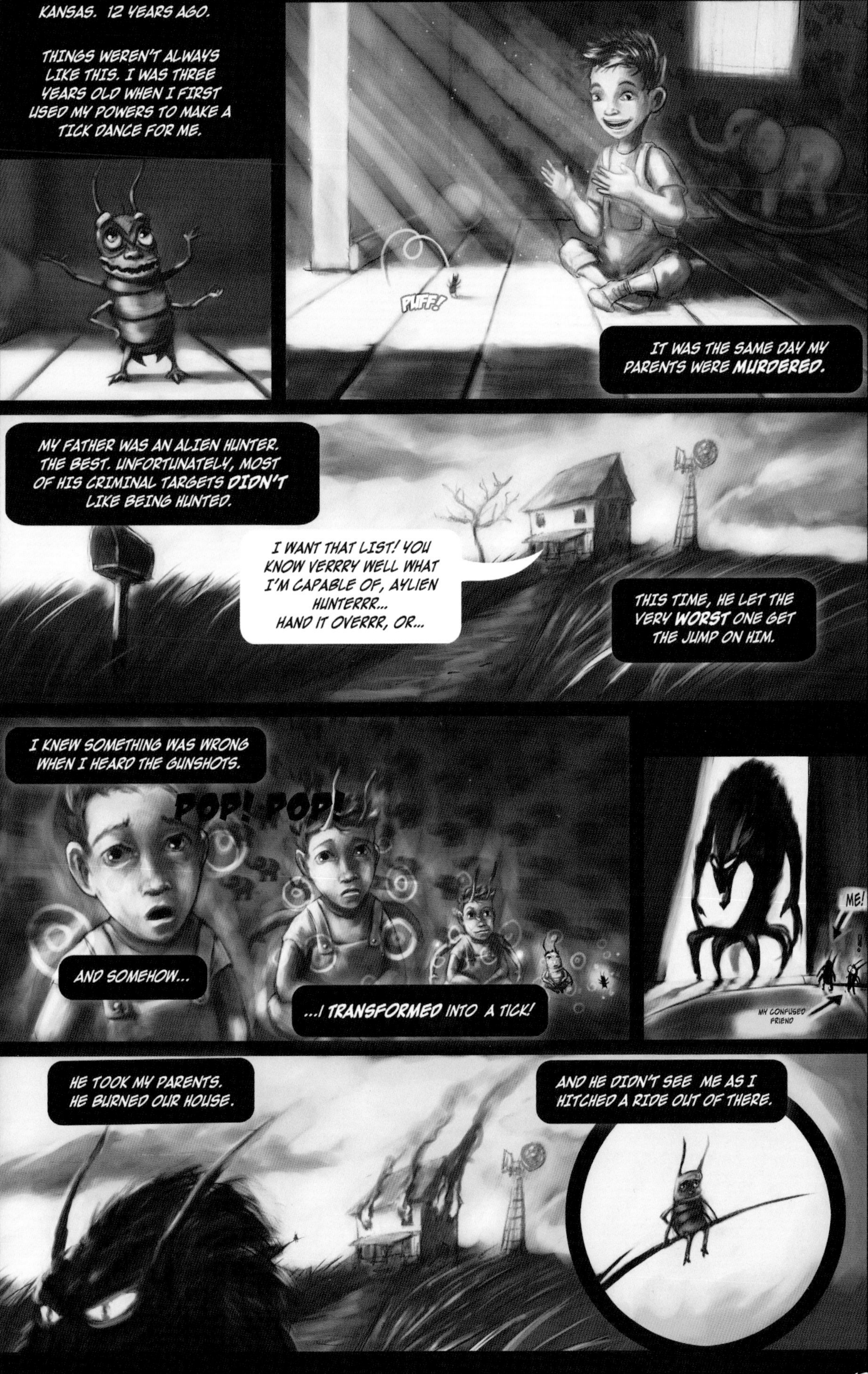
KANSAS. 12 YEARS AGO.
THINGS WEREN'T ALWAYS LIKE THIS. I WAS THREE YEARS OLD WHEN I FIRST USED MY POWERS TO MAKE A TICK DANCE FOR ME.
PUFF!
IT WAS THE SAME DAY MY PARENTS WERE MURDERED.
MY FATHER WAS AN ALIEN HUNTER. THE BEST. UNFORTUNATELY, MOST OF HIS CRIMINAL TARGETS DIDN'T LIKE BEING HUNTED.
I WANT THAT LIST! YOU KNOW VERRRY WELL WHAT I'M CAPABLE OF, AYLIEN HUNTERRR... HAND IT OVERRR, OR...
THIS TIME, HE LET THE VERY WORST ONE GET THE JUMP ON HIM.
I KNEW SOMETHING WAS WRONG WHEN I HEARD THE GUNSHOTS.
POP! POP!
AND SOMEHOW...
...I TRANSFORMED INTO A TICK!
ME!
MY CONFUSED FRIEND
HE TOOK MY PARENTS. HE BURNED OUR HOUSE.
AND HE DIDN'T SEE ME AS I HITCHED A RIDE OUT OF THERE.

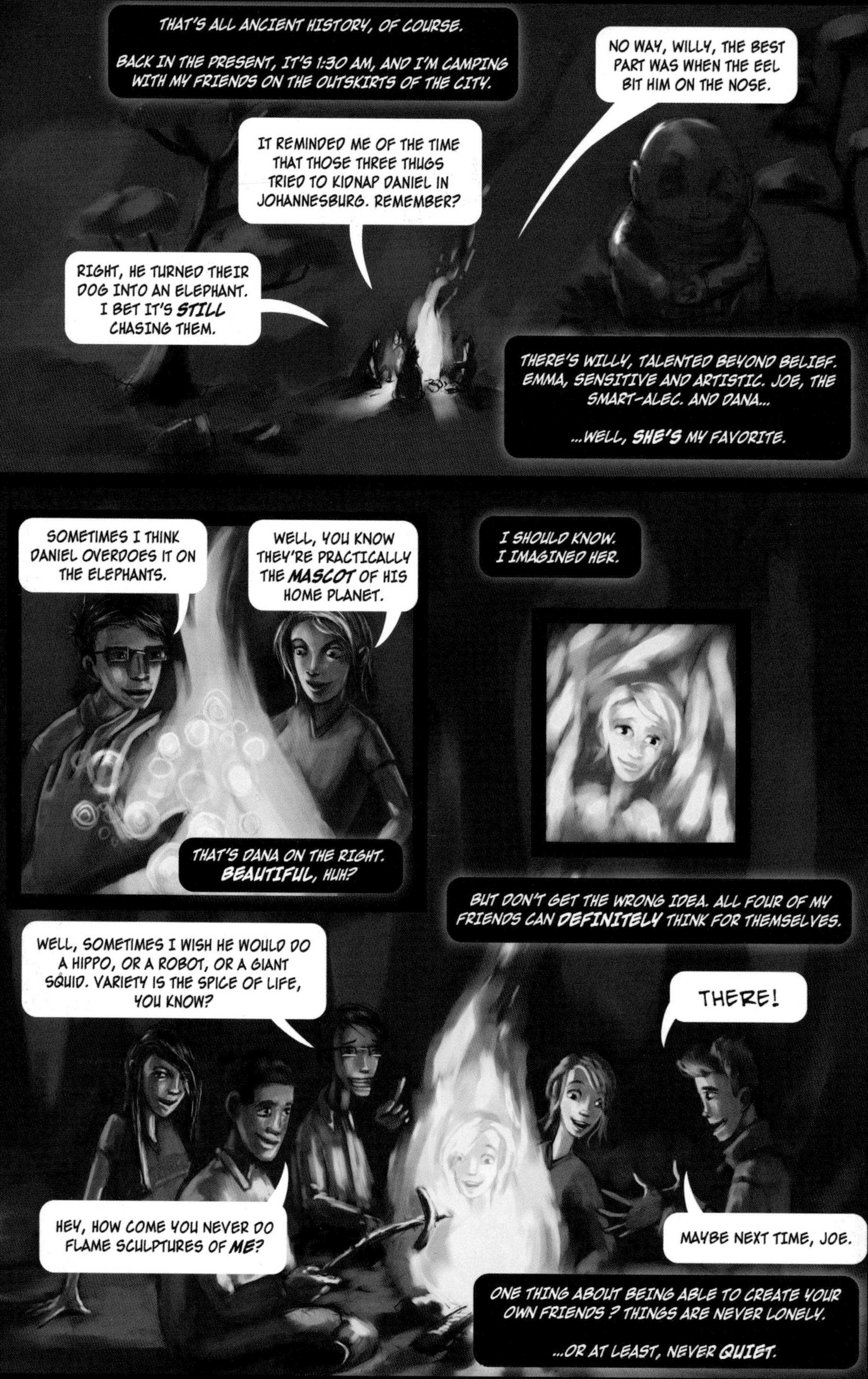
THAT'S ALL ANCIENT HISTORY, OF COURSE.
BACK IN THE PRESENT, IT'S 1:30 AM, AND I'M CAMPING WITH MY FRIENDS ON THE OUTSKIRTS OF THE CITY.
NO WAY, WILLY, THE BEST PART WAS WHEN THE EEL BIT HIM ON THE NOSE.
IT REMINDED ME OF THE TIME THAT THOSE THREE THUGS TRIED TO KIDNAP DANIEL IN JOHANNESBURG. REMEMBER?
RIGHT, HE TURNED THEIR DOG INTO AN ELEPHANT. I BET IT'S STILL CHASING THEM.
THERE'S WILLY, TALENTED BEYOND BELIEF. EMMA, SENSITIVE AND ARTISTIC. JOE, THE SMART-ALEC. AND DANA...
...WELL, SHE'S MY FAVORITE.
SOMETIMES I THINK DANIEL OVERDOES IT ON THE ELEPHANTS.
WELL, YOU KNOW THEY'RE PRACTICALLY THE MASCOT OF HIS HOME PLANET.
THAT'S DANA ON THE RIGHT. BEAUTIFUL, HUH?
I SHOULD KNOW. I IMAGINED HER.
BUT DON'T GET THE WRONG IDEA. ALL FOUR OF MY FRIENDS CAN DEFINITELY THINK FOR THEMSELVES.
WELL, SOMETIMES I WISH HE WOULD DO A HIPPO, OR A ROBOT, OR A GIANT SQUID. VARIETY IS THE SPICE OF LIFE, YOU KNOW?
THERE!
HEY, HOW COME YOU NEVER DO FLAME SCULPTURES OF ME?
MAYBE NEXT TIME, JOE.
ONE THING ABOUT BEING ABLE TO CREATE YOUR OWN FRIENDS ? THINGS ARE NEVER LONELY.
...OR AT LEAST, NEVER QUIET.

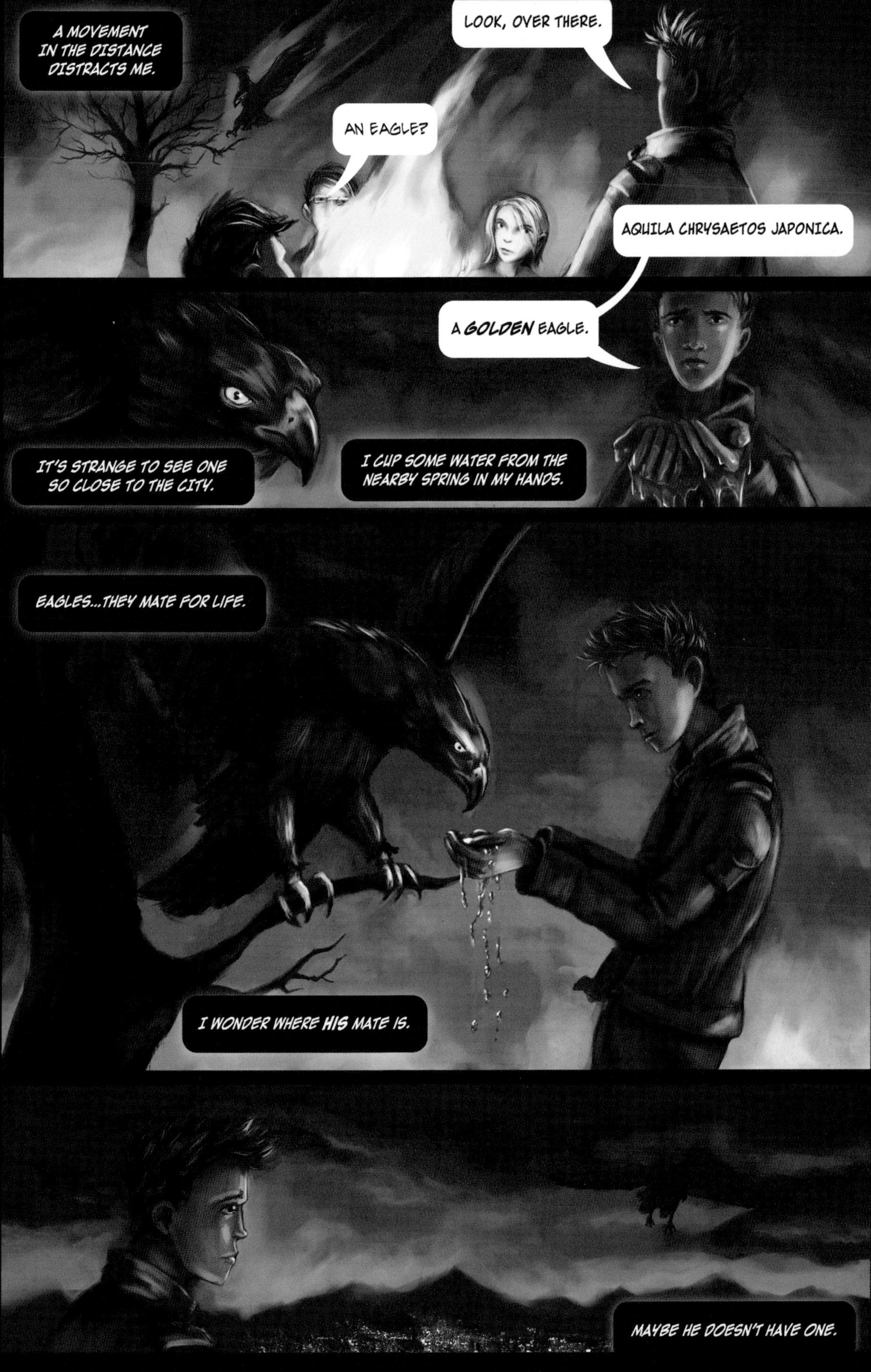
A MOVEMENT IN THE DISTANCE DISTRACTS ME.
LOOK, OVER THERE.
AN EAGLE?
AQUILA CHRYSAETOS JAPONICA.
A GOLDEN EAGLE.
IT'S STRANGE TO SEE ONE SO CLOSE TO THE CITY.
I CUP SOME WATER FROM THE NEARBY SPRING IN MY HANDS.
EAGLES...THEY MATE FOR LIFE.
I WONDER WHERE HIS MATE IS.
MAYBE HE DOESN'T HAVE ONE.

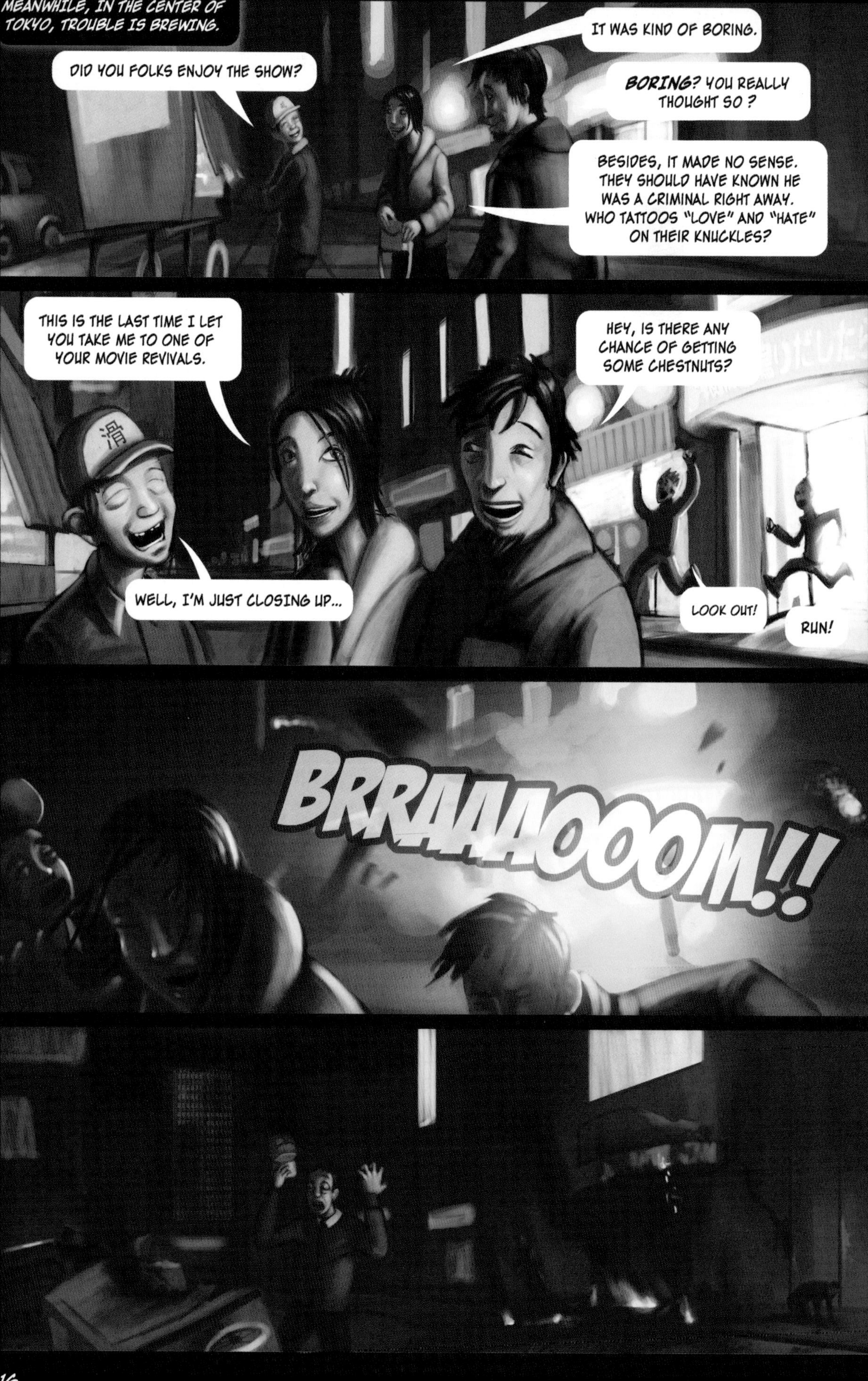
MEANWHILE, IN THE CENTER OF TOKYO, TROUBLE IS BREWING.
DID YOU FOLKS ENJOY THE SHOW?
IT WAS KIND OF BORING.
BORING? YOU REALLY THOUGHT SO ?
BESIDES, IT MADE NO SENSE. THEY SHOULD HAVE KNOWN HE WAS A CRIMINAL RIGHT AWAY. WHO TATTOOS "LOVE" AND "HATE" ON THEIR KNUCKLES?
THIS IS THE LAST TIME I LET YOU TAKE ME TO ONE OF YOUR MOVIE REVIVALS.
HEY, IS THERE ANY CHANCE OF GETTING SOME CHESTNUTS?
WELL, I'M JUST CLOSING UP...
LOOK OUT!
RUN!
BRRAAAOOOM!!

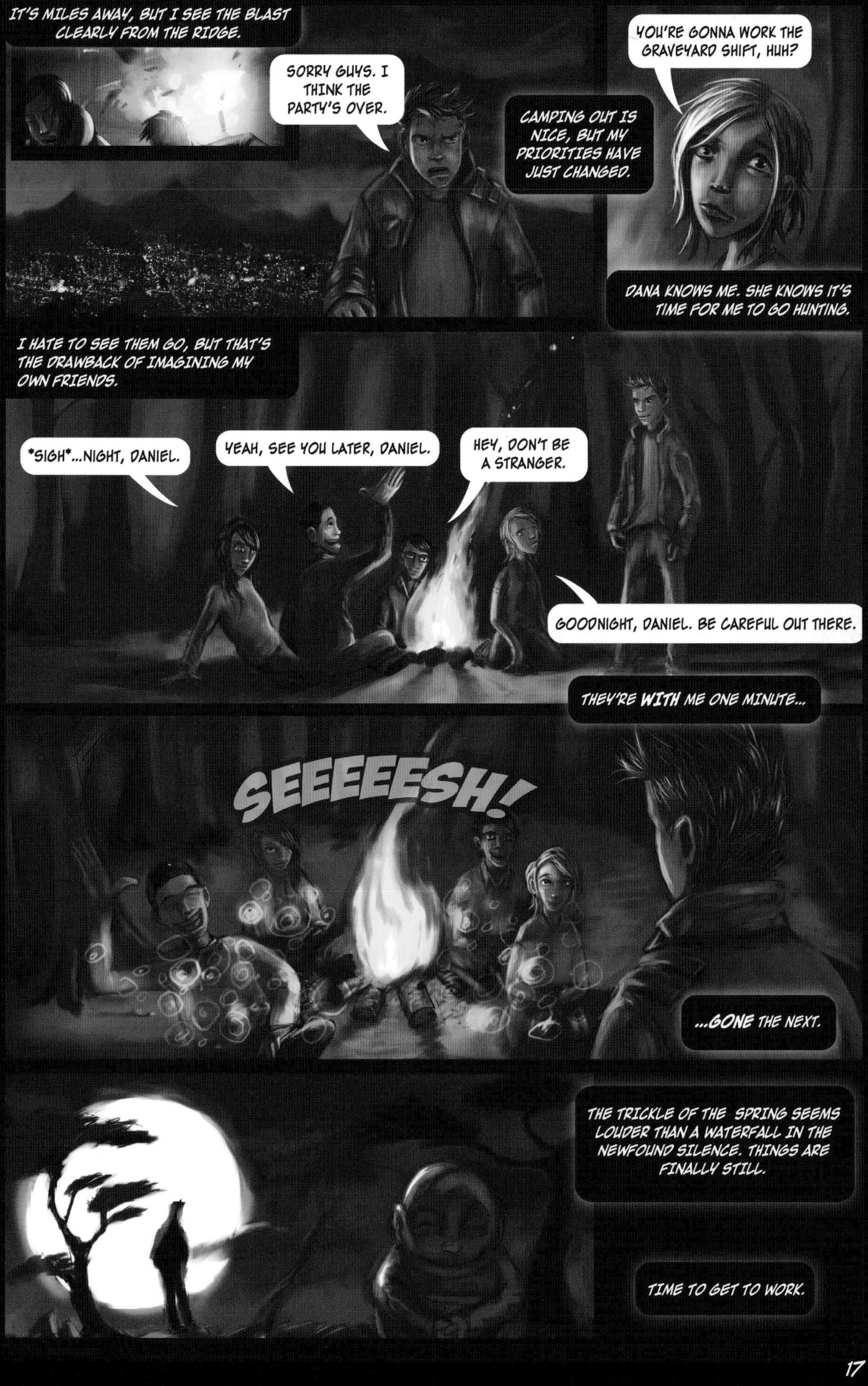
IT'S MILES AWAY, BUT I SEE THE BLAST CLEARLY FROM THE RIDGE.
SORRY GUYS. I THINK THE PARTY'S OVER.
CAMPING OUT IS NICE, BUT MY PRIORITIES HAVE JUST CHANGED.
YOU'RE GONNA WORK THE GRAVEYARD SHIFT, HUH?
DANA KNOWS ME. SHE KNOWS IT'S TIME FOR ME TO GO HUNTING.
I HATE TO SEE THEM GO, BUT THAT'S THE DRAWBACK OF IMAGINING MY OWN FRIENDS.
SIGH...NIGHT, DANIEL.
YEAH, SEE YOU LATER, DANIEL.
HEY, DON'T BE A STRANGER.
GOODNIGHT, DANIEL. BE CAREFUL OUT THERE.
THEY'RE WITH ME ONE MINUTE...
SEEEEEESH!
...GONE THE NEXT.
THE TRICKLE OF THE SPRING SEEMS LOUDER THAN A WATERFALL IN THE NEWFOUND SILENCE. THINGS ARE FINALLY STILL.
TIME TO GET TO WORK.

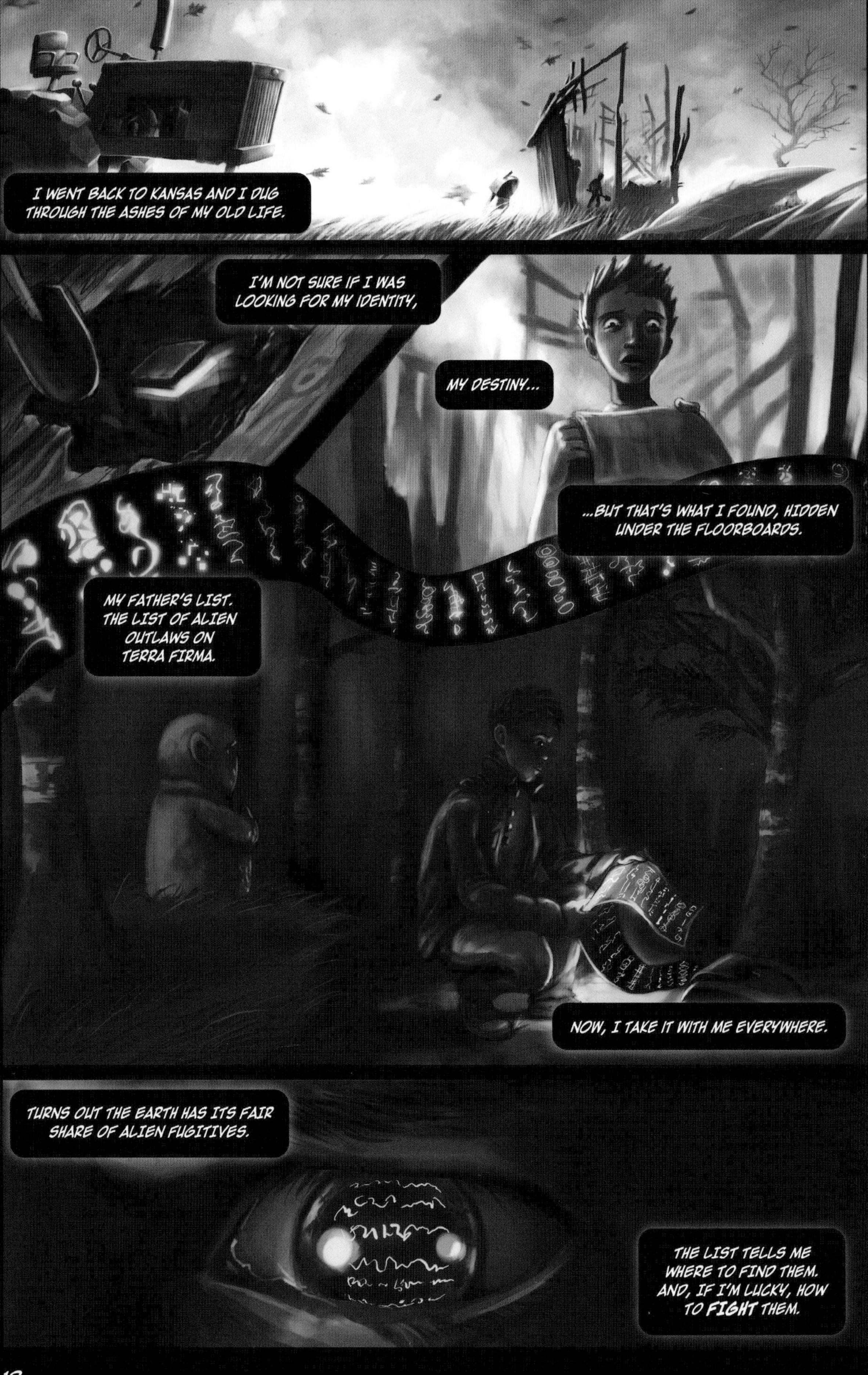
I WENT BACK TO KANSAS AND I DUG THROUGH THE ASHES OF MY OLD LIFE.
I'M NOT SURE IF I WAS LOOKING FOR MY IDENTITY,
MY DESTINY...
...BUT THAT'S WHAT I FOUND, HIDDEN UNDER THE FLOORBOARDS.
MY FATHER'S LIST. THE LIST OF ALIEN OUTLAWS ON TERRA FIRMA.
NOW, I TAKE IT WITH ME EVERYWHERE.
TURNS OUT THE EARTH HAS ITS FAIR SHARE OF ALIEN FUGITIVES.
THE LIST TELLS ME WHERE TO FIND THEM. AND, IF I'M LUCKY, HOW TO **FIGHT** THEM.

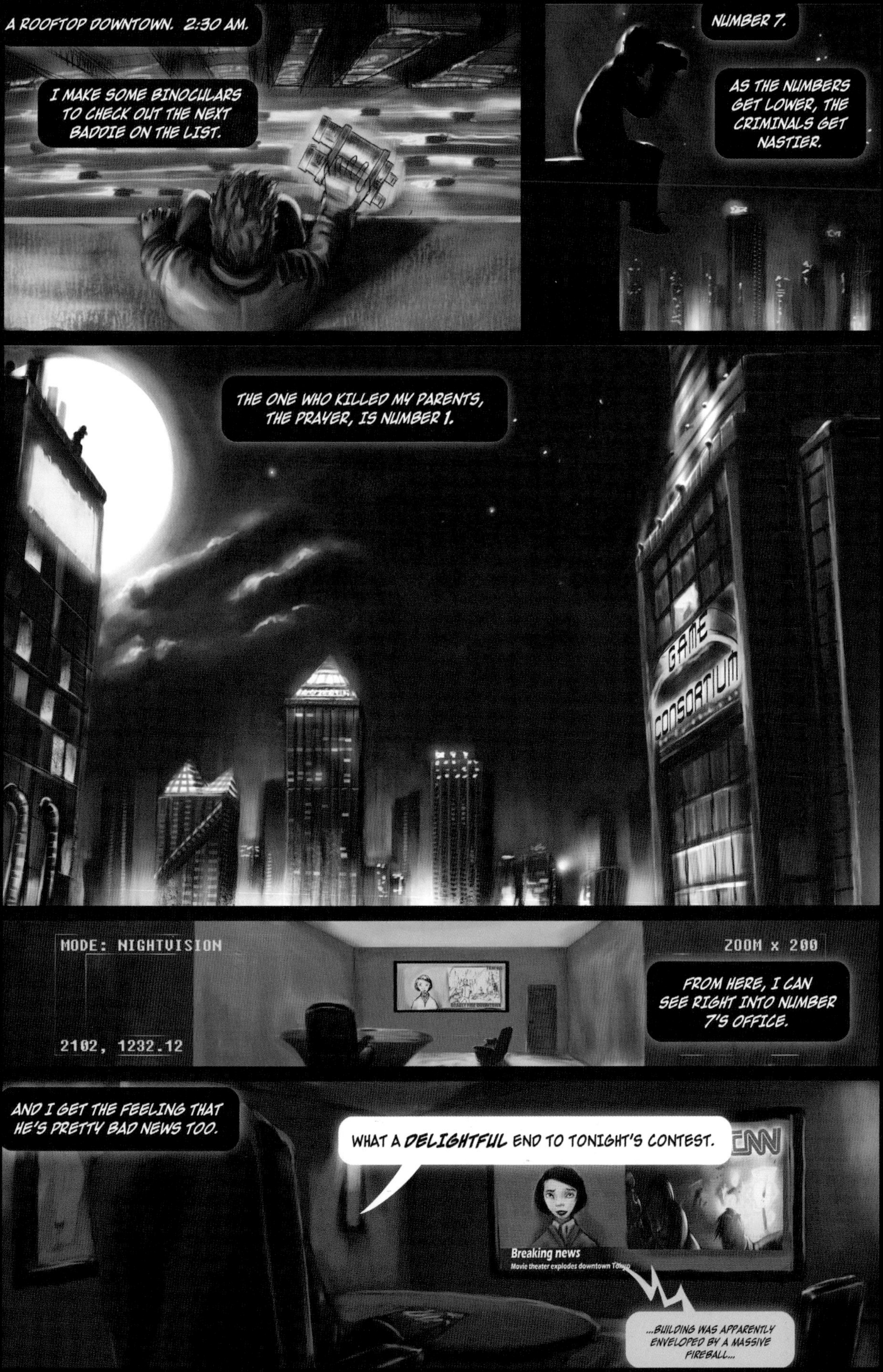
A ROOFTOP DOWNTOWN. 2:30 AM.
I MAKE SOME BINOCULARS TO CHECK OUT THE NEXT BADDIE ON THE LIST.
NUMBER 7.
AS THE NUMBERS GET LOWER, THE CRIMINALS GET NASTIER.
THE ONE WHO KILLED MY PARENTS, THE PRAYER, IS NUMBER 1.
GAME CONSORTIUM
MODE: NIGHTVISION
ZOOM x 200
2102, 1232.12
FROM HERE, I CAN SEE RIGHT INTO NUMBER 7'S OFFICE.
AND I GET THE FEELING THAT HE'S PRETTY BAD NEWS TOO.
WHAT A DELIGHTFUL END TO TONIGHT'S CONTEST.
Breaking news
Movie theater explodes downtown Tokyo
...BUILDING WAS APPARENTLY ENVELOPED BY A MASSIVE FIREBALL...

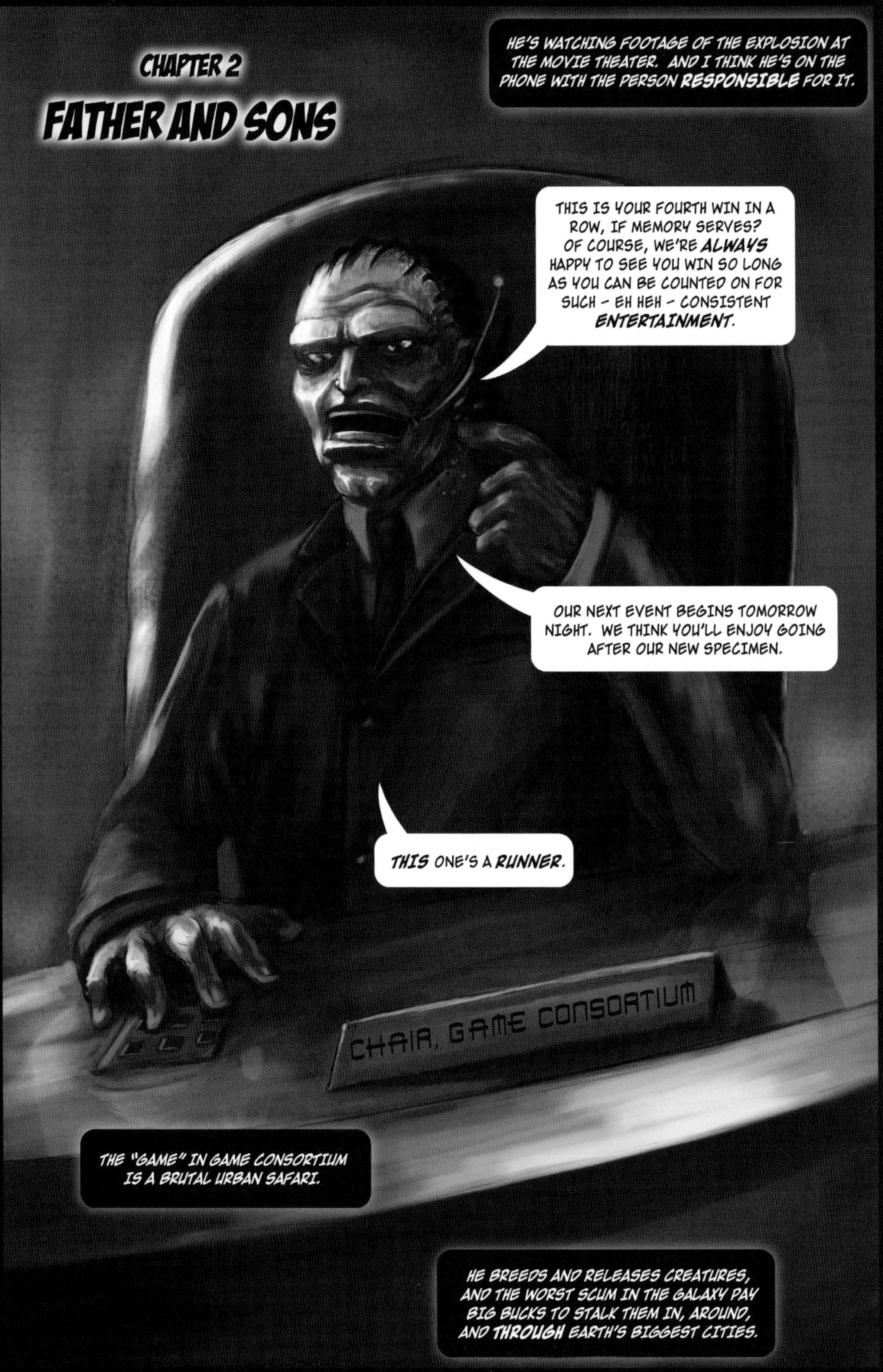
CHAPTER 2
FATHER AND SONS
HE'S WATCHING FOOTAGE OF THE EXPLOSION AT THE MOVIE THEATER. AND I THINK HE'S ON THE PHONE WITH THE PERSON RESPONSIBLE FOR IT.
THIS IS YOUR FOURTH WIN IN A ROW, IF MEMORY SERVES? OF COURSE, WE'RE ALWAYS HAPPY TO SEE YOU WIN SO LONG AS YOU CAN BE COUNTED ON FOR SUCH - EH HEH - CONSISTENT ENTERTAINMENT.
OUR NEXT EVENT BEGINS TOMORROW NIGHT. WE THINK YOU'LL ENJOY GOING AFTER OUR NEW SPECIMEN.
THIS ONE'S A RUNNER.
CHAIR, GAME CONSORTIUM
THE "GAME" IN GAME CONSORTIUM IS A BRUTAL URBAN SAFARI.
HE BREEDS AND RELEASES CREATURES, AND THE WORST SCUM IN THE GALAXY PAY BIG BUCKS TO STALK THEM IN, AROUND, AND THROUGH EARTH'S BIGGEST CITIES.

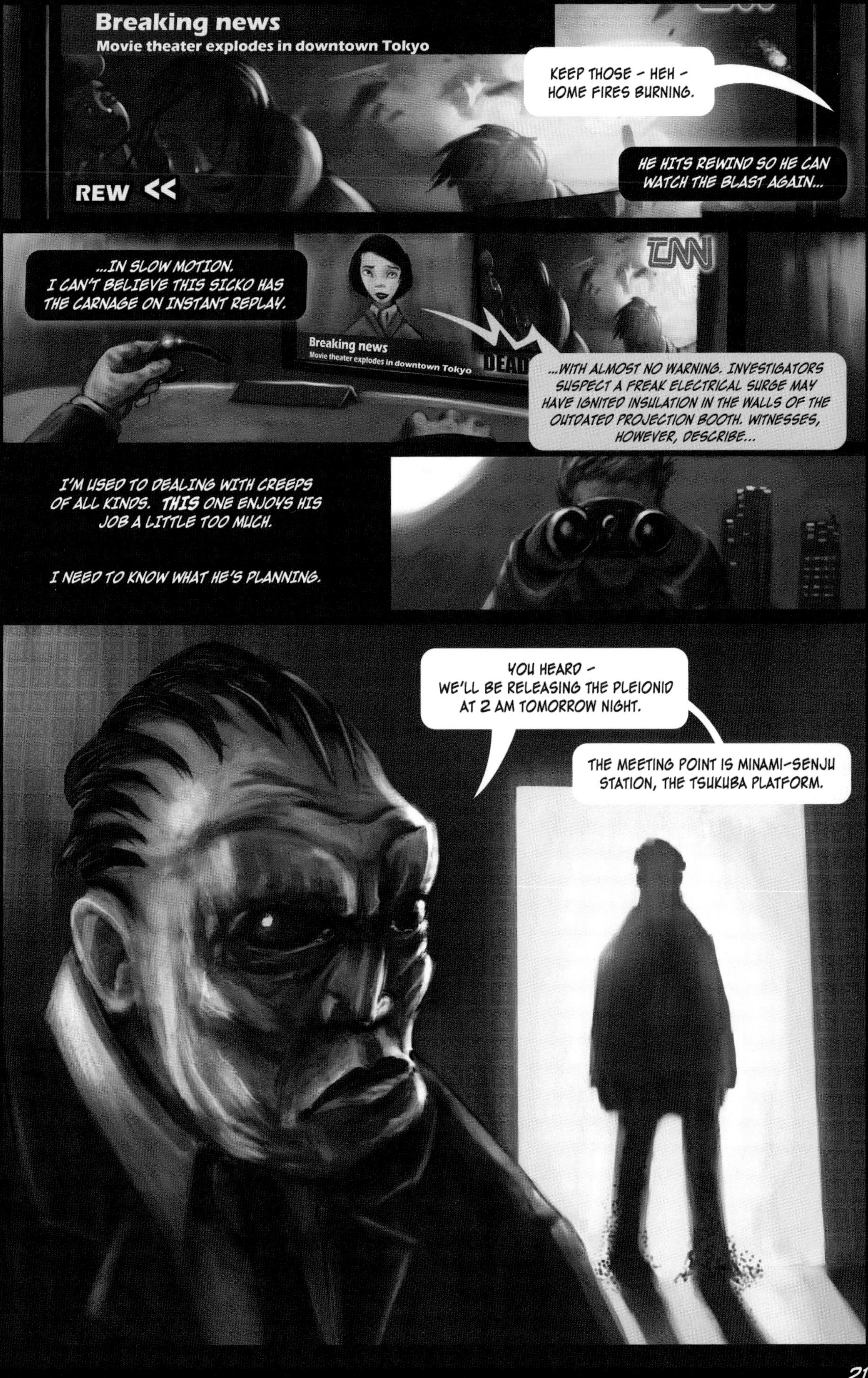
Breaking news
Movie theater explodes in downtown Tokyo
KEEP THOSE - HEH - HOME FIRES BURNING.
REW <<
HE HITS REWIND SO HE CAN WATCH THE BLAST AGAIN...
...IN SLOW MOTION. I CAN'T BELIEVE THIS SICKO HAS THE CARNAGE ON INSTANT REPLAY.
TNN
Breaking news
Movie theater explodes in downtown Tokyo
...WITH ALMOST NO WARNING. INVESTIGATORS SUSPECT A FREAK ELECTRICAL SURGE MAY HAVE IGNITED INSULATION IN THE WALLS OF THE OUTDATED PROJECTION BOOTH. WITNESSES, HOWEVER, DESCRIBE...
I'M USED TO DEALING WITH CREEPS OF ALL KINDS. **THIS** ONE ENJOYS HIS JOB A LITTLE TOO MUCH.
I NEED TO KNOW WHAT HE'S PLANNING.
YOU HEARD - WE'LL BE RELEASING THE PLEIONID AT 2 AM TOMORROW NIGHT.
THE MEETING POINT IS MINAMI-SENJU STATION, THE TSUKUBA PLATFORM.

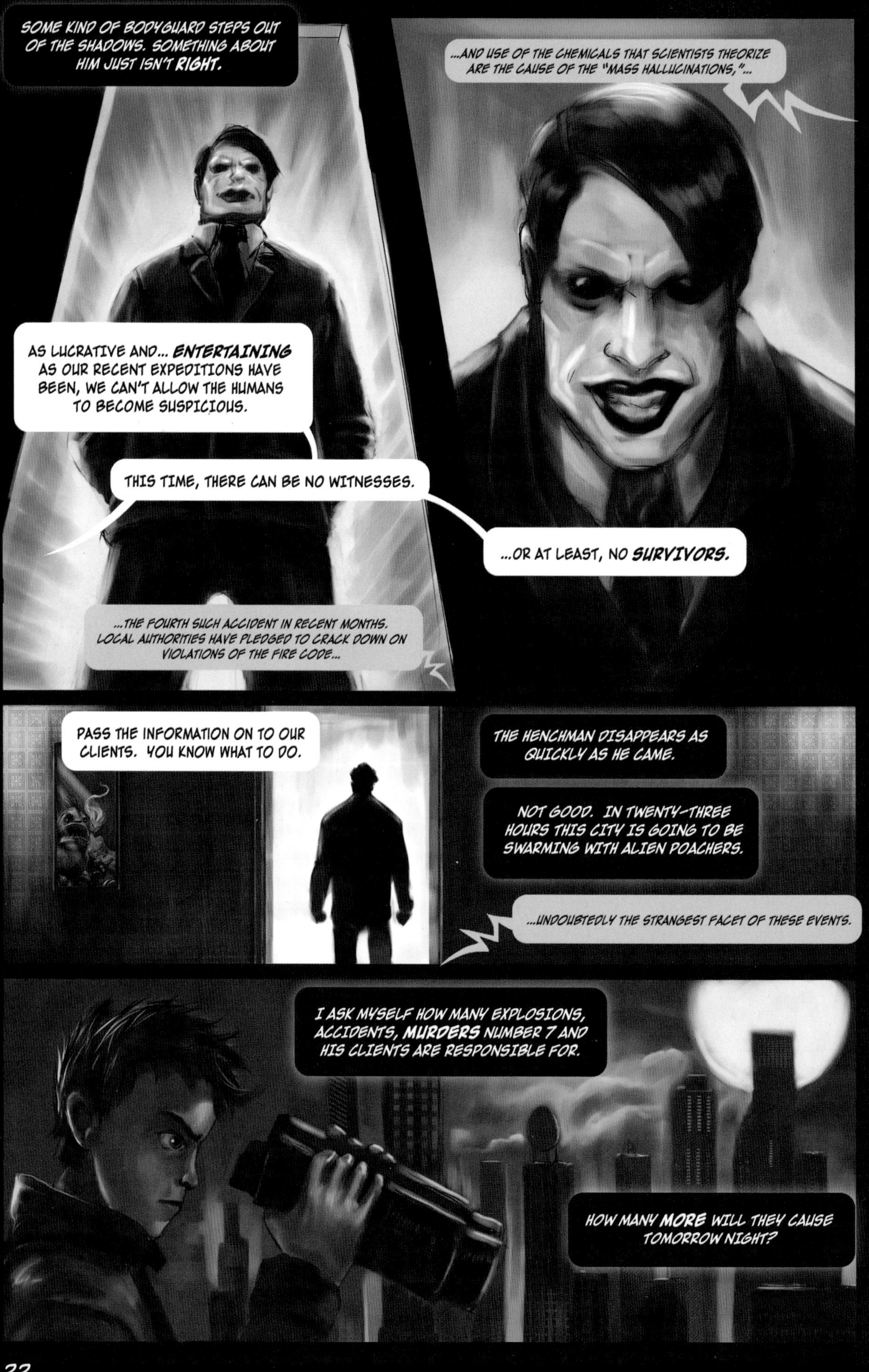
SOME KIND OF BODYGUARD STEPS OUT OF THE SHADOWS. SOMETHING ABOUT HIM JUST ISN'T RIGHT.
...AND USE OF THE CHEMICALS THAT SCIENTISTS THEORIZE ARE THE CAUSE OF THE "MASS HALLUCINATIONS,"...
AS LUCRATIVE AND... ENTERTAINING AS OUR RECENT EXPEDITIONS HAVE BEEN, WE CAN'T ALLOW THE HUMANS TO BECOME SUSPICIOUS.
THIS TIME, THERE CAN BE NO WITNESSES.
...OR AT LEAST, NO SURVIVORS.
...THE FOURTH SUCH ACCIDENT IN RECENT MONTHS. LOCAL AUTHORITIES HAVE PLEDGED TO CRACK DOWN ON VIOLATIONS OF THE FIRE CODE...
PASS THE INFORMATION ON TO OUR CLIENTS. YOU KNOW WHAT TO DO.
THE HENCHMAN DISAPPEARS AS QUICKLY AS HE CAME.
NOT GOOD. IN TWENTY-THREE HOURS THIS CITY IS GOING TO BE SWARMING WITH ALIEN POACHERS.
...UNDOUBTEDLY THE STRANGEST FACET OF THESE EVENTS.
I ASK MYSELF HOW MANY EXPLOSIONS, ACCIDENTS, MURDERS NUMBER 7 AND HIS CLIENTS ARE RESPONSIBLE FOR.
HOW MANY MORE WILL THEY CAUSE TOMORROW NIGHT?

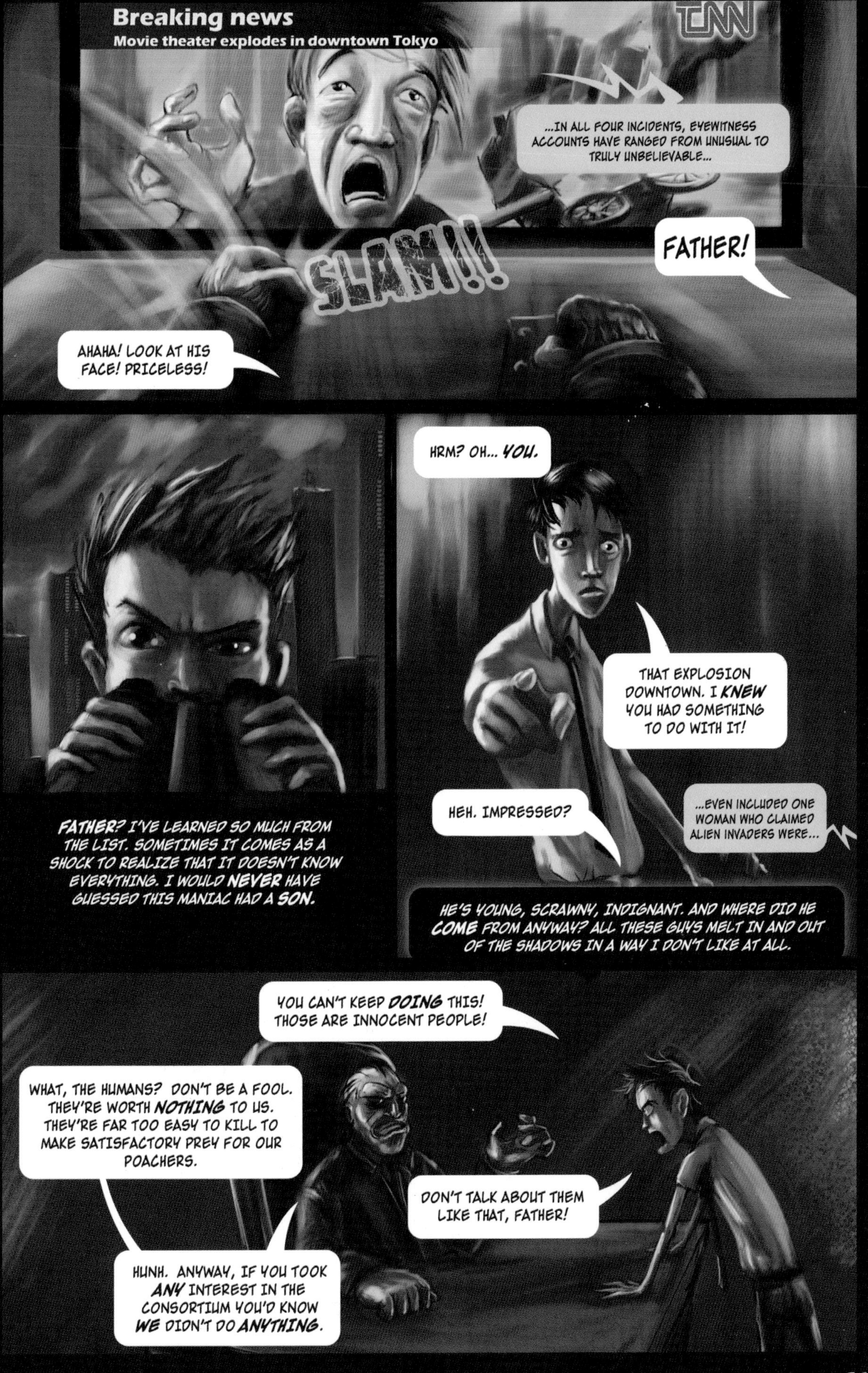
Breaking news
Movie theater explodes in downtown Tokyo
TNN
...IN ALL FOUR INCIDENTS, EYEWITNESS ACCOUNTS HAVE RANGED FROM UNUSUAL TO TRULY UNBELIEVABLE...
SLAM!!
FATHER!
AHAHA! LOOK AT HIS FACE! PRICELESS!
FATHER? I'VE LEARNED SO MUCH FROM THE LIST. SOMETIMES IT COMES AS A SHOCK TO REALIZE THAT IT DOESN'T KNOW EVERYTHING. I WOULD NEVER HAVE GUESSED THIS MANIAC HAD A SON.
HRM? OH... YOU.
THAT EXPLOSION DOWNTOWN. I KNEW YOU HAD SOMETHING TO DO WITH IT!
HEH. IMPRESSED?
...EVEN INCLUDED ONE WOMAN WHO CLAIMED ALIEN INVADERS WERE...
HE'S YOUNG, SCRAWNY, INDIGNANT. AND WHERE DID HE COME FROM ANYWAY? ALL THESE GUYS MELT IN AND OUT OF THE SHADOWS IN A WAY I DON'T LIKE AT ALL.
YOU CAN'T KEEP DOING THIS! THOSE ARE INNOCENT PEOPLE!
WHAT, THE HUMANS? DON'T BE A FOOL. THEY'RE WORTH NOTHING TO US. THEY'RE FAR TOO EASY TO KILL TO MAKE SATISFACTORY PREY FOR OUR POACHERS.
DON'T TALK ABOUT THEM LIKE THAT, FATHER!
HUNH. ANYWAY, IF YOU TOOK ANY INTEREST IN THE CONSORTIUM YOU'D KNOW WE DIDN'T DO ANYTHING.

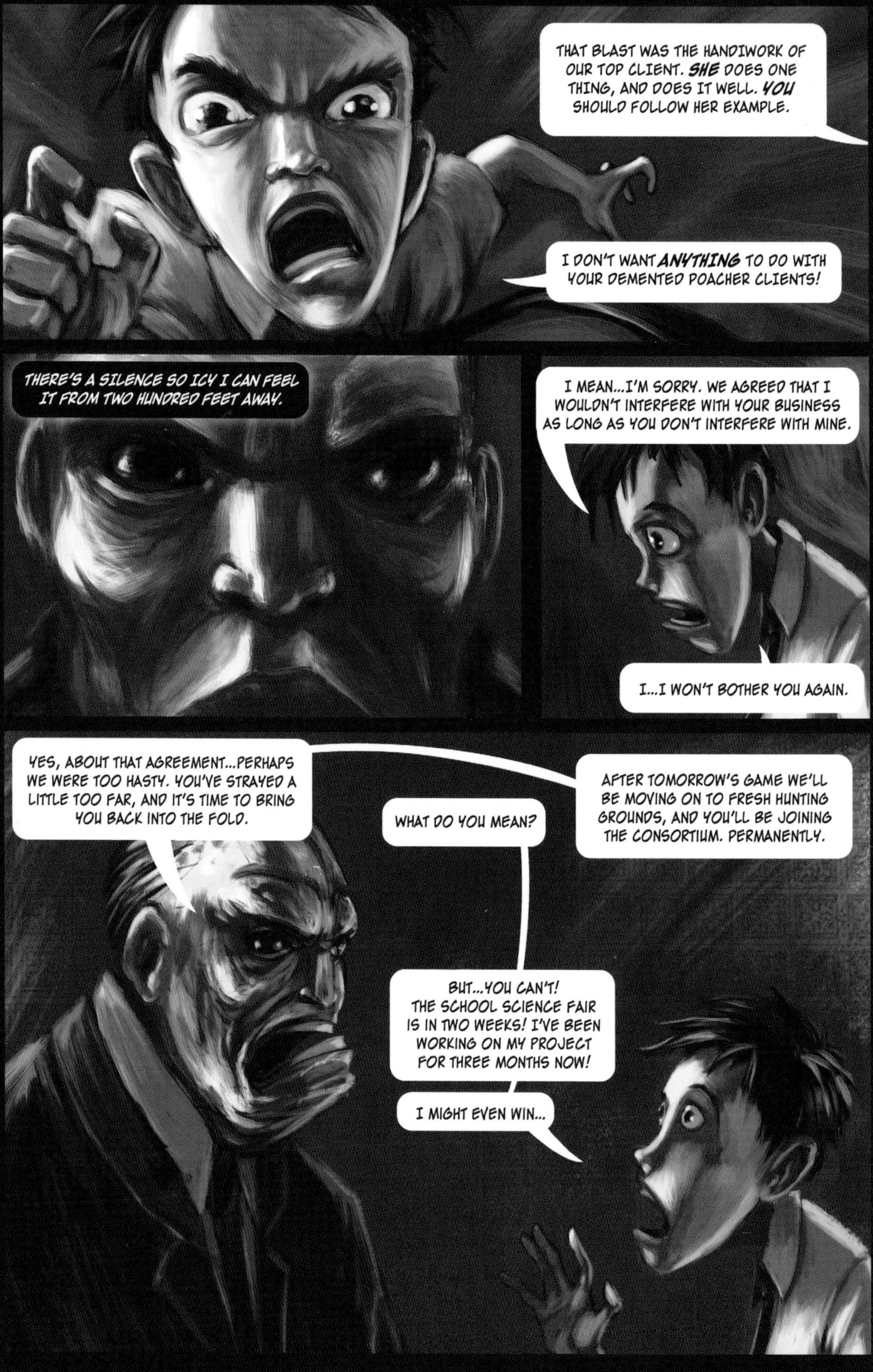
THAT BLAST WAS THE HANDIWORK OF OUR TOP CLIENT. *SHE* DOES ONE THING, AND DOES IT WELL. *YOU* SHOULD FOLLOW HER EXAMPLE.
I DON'T WANT ***ANYTHING*** TO DO WITH YOUR DEMENTED POACHER CLIENTS!
THERE'S A SILENCE SO ICY I CAN FEEL IT FROM TWO HUNDRED FEET AWAY.
I MEAN...I'M SORRY. WE AGREED THAT I WOULDN'T INTERFERE WITH YOUR BUSINESS AS LONG AS YOU DON'T INTERFERE WITH MINE.
I...I WON'T BOTHER YOU AGAIN.
YES, ABOUT THAT AGREEMENT...PERHAPS WE WERE TOO HASTY. YOU'VE STRAYED A LITTLE TOO FAR, AND IT'S TIME TO BRING YOU BACK INTO THE FOLD.
AFTER TOMORROW'S GAME WE'LL BE MOVING ON TO FRESH HUNTING GROUNDS, AND YOU'LL BE JOINING THE CONSORTIUM. PERMANENTLY.
WHAT DO YOU MEAN?
BUT...YOU CAN'T! THE SCHOOL SCIENCE FAIR IS IN TWO WEEKS! I'VE BEEN WORKING ON MY PROJECT FOR THREE MONTHS NOW!
I MIGHT EVEN WIN...

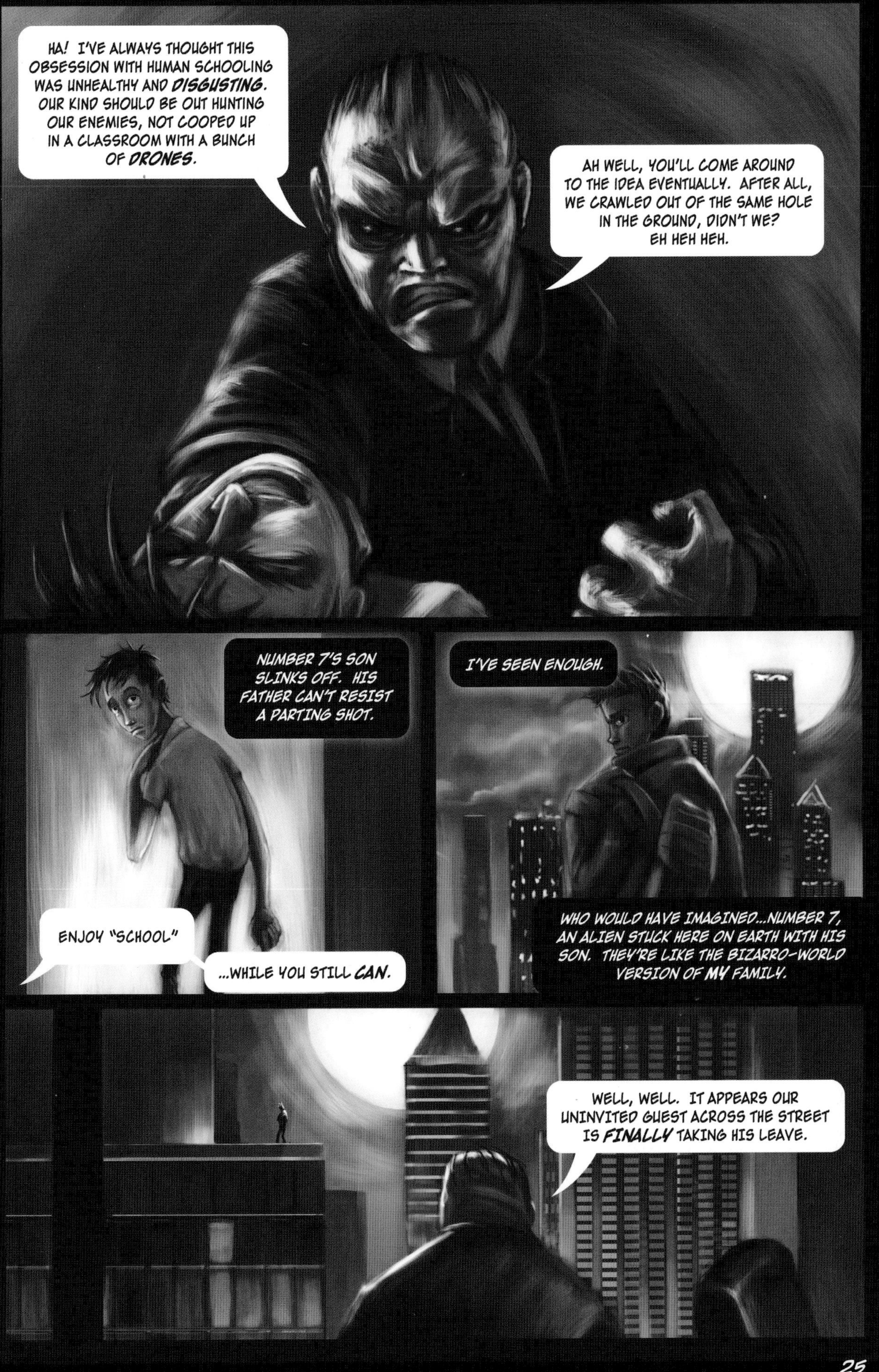
HA! I'VE ALWAYS THOUGHT THIS OBSESSION WITH HUMAN SCHOOLING WAS UNHEALTHY AND DISGUSTING. OUR KIND SHOULD BE OUT HUNTING OUR ENEMIES, NOT COOPED UP IN A CLASSROOM WITH A BUNCH OF DRONES.
AH WELL, YOU'LL COME AROUND TO THE IDEA EVENTUALLY. AFTER ALL, WE CRAWLED OUT OF THE SAME HOLE IN THE GROUND, DIDN'T WE? EH HEH HEH.
NUMBER 7'S SON SLINKS OFF. HIS FATHER CAN'T RESIST A PARTING SHOT.
ENJOY "SCHOOL"
...WHILE YOU STILL CAN.
I'VE SEEN ENOUGH.
WHO WOULD HAVE IMAGINED...NUMBER 7, AN ALIEN STUCK HERE ON EARTH WITH HIS SON. THEY'RE LIKE THE BIZARRO-WORLD VERSION OF MY FAMILY.
WELL, WELL. IT APPEARS OUR UNINVITED GUEST ACROSS THE STREET IS FINALLY TAKING HIS LEAVE.

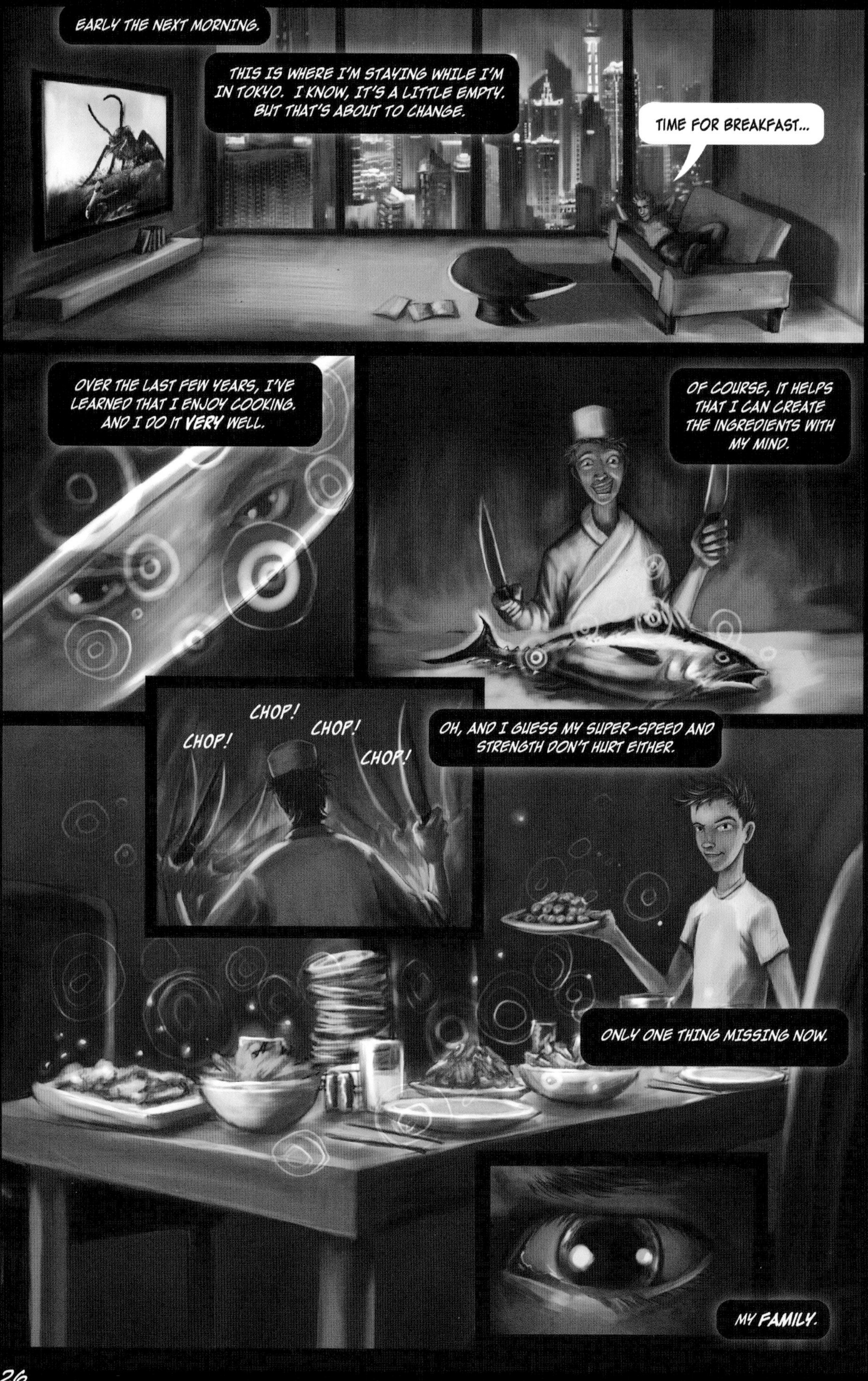
EARLY THE NEXT MORNING.
THIS IS WHERE I'M STAYING WHILE I'M IN TOKYO. I KNOW, IT'S A LITTLE EMPTY. BUT THAT'S ABOUT TO CHANGE.
TIME FOR BREAKFAST...
OVER THE LAST FEW YEARS, I'VE LEARNED THAT I ENJOY COOKING. AND I DO IT VERY WELL.
OF COURSE, IT HELPS THAT I CAN CREATE THE INGREDIENTS WITH MY MIND.
CHOP!
CHOP!
CHOP!
CHOP!
OH, AND I GUESS MY SUPER-SPEED AND STRENGTH DON'T HURT EITHER.
ONLY ONE THING MISSING NOW.
MY FAMILY.

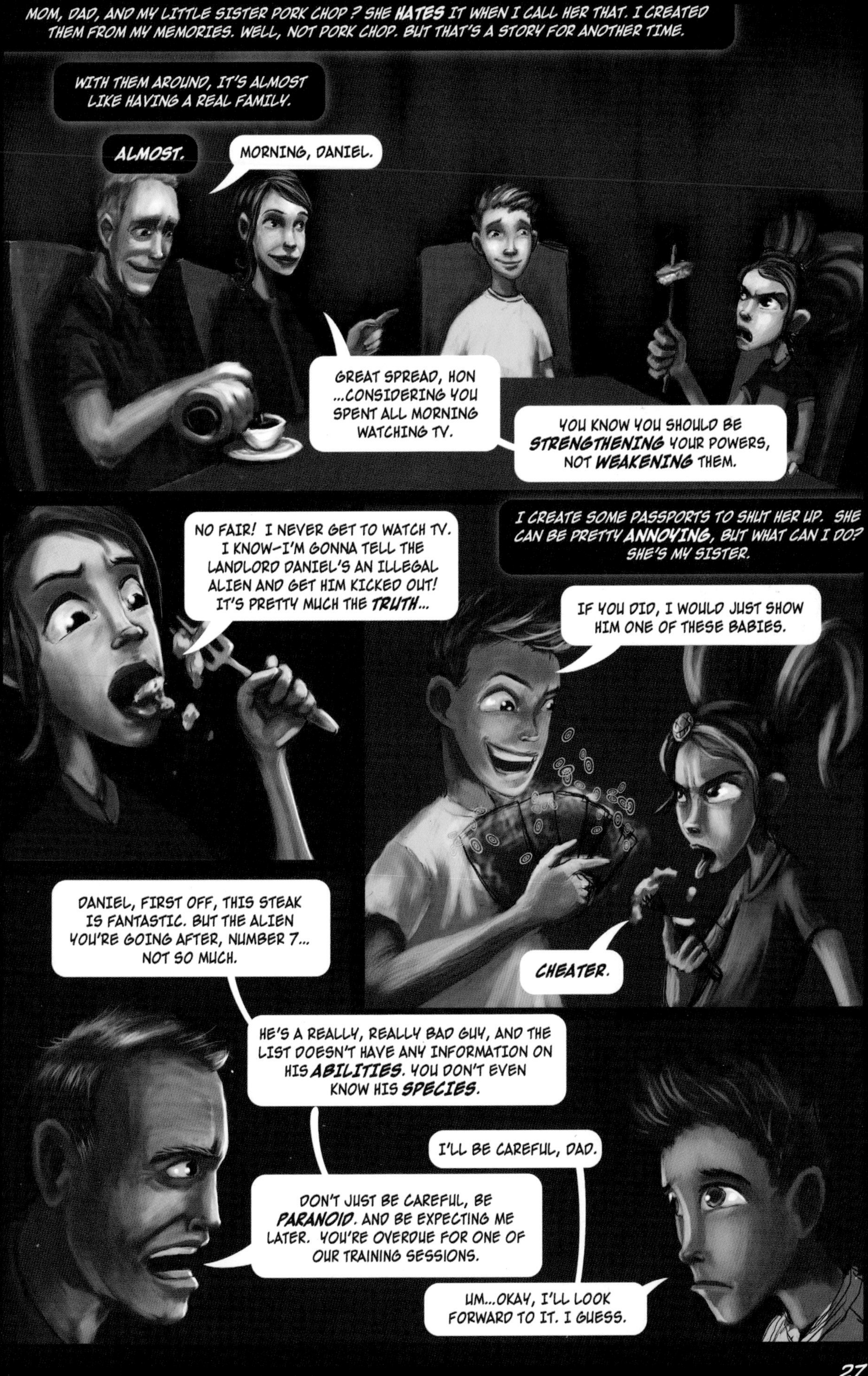
MOM, DAD, AND MY LITTLE SISTER PORK CHOP ? SHE HATES IT WHEN I CALL HER THAT. I CREATED THEM FROM MY MEMORIES. WELL, NOT PORK CHOP. BUT THAT'S A STORY FOR ANOTHER TIME.
WITH THEM AROUND, IT'S ALMOST LIKE HAVING A REAL FAMILY.
ALMOST.
MORNING, DANIEL.
GREAT SPREAD, HON ...CONSIDERING YOU SPENT ALL MORNING WATCHING TV.
YOU KNOW YOU SHOULD BE STRENGTHENING YOUR POWERS, NOT WEAKENING THEM.
NO FAIR! I NEVER GET TO WATCH TV. I KNOW–I'M GONNA TELL THE LANDLORD DANIEL'S AN ILLEGAL ALIEN AND GET HIM KICKED OUT! IT'S PRETTY MUCH THE TRUTH...
I CREATE SOME PASSPORTS TO SHUT HER UP. SHE CAN BE PRETTY ANNOYING, BUT WHAT CAN I DO? SHE'S MY SISTER.
IF YOU DID, I WOULD JUST SHOW HIM ONE OF THESE BABIES.
CHEATER.
DANIEL, FIRST OFF, THIS STEAK IS FANTASTIC. BUT THE ALIEN YOU'RE GOING AFTER, NUMBER 7... NOT SO MUCH.
HE'S A REALLY, REALLY BAD GUY, AND THE LIST DOESN'T HAVE ANY INFORMATION ON HIS ABILITIES. YOU DON'T EVEN KNOW HIS SPECIES.
I'LL BE CAREFUL, DAD.
DON'T JUST BE CAREFUL, BE PARANOID. AND BE EXPECTING ME LATER. YOU'RE OVERDUE FOR ONE OF OUR TRAINING SESSIONS.
UM...OKAY, I'LL LOOK FORWARD TO IT. I GUESS.

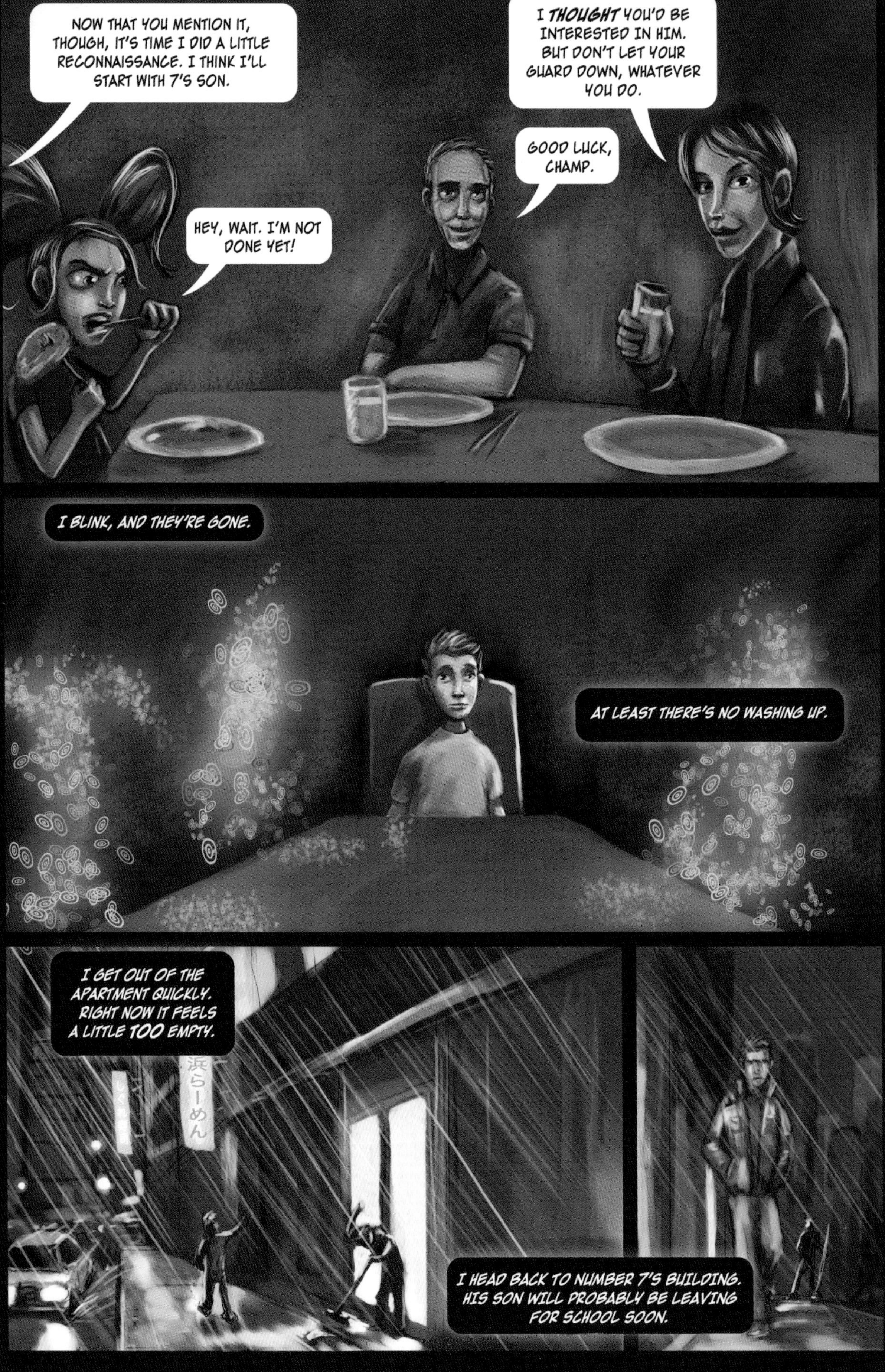
NOW THAT YOU MENTION IT, THOUGH, IT'S TIME I DID A LITTLE RECONNAISSANCE. I THINK I'LL START WITH 7'S SON.
HEY, WAIT. I'M NOT DONE YET!
GOOD LUCK, CHAMP.
I **THOUGHT** YOU'D BE INTERESTED IN HIM. BUT DON'T LET YOUR GUARD DOWN, WHATEVER YOU DO.
I BLINK, AND THEY'RE GONE.
AT LEAST THERE'S NO WASHING UP.
I GET OUT OF THE APARTMENT QUICKLY. RIGHT NOW IT FEELS A LITTLE **TOO** EMPTY.
浜らーめん
I HEAD BACK TO NUMBER 7'S BUILDING. HIS SON WILL PROBABLY BE LEAVING FOR SCHOOL SOON.

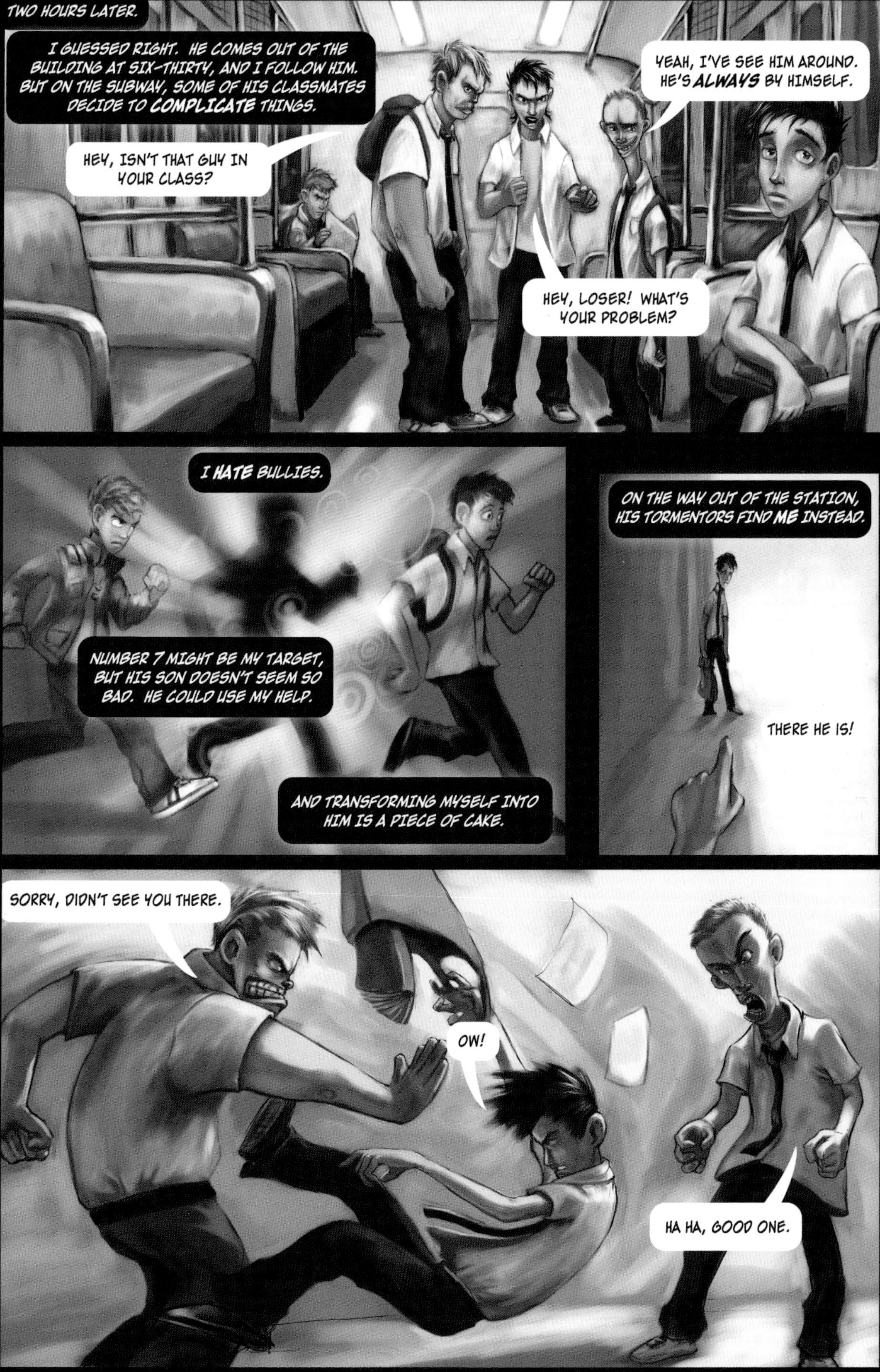
TWO HOURS LATER.
I GUESSED RIGHT. HE COMES OUT OF THE BUILDING AT SIX-THIRTY, AND I FOLLOW HIM. BUT ON THE SUBWAY, SOME OF HIS CLASSMATES DECIDE TO COMPLICATE THINGS.
HEY, ISN'T THAT GUY IN YOUR CLASS?
YEAH, I'VE SEE HIM AROUND. HE'S ALWAYS BY HIMSELF.
HEY, LOSER! WHAT'S YOUR PROBLEM?
I HATE BULLIES.
NUMBER 7 MIGHT BE MY TARGET, BUT HIS SON DOESN'T SEEM SO BAD. HE COULD USE MY HELP.
AND TRANSFORMING MYSELF INTO HIM IS A PIECE OF CAKE.
ON THE WAY OUT OF THE STATION, HIS TORMENTORS FIND ME INSTEAD.
THERE HE IS!
SORRY, DIDN'T SEE YOU THERE.
OW!
HA HA, GOOD ONE.

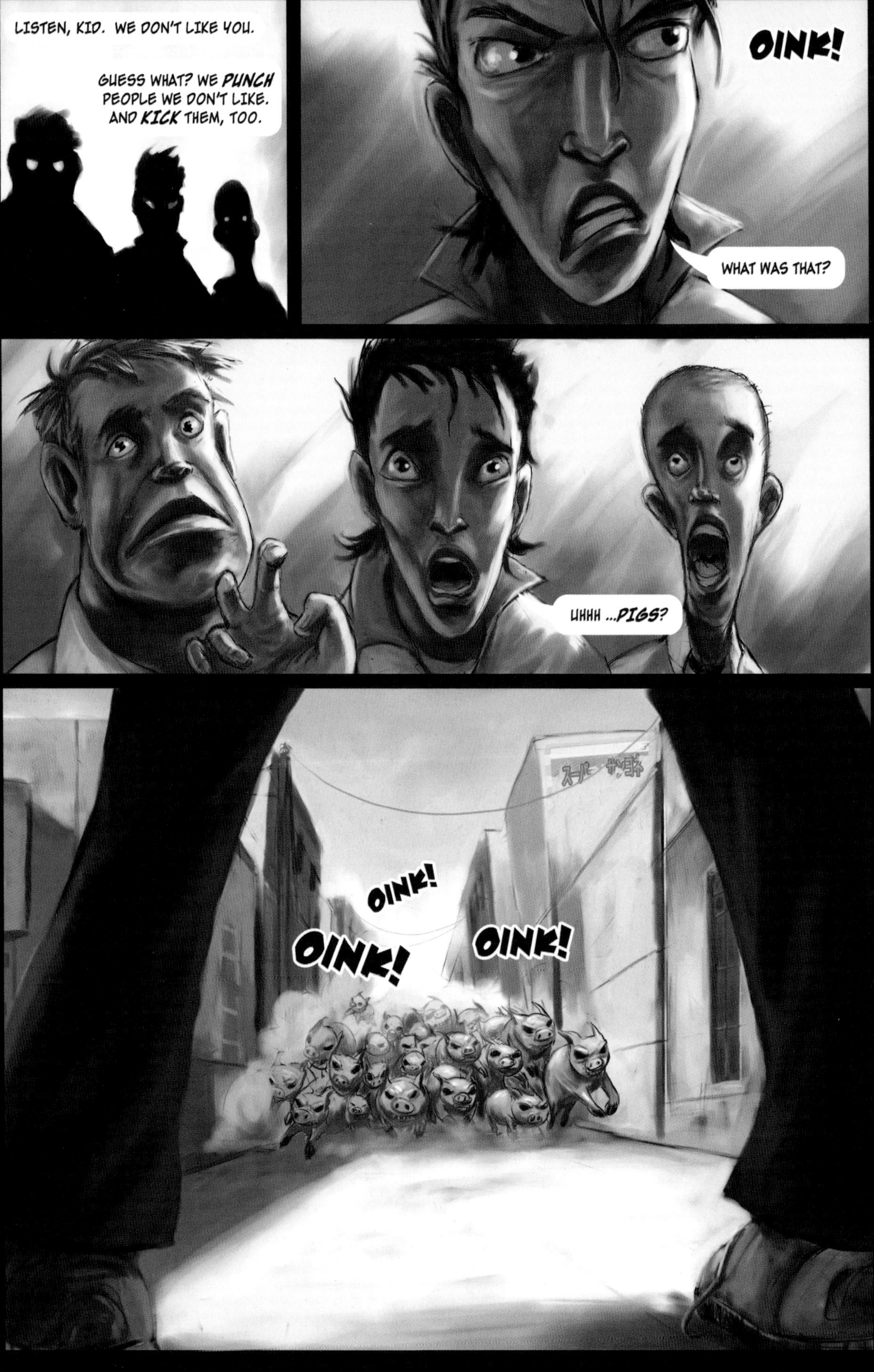
LISTEN, KID. WE DON'T LIKE YOU.
GUESS WHAT? WE PUNCH PEOPLE WE DON'T LIKE. AND KICK THEM, TOO.
OINK!
WHAT WAS THAT?
UHHH ...PIGS?
OINK!
OINK!
OINK!

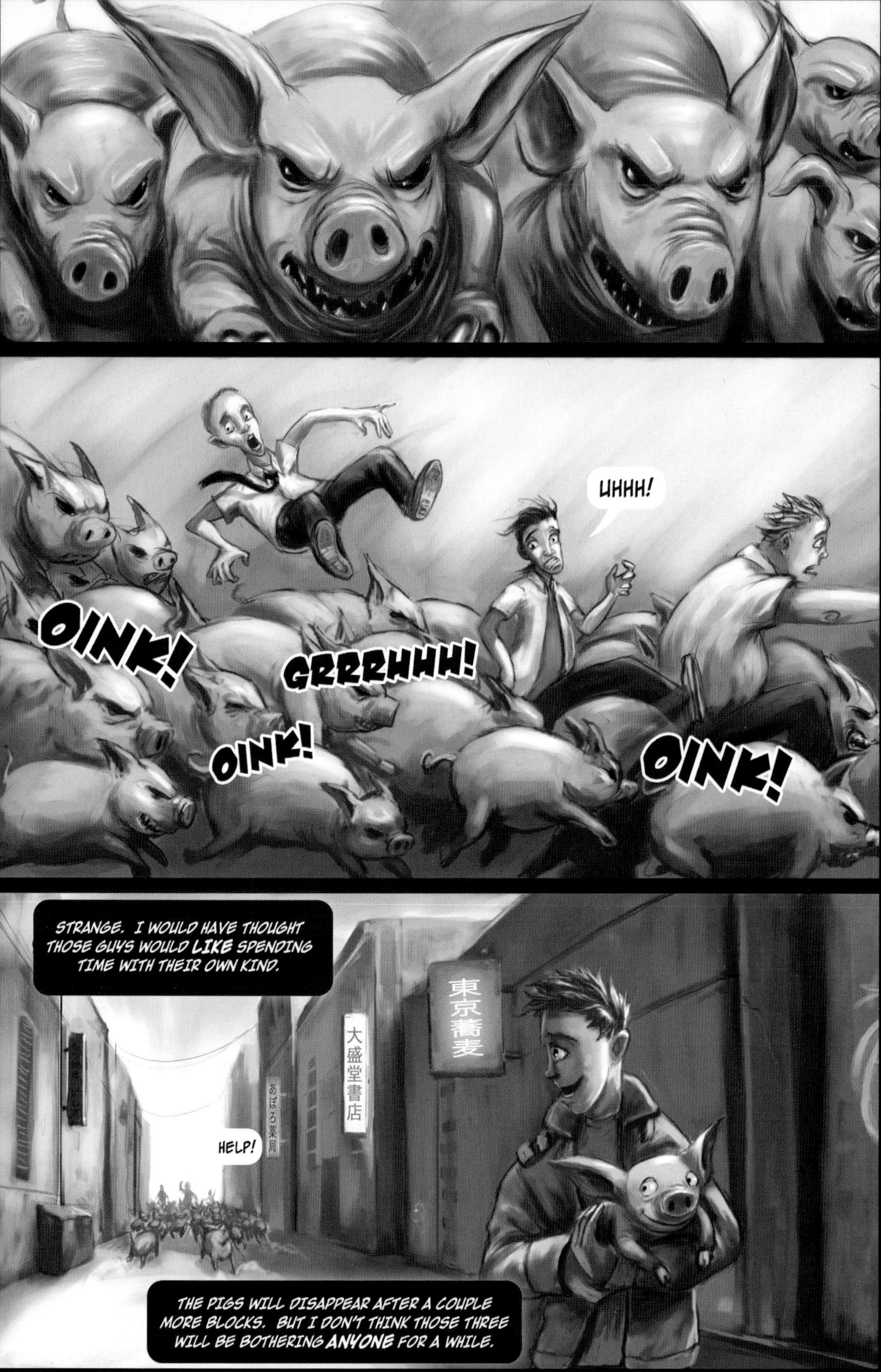
UHHH!
OINK!
GRRRHHH!
OINK!
OINK!
STRANGE. I WOULD HAVE THOUGHT THOSE GUYS WOULD **LIKE** SPENDING TIME WITH THEIR OWN KIND.
東京蕎麦
大盛堂書店
あぼろ薬局
HELP!
THE PIGS WILL DISAPPEAR AFTER A COUPLE MORE BLOCKS. BUT I DON'T THINK THOSE THREE WILL BE BOTHERING **ANYONE** FOR A WHILE.

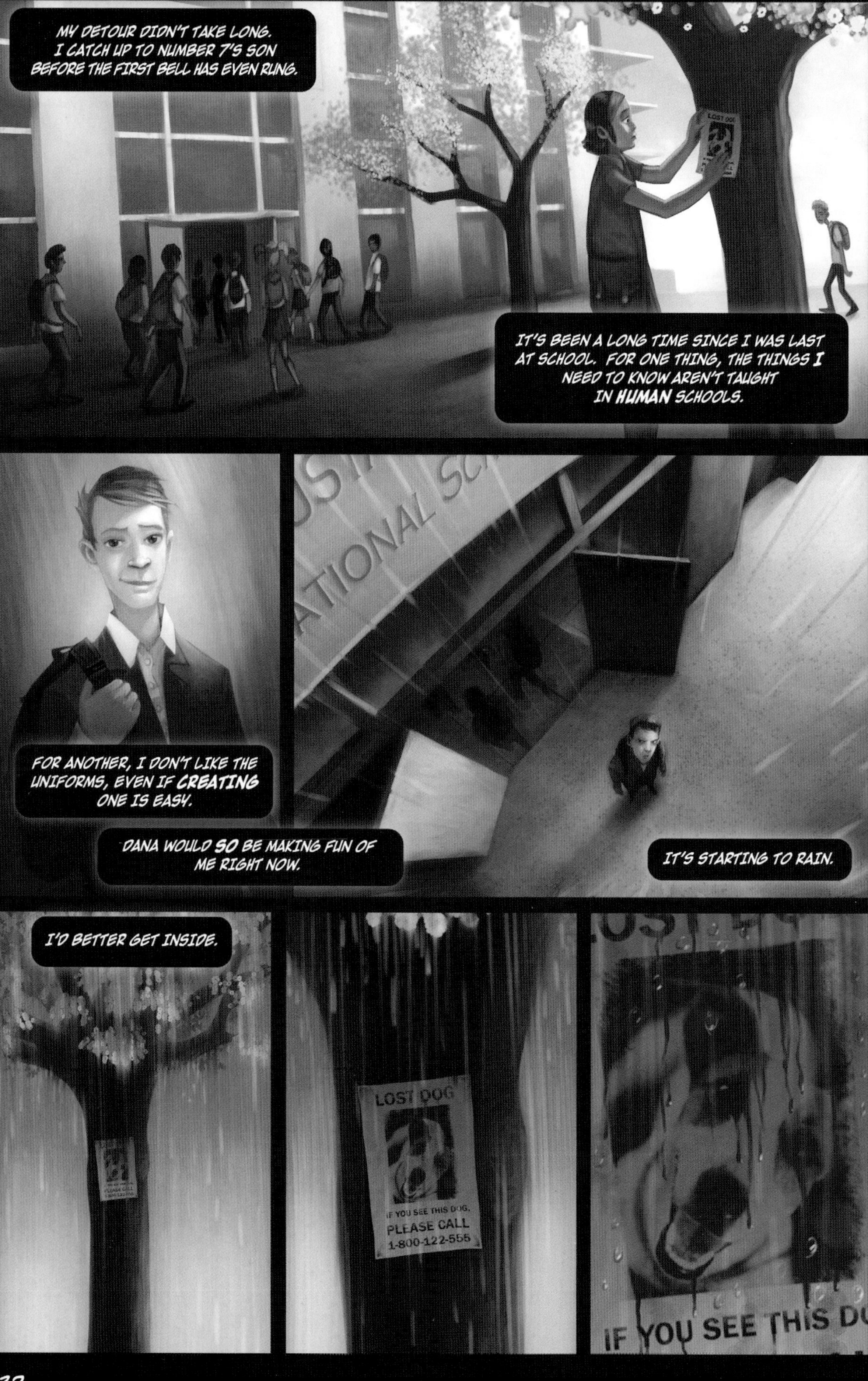
MY DETOUR DIDN'T TAKE LONG. I CATCH UP TO NUMBER 7'S SON BEFORE THE FIRST BELL HAS EVEN RUNG.
LOST DOG
IT'S BEEN A LONG TIME SINCE I WAS LAST AT SCHOOL. FOR ONE THING, THE THINGS I NEED TO KNOW AREN'T TAUGHT IN HUMAN SCHOOLS.
FOR ANOTHER, I DON'T LIKE THE UNIFORMS, EVEN IF CREATING ONE IS EASY.
DANA WOULD SO BE MAKING FUN OF ME RIGHT NOW.
IT'S STARTING TO RAIN.
I'D BETTER GET INSIDE.
LOST DOG
IF YOU SEE THIS DOG,
PLEASE CALL
1-800-122-555
IF YOU SEE THIS D

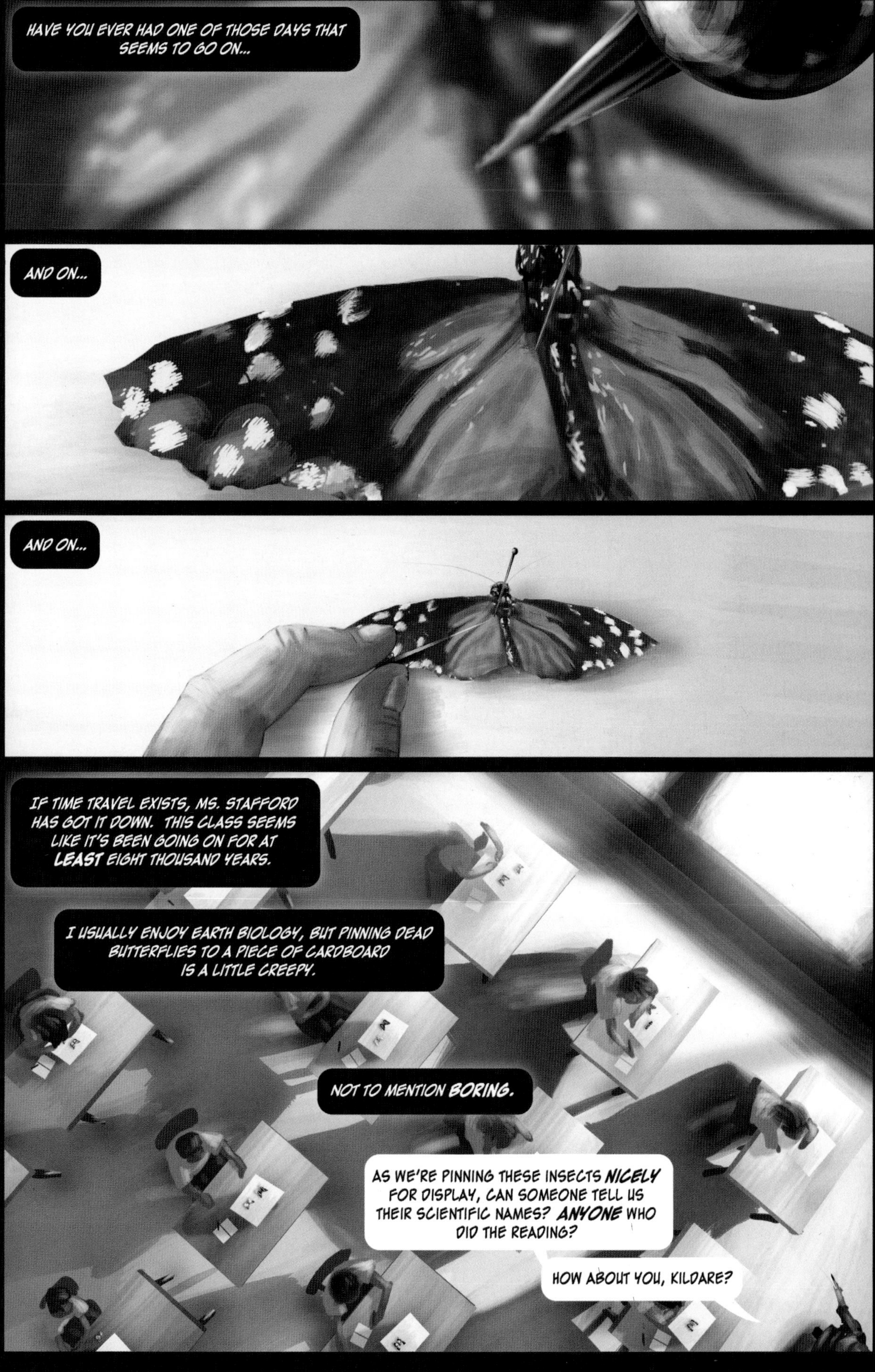
HAVE YOU EVER HAD ONE OF THOSE DAYS THAT SEEMS TO GO ON...
AND ON...
AND ON...
IF TIME TRAVEL EXISTS, MS. STAFFORD HAS GOT IT DOWN. THIS CLASS SEEMS LIKE IT'S BEEN GOING ON FOR AT LEAST EIGHT THOUSAND YEARS.
I USUALLY ENJOY EARTH BIOLOGY, BUT PINNING DEAD BUTTERFLIES TO A PIECE OF CARDBOARD IS A LITTLE CREEPY.
NOT TO MENTION BORING.
AS WE'RE PINNING THESE INSECTS NICELY FOR DISPLAY, CAN SOMEONE TELL US THEIR SCIENTIFIC NAMES? ANYONE WHO DID THE READING?
HOW ABOUT YOU, KILDARE?

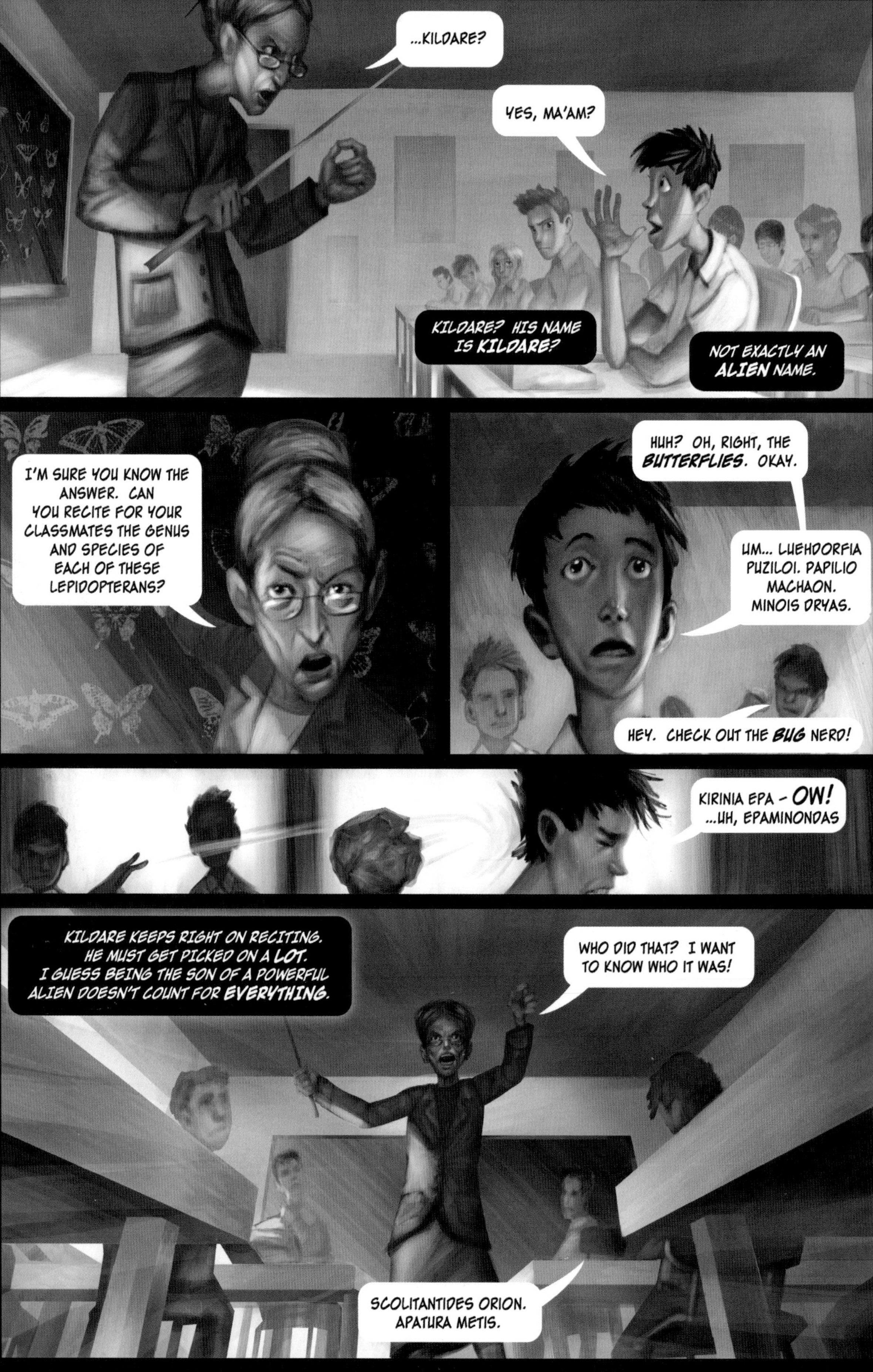
...KILDARE?
YES, MA'AM?
KILDARE? HIS NAME IS KILDARE?
NOT EXACTLY AN ALIEN NAME.
I'M SURE YOU KNOW THE ANSWER. CAN YOU RECITE FOR YOUR CLASSMATES THE GENUS AND SPECIES OF EACH OF THESE LEPIDOPTERANS?
HUH? OH, RIGHT, THE BUTTERFLIES. OKAY.
UM... LUEHDORFIA PUZILOI. PAPILIO MACHAON. MINOIS DRYAS.
HEY. CHECK OUT THE BUG NERD!
KIRINIA EPA - OW! ...UH, EPAMINONDAS
KILDARE KEEPS RIGHT ON RECITING. HE MUST GET PICKED ON A LOT. I GUESS BEING THE SON OF A POWERFUL ALIEN DOESN'T COUNT FOR EVERYTHING.
WHO DID THAT? I WANT TO KNOW WHO IT WAS!
SCOLITANTIDES ORION. APATURA METIS.

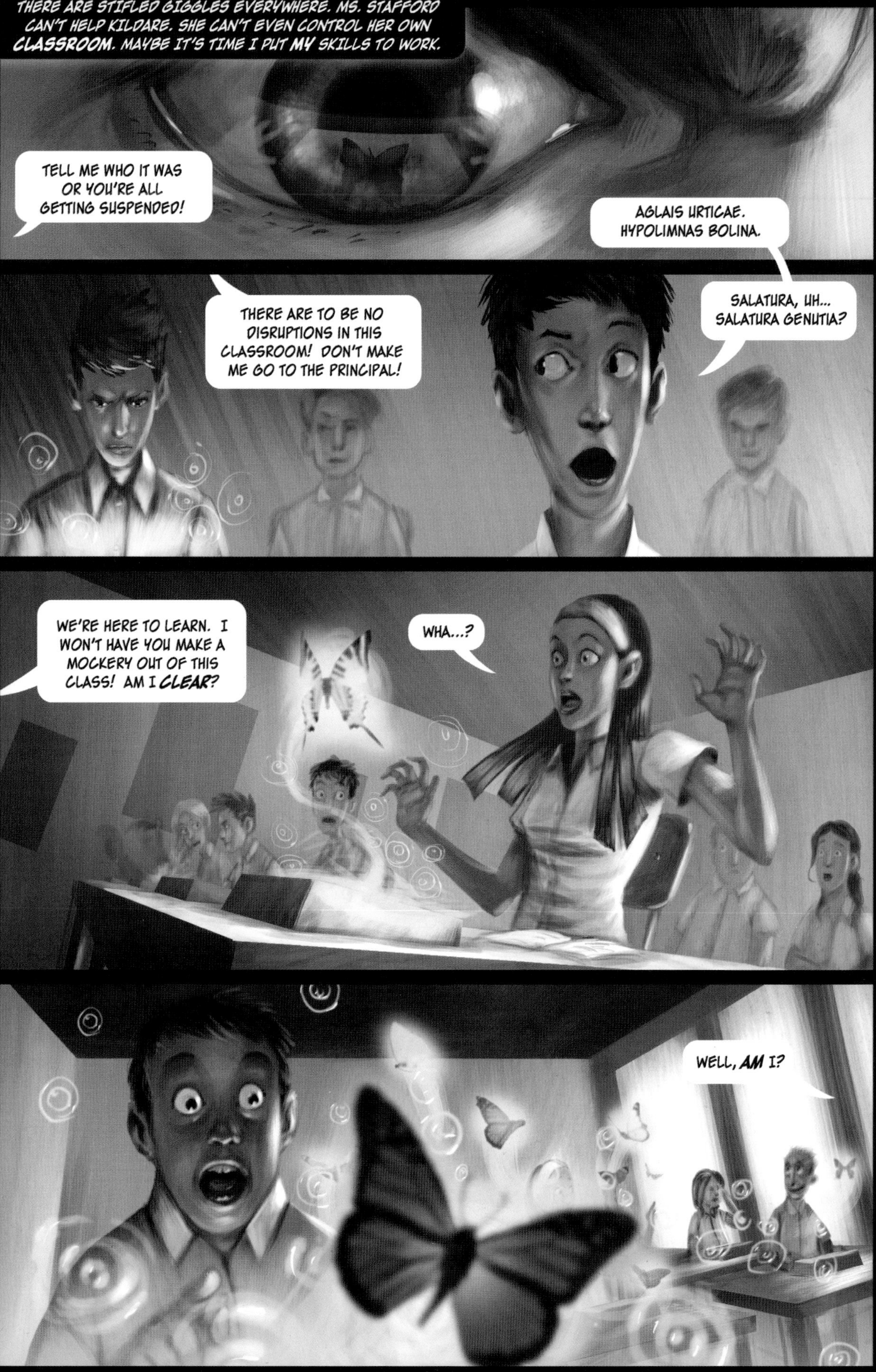
THERE ARE STIFLED GIGGLES EVERYWHERE. MS. STAFFORD CAN'T HELP KILDARE. SHE CAN'T EVEN CONTROL HER OWN CLASSROOM. MAYBE IT'S TIME I PUT MY SKILLS TO WORK.
TELL ME WHO IT WAS OR YOU'RE ALL GETTING SUSPENDED!
AGLAIS URTICAE. HYPOLIMNAS BOLINA.
THERE ARE TO BE NO DISRUPTIONS IN THIS CLASSROOM! DON'T MAKE ME GO TO THE PRINCIPAL!
SALATURA, UH... SALATURA GENUTIA?
WE'RE HERE TO LEARN. I WON'T HAVE YOU MAKE A MOCKERY OUT OF THIS CLASS! AM I CLEAR?
WHA...?
WELL, AM I?

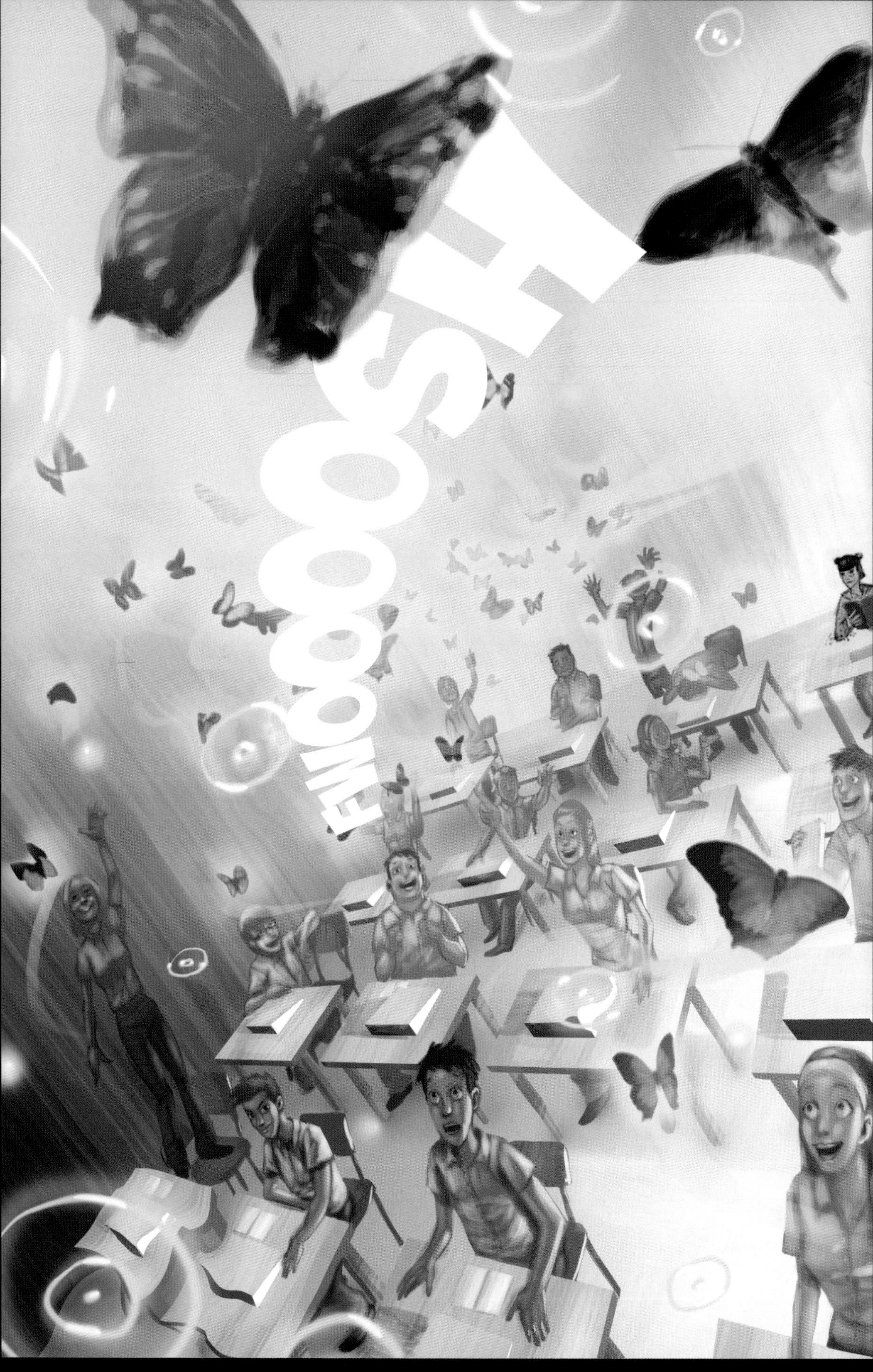
FWOOOOOSH

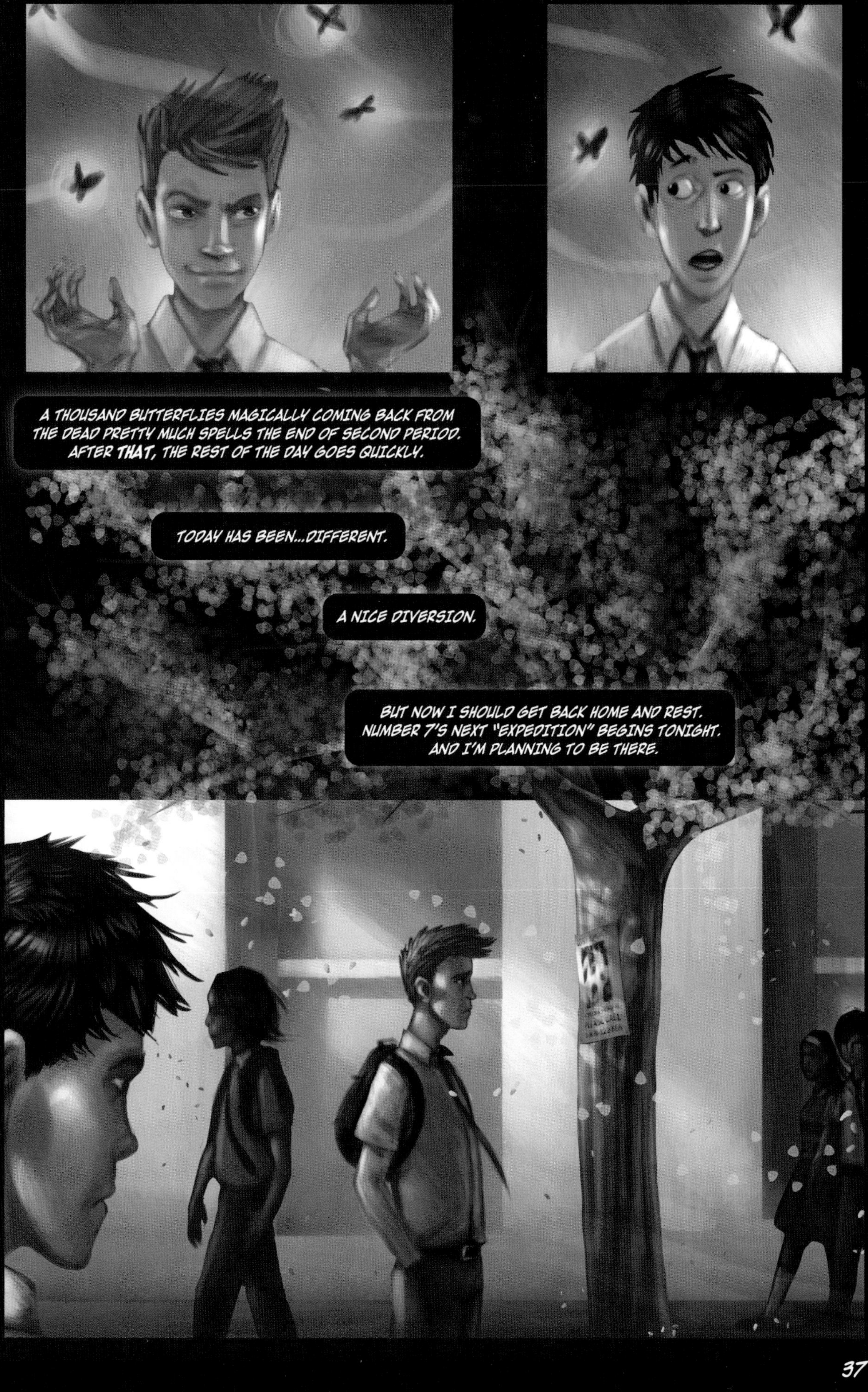
A THOUSAND BUTTERFLIES MAGICALLY COMING BACK FROM THE DEAD PRETTY MUCH SPELLS THE END OF SECOND PERIOD. AFTER **THAT,** THE REST OF THE DAY GOES QUICKLY.
TODAY HAS BEEN...DIFFERENT.
A NICE DIVERSION.
BUT NOW I SHOULD GET BACK HOME AND REST. NUMBER 7'S NEXT "EXPEDITION" BEGINS TONIGHT. AND I'M PLANNING TO BE THERE.

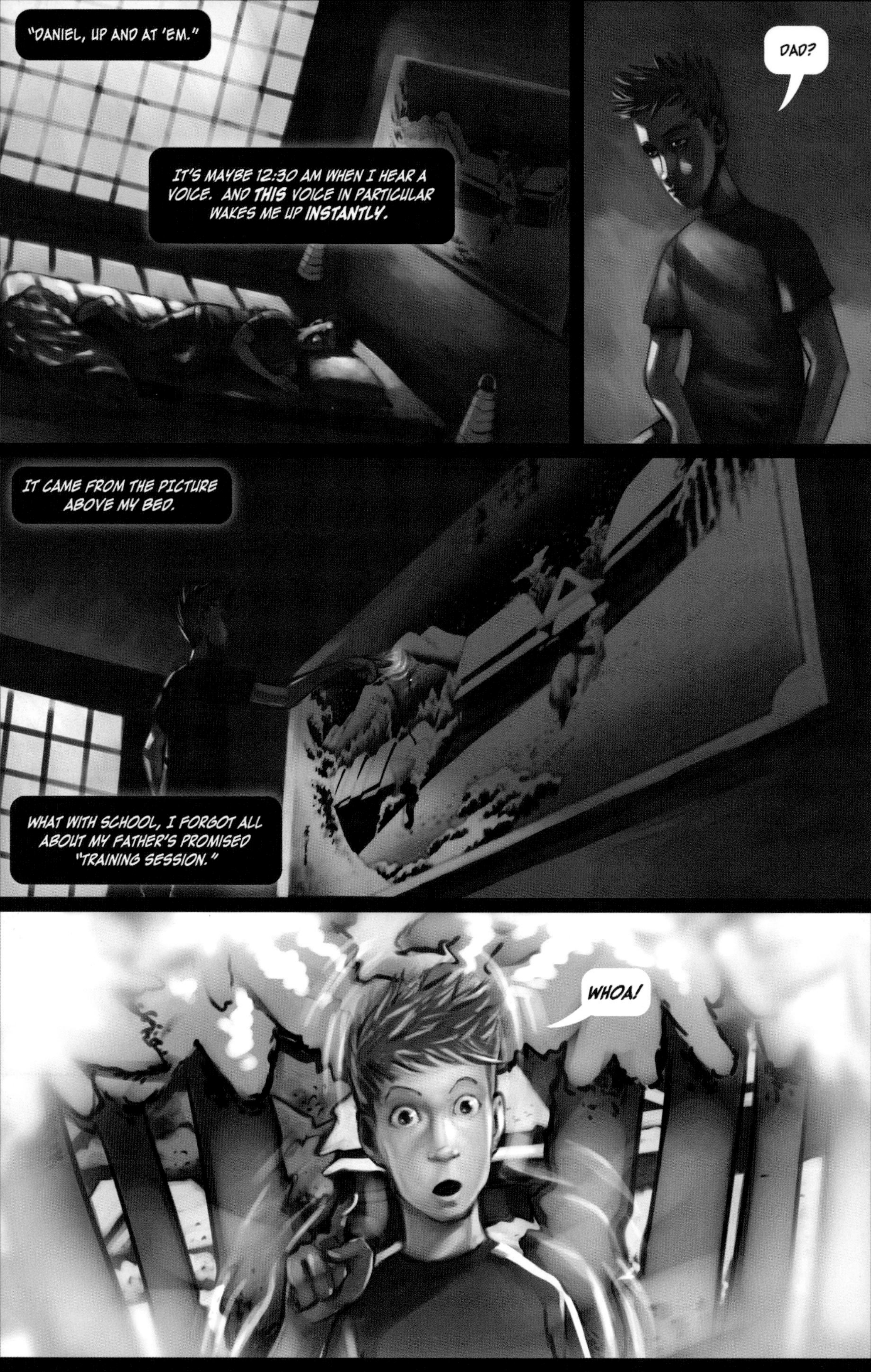
"DANIEL, UP AND AT 'EM."
IT'S MAYBE 12:30 AM WHEN I HEAR A VOICE. AND THIS VOICE IN PARTICULAR WAKES ME UP INSTANTLY.
DAD?
IT CAME FROM THE PICTURE ABOVE MY BED.
WHAT WITH SCHOOL, I FORGOT ALL ABOUT MY FATHER'S PROMISED "TRAINING SESSION."
WHOA!

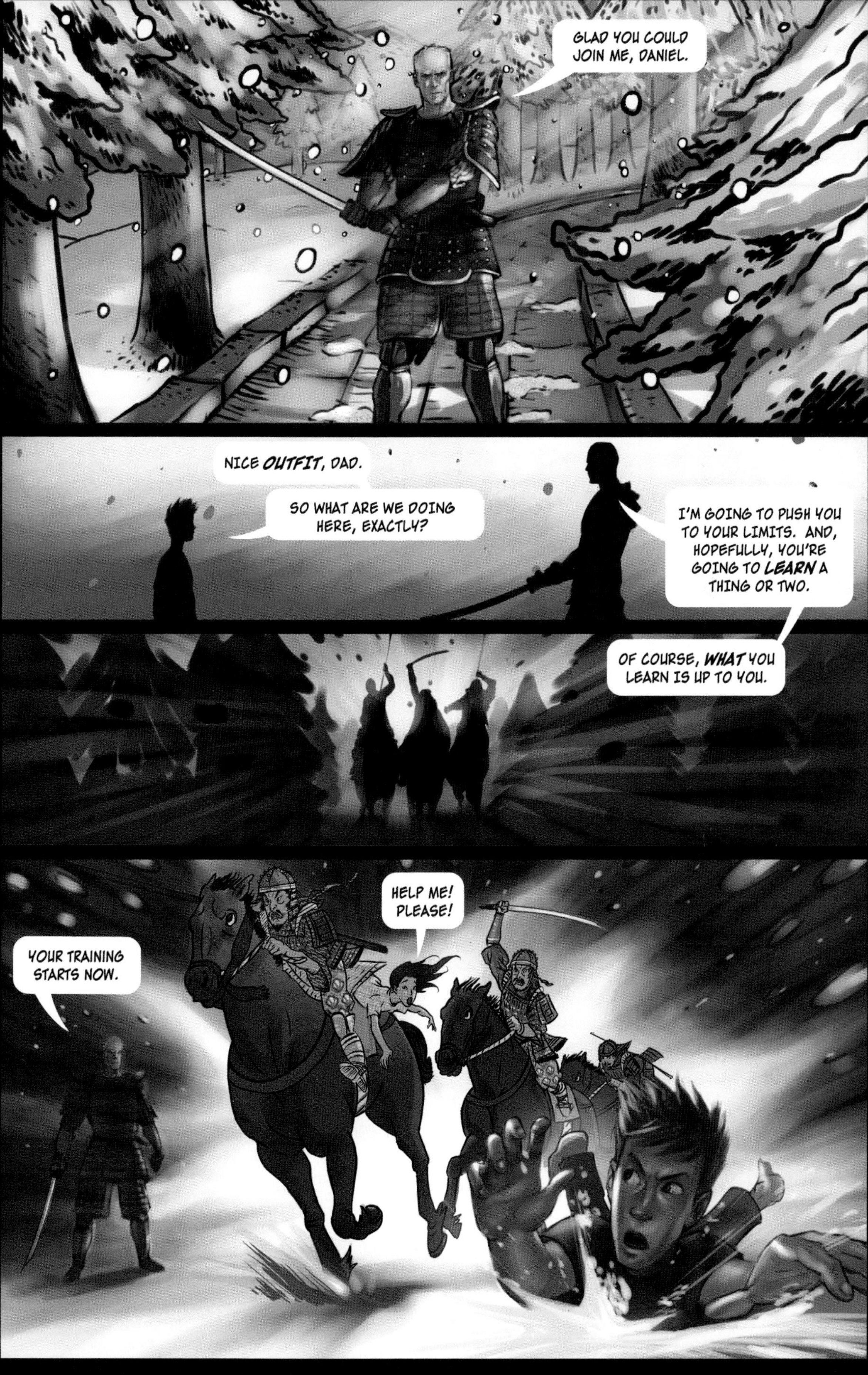
GLAD YOU COULD JOIN ME, DANIEL.
NICE OUTFIT, DAD.
SO WHAT ARE WE DOING HERE, EXACTLY?
I'M GOING TO PUSH YOU TO YOUR LIMITS. AND, HOPEFULLY, YOU'RE GOING TO LEARN A THING OR TWO.
OF COURSE, WHAT YOU LEARN IS UP TO YOU.
YOUR TRAINING STARTS NOW.
HELP ME! PLEASE!

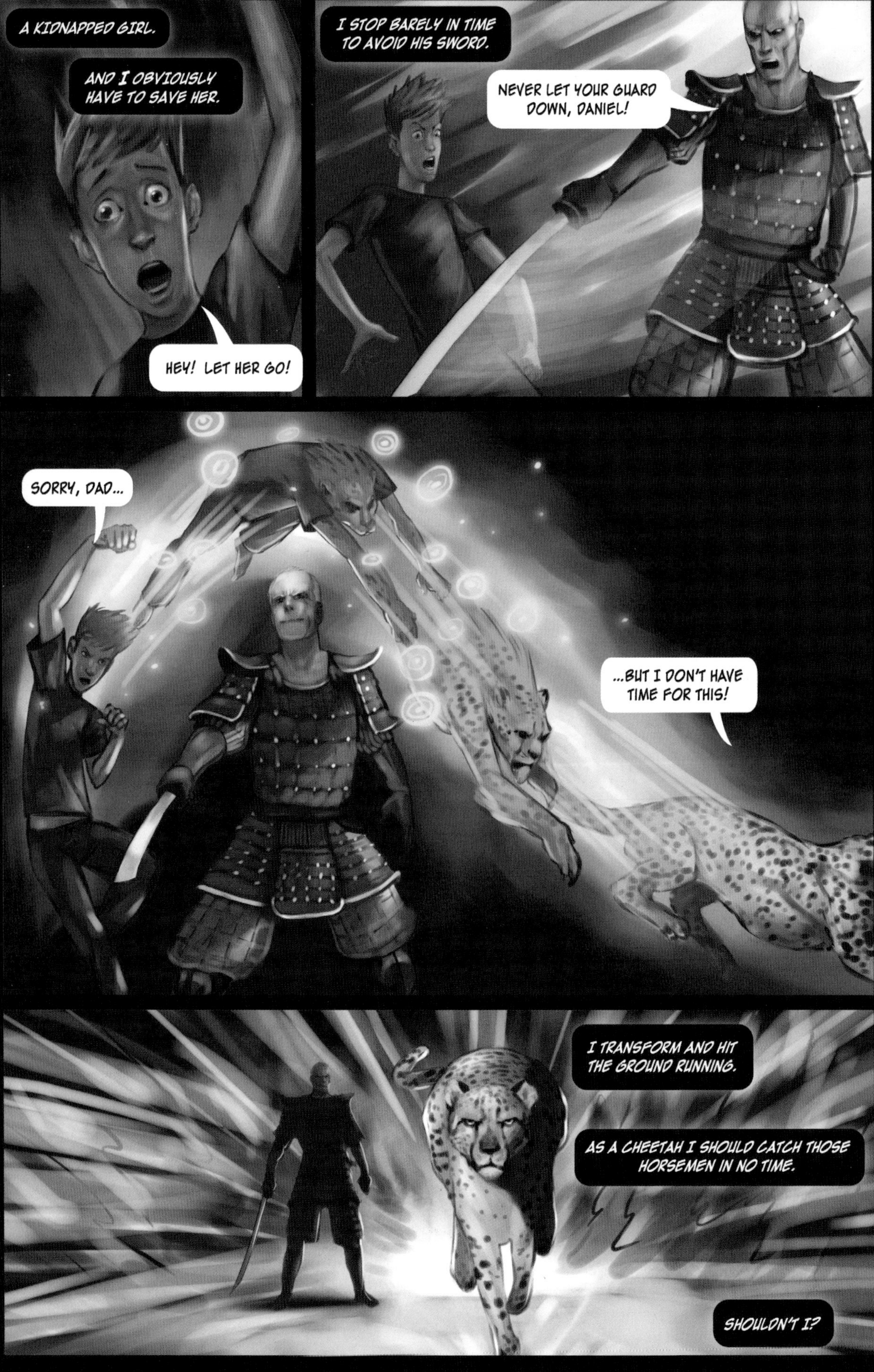
A KIDNAPPED GIRL.
AND I OBVIOUSLY HAVE TO SAVE HER.
HEY! LET HER GO!
I STOP BARELY IN TIME TO AVOID HIS SWORD.
NEVER LET YOUR GUARD DOWN, DANIEL!
SORRY, DAD...
...BUT I DON'T HAVE TIME FOR THIS!
I TRANSFORM AND HIT THE GROUND RUNNING.
AS A CHEETAH I SHOULD CATCH THOSE HORSEMEN IN NO TIME.
SHOULDN'T I?

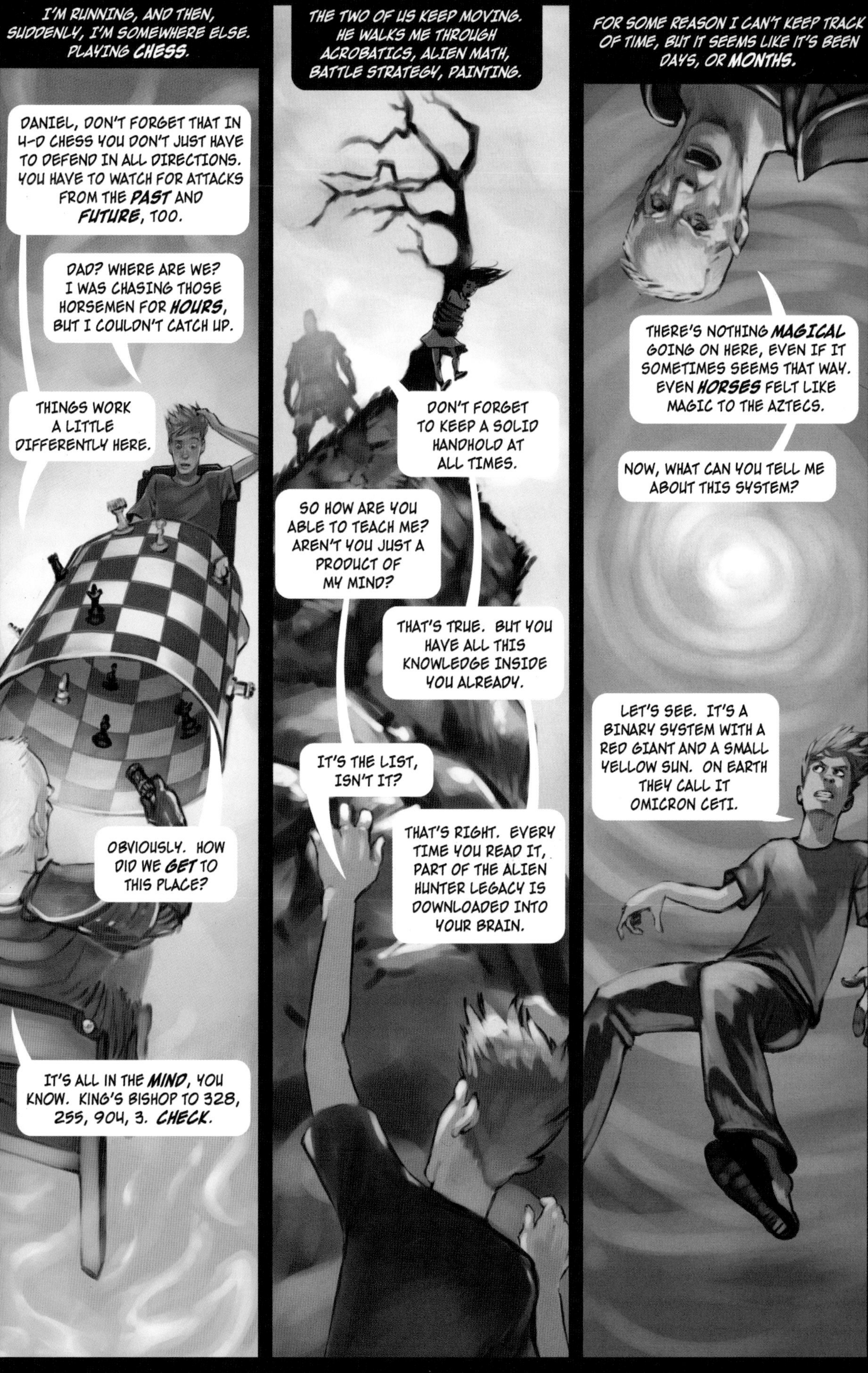
I'M RUNNING, AND THEN, SUDDENLY, I'M SOMEWHERE ELSE. PLAYING CHESS.
DANIEL, DON'T FORGET THAT IN 4-D CHESS YOU DON'T JUST HAVE TO DEFEND IN ALL DIRECTIONS. YOU HAVE TO WATCH FOR ATTACKS FROM THE PAST AND FUTURE, TOO.
DAD? WHERE ARE WE? I WAS CHASING THOSE HORSEMEN FOR HOURS, BUT I COULDN'T CATCH UP.
THINGS WORK A LITTLE DIFFERENTLY HERE.
OBVIOUSLY. HOW DID WE GET TO THIS PLACE?
IT'S ALL IN THE MIND, YOU KNOW. KING'S BISHOP TO 328, 255, 904, 3. CHECK.
THE TWO OF US KEEP MOVING. HE WALKS ME THROUGH ACROBATICS, ALIEN MATH, BATTLE STRATEGY, PAINTING.
DON'T FORGET TO KEEP A SOLID HANDHOLD AT ALL TIMES.
SO HOW ARE YOU ABLE TO TEACH ME? AREN'T YOU JUST A PRODUCT OF MY MIND?
THAT'S TRUE. BUT YOU HAVE ALL THIS KNOWLEDGE INSIDE YOU ALREADY.
IT'S THE LIST, ISN'T IT?
THAT'S RIGHT. EVERY TIME YOU READ IT, PART OF THE ALIEN HUNTER LEGACY IS DOWNLOADED INTO YOUR BRAIN.
FOR SOME REASON I CAN'T KEEP TRACK OF TIME, BUT IT SEEMS LIKE IT'S BEEN DAYS, OR MONTHS.
THERE'S NOTHING MAGICAL GOING ON HERE, EVEN IF IT SOMETIMES SEEMS THAT WAY. EVEN HORSES FELT LIKE MAGIC TO THE AZTECS.
NOW, WHAT CAN YOU TELL ME ABOUT THIS SYSTEM?
LET'S SEE. IT'S A BINARY SYSTEM WITH A RED GIANT AND A SMALL YELLOW SUN. ON EARTH THEY CALL IT OMICRON CETI.

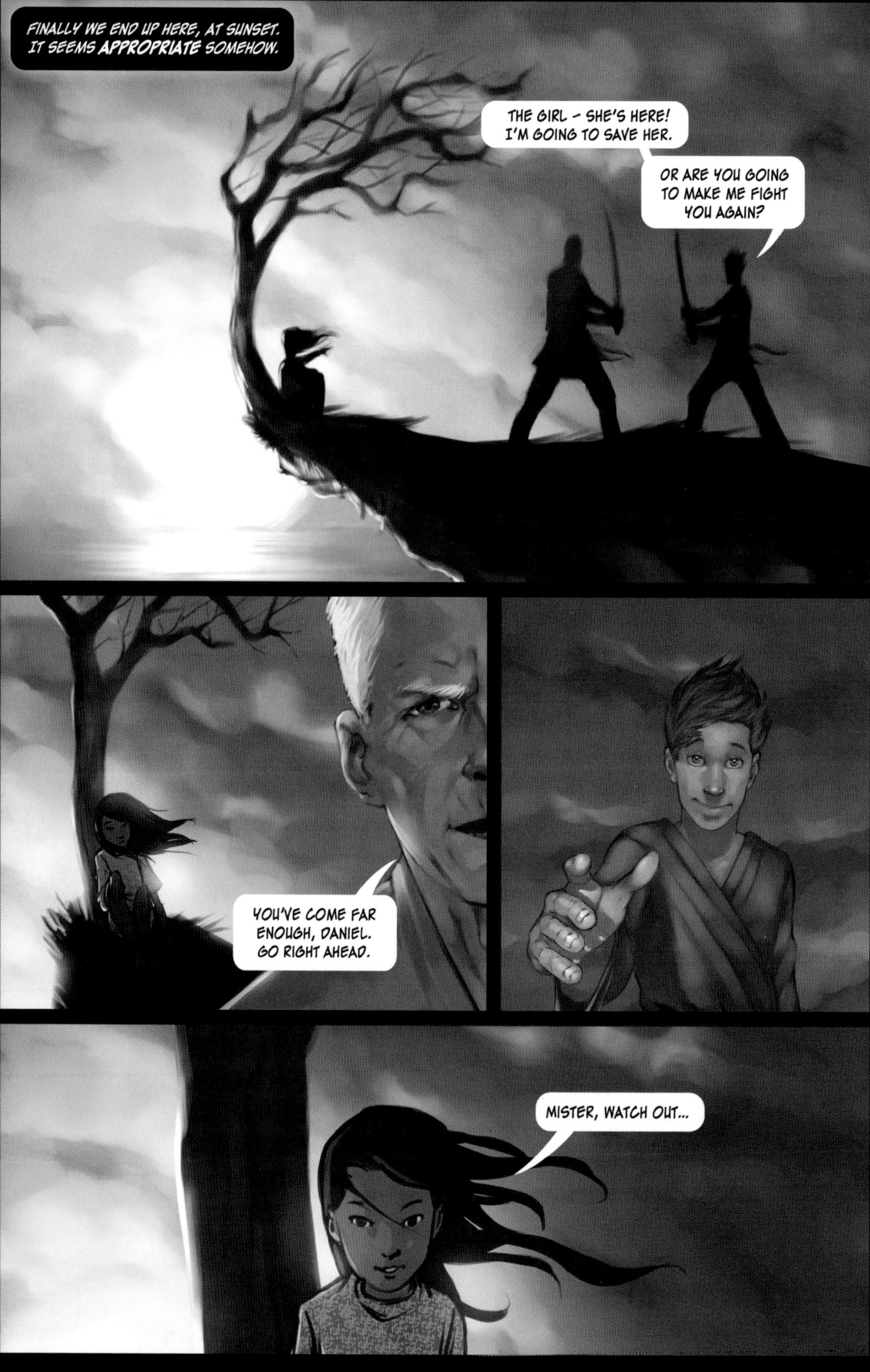
FINALLY WE END UP HERE, AT SUNSET. IT SEEMS APPROPRIATE SOMEHOW.
THE GIRL - SHE'S HERE! I'M GOING TO SAVE HER.
OR ARE YOU GOING TO MAKE ME FIGHT YOU AGAIN?
YOU'VE COME FAR ENOUGH, DANIEL. GO RIGHT AHEAD.
MISTER, WATCH OUT...

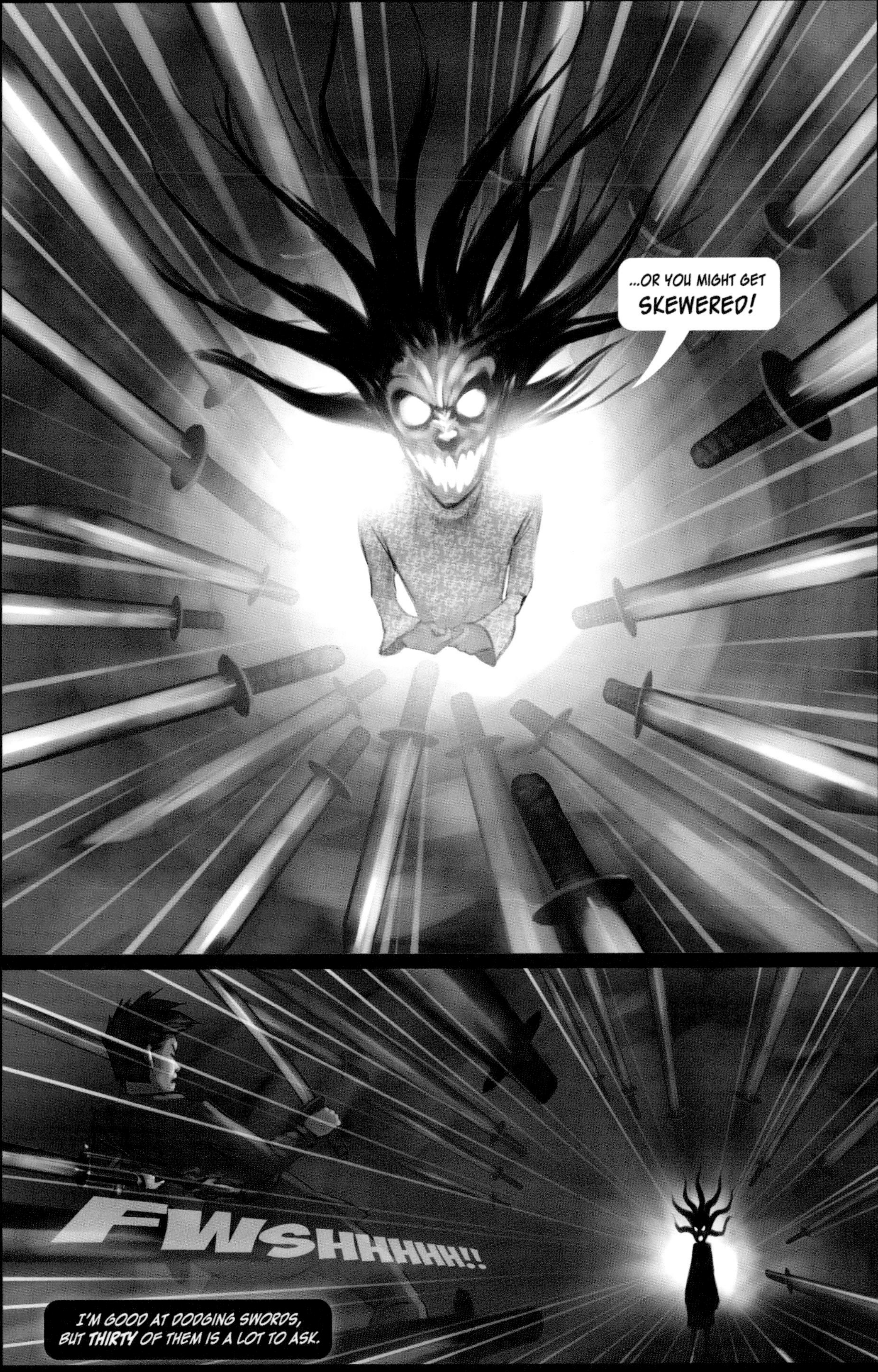
...OR YOU MIGHT GET SKEWERED!
FWSHHHHH!!
I'M GOOD AT DODGING SWORDS, BUT THIRTY OF THEM IS A LOT TO ASK.

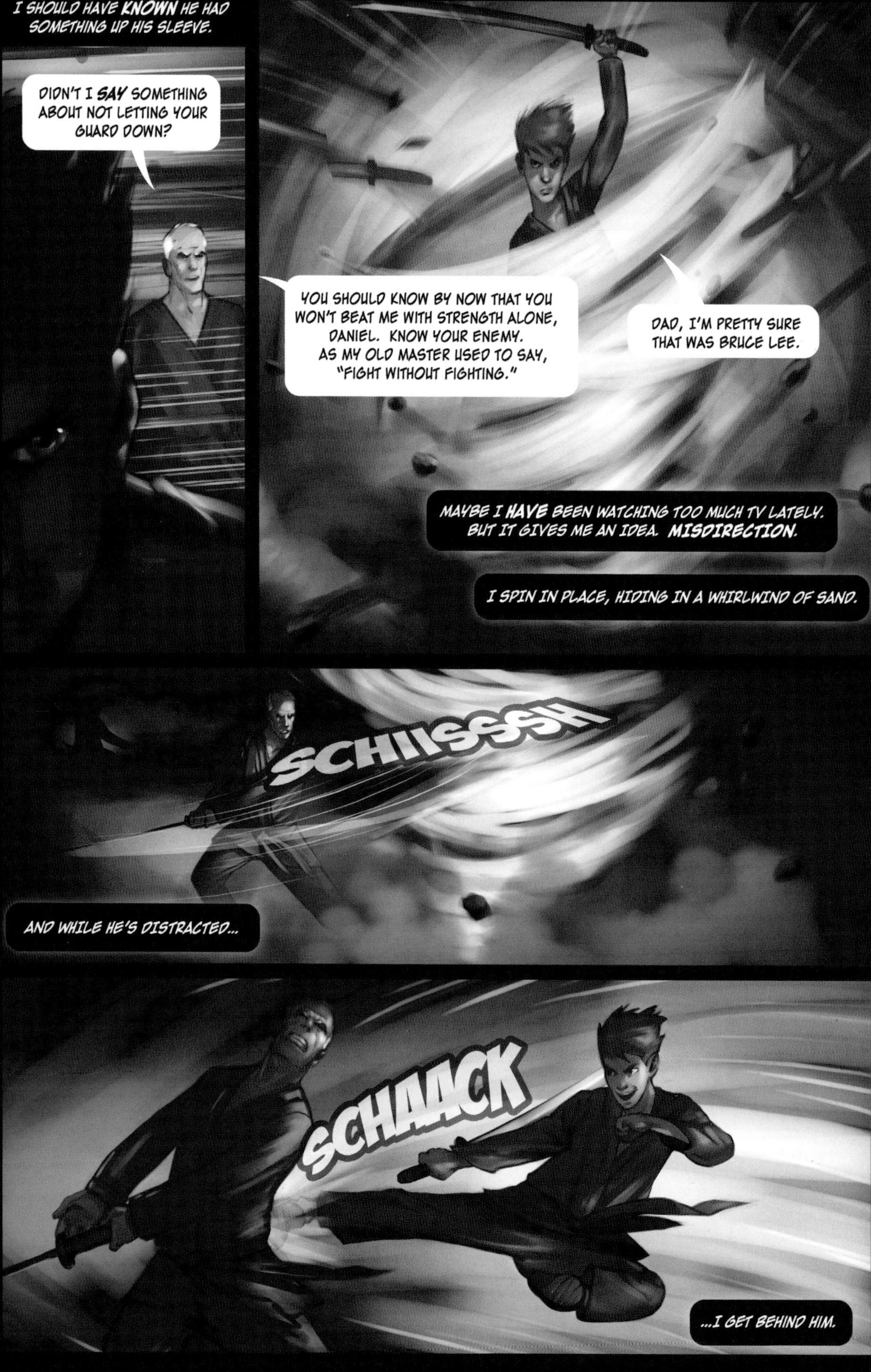
I SHOULD HAVE KNOWN HE HAD SOMETHING UP HIS SLEEVE.
DIDN'T I SAY SOMETHING ABOUT NOT LETTING YOUR GUARD DOWN?
YOU SHOULD KNOW BY NOW THAT YOU WON'T BEAT ME WITH STRENGTH ALONE, DANIEL. KNOW YOUR ENEMY. AS MY OLD MASTER USED TO SAY, "FIGHT WITHOUT FIGHTING."
DAD, I'M PRETTY SURE THAT WAS BRUCE LEE.
MAYBE I HAVE BEEN WATCHING TOO MUCH TV LATELY. BUT IT GIVES ME AN IDEA. MISDIRECTION.
I SPIN IN PLACE, HIDING IN A WHIRLWIND OF SAND.
SCHIISSSH
AND WHILE HE'S DISTRACTED...
SCHAACK
...I GET BEHIND HIM.

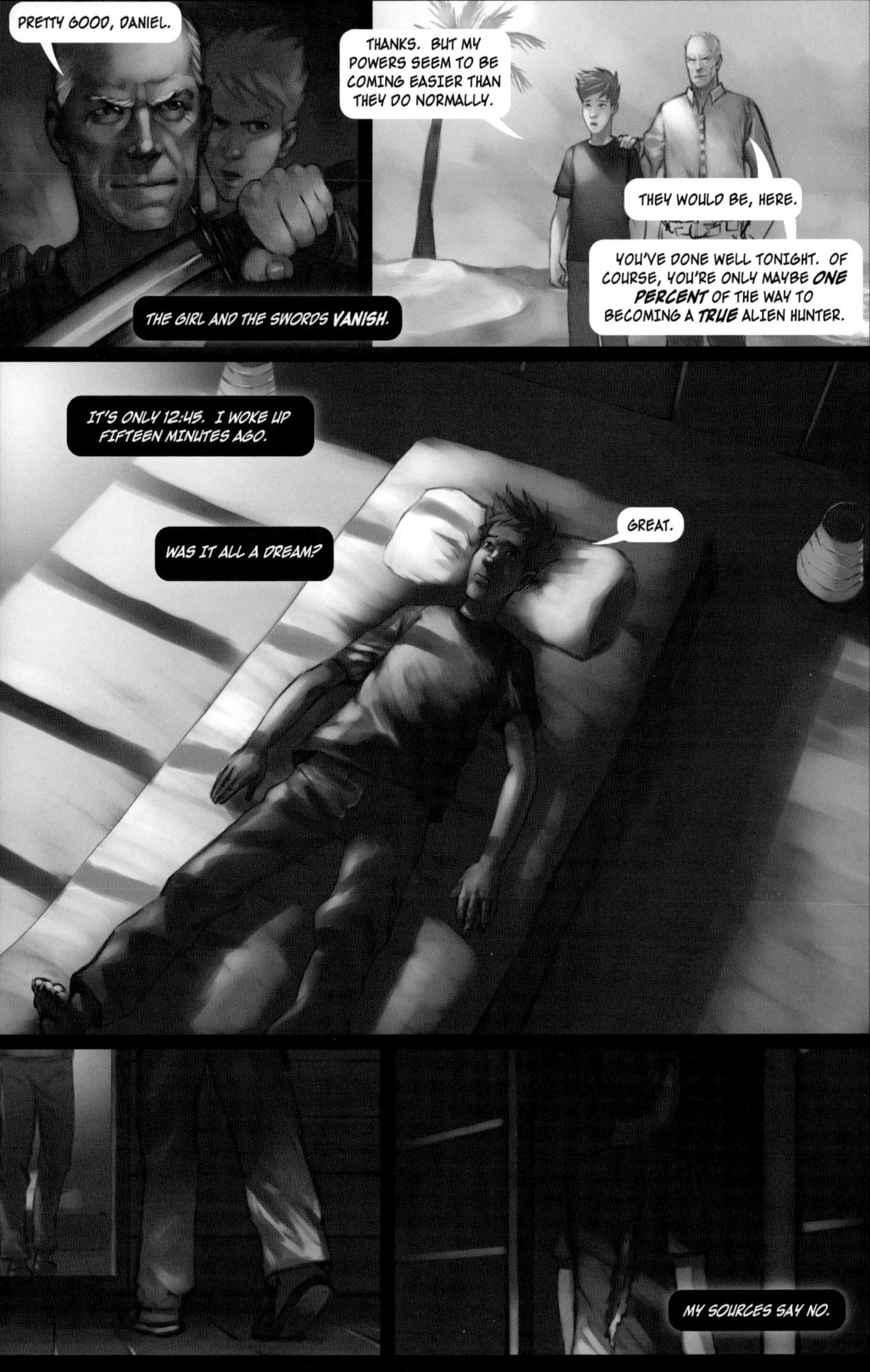

PRETTY GOOD, DANIEL.
THE GIRL AND THE SWORDS VANISH.
THANKS. BUT MY POWERS SEEM TO BE COMING EASIER THAN THEY DO NORMALLY.
THEY WOULD BE, HERE.
YOU'VE DONE WELL TONIGHT. OF COURSE, YOU'RE ONLY MAYBE ONE PERCENT OF THE WAY TO BECOMING A TRUE ALIEN HUNTER.
IT'S ONLY 12:45. I WOKE UP FIFTEEN MINUTES AGO.
WAS IT ALL A DREAM?
GREAT.
MY SOURCES SAY NO.

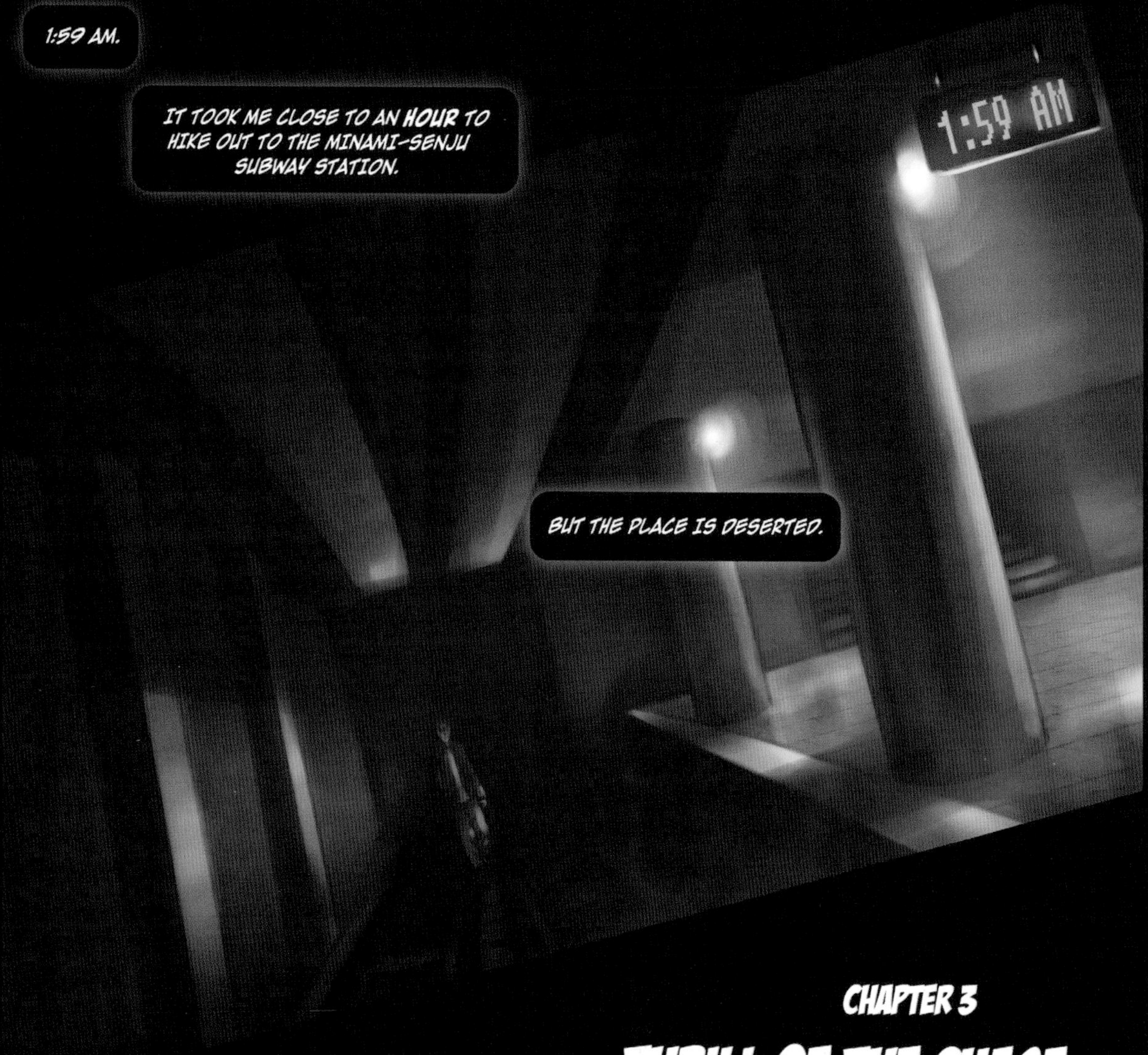
1:59 AM.
IT TOOK ME CLOSE TO AN HOUR TO HIKE OUT TO THE MINAMI-SENJU SUBWAY STATION.
1:59 AM
BUT THE PLACE IS DESERTED.

CHAPTER 3

THRILL OF THE CHASE

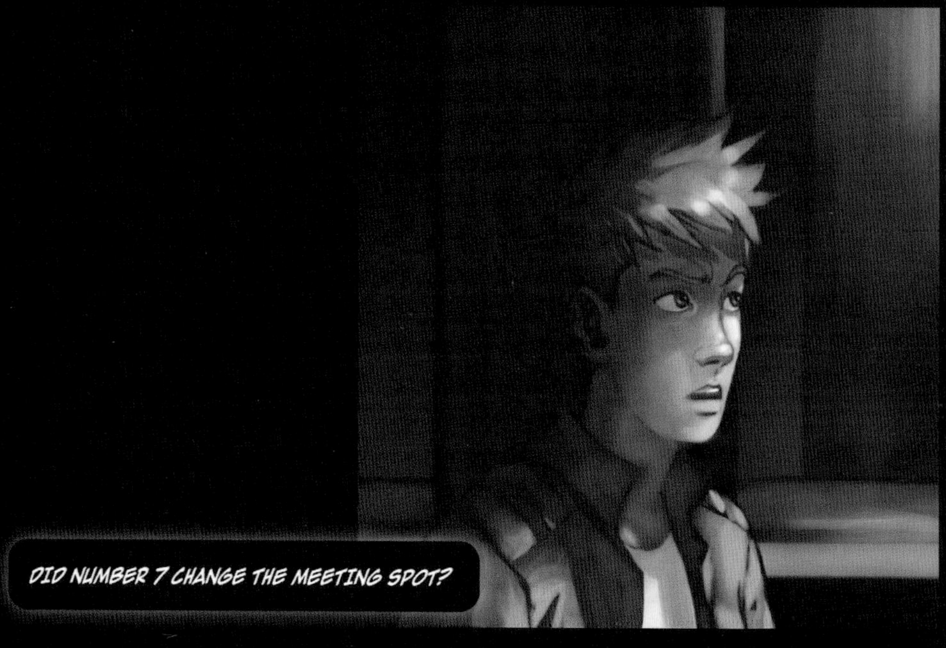
DID NUMBER 7 CHANGE THE MEETING SPOT?

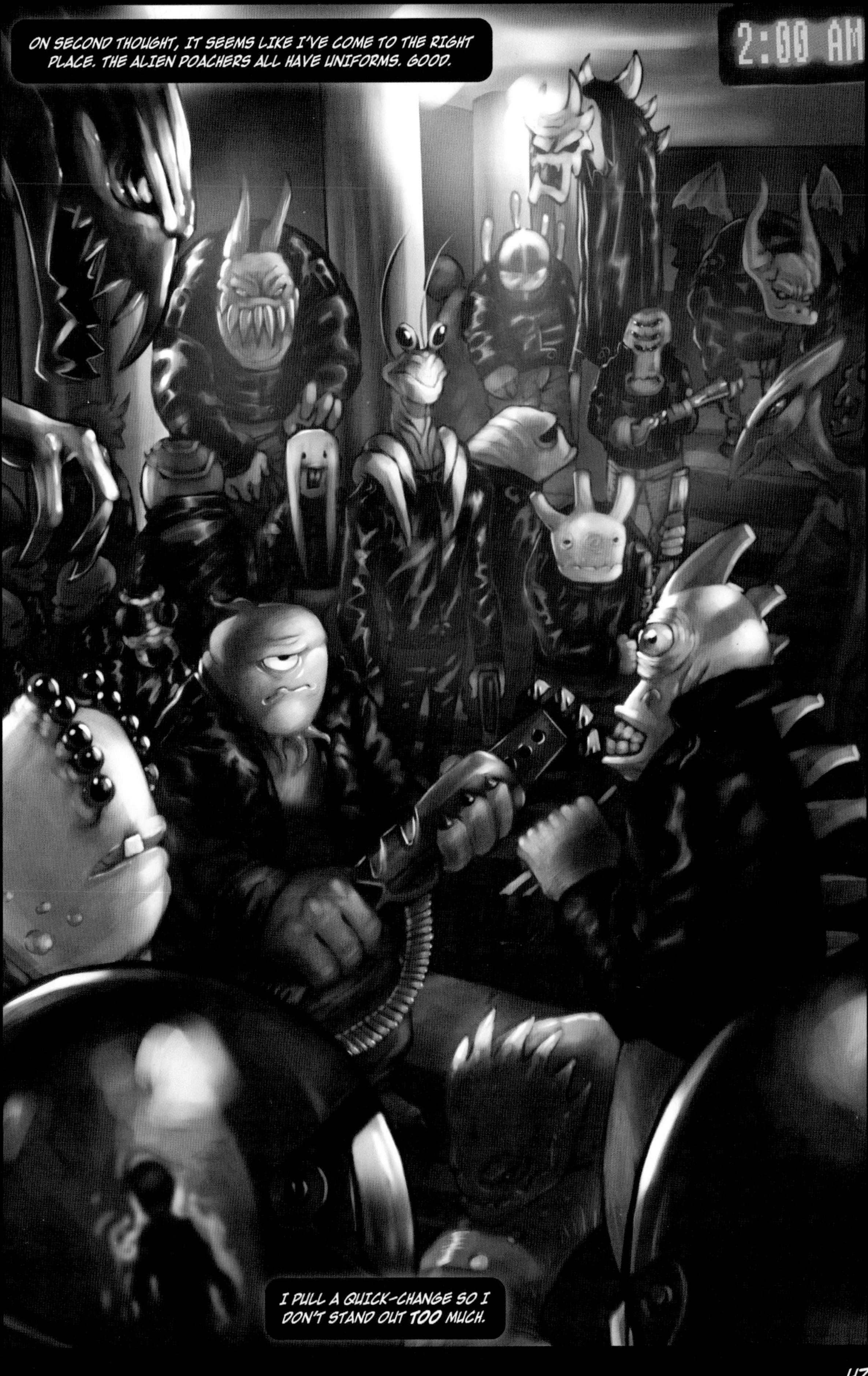
ON SECOND THOUGHT, IT SEEMS LIKE I'VE COME TO THE RIGHT PLACE. THE ALIEN POACHERS ALL HAVE UNIFORMS. GOOD.
2:00 AM
I PULL A QUICK-CHANGE SO I DON'T STAND OUT **TOO** MUCH.

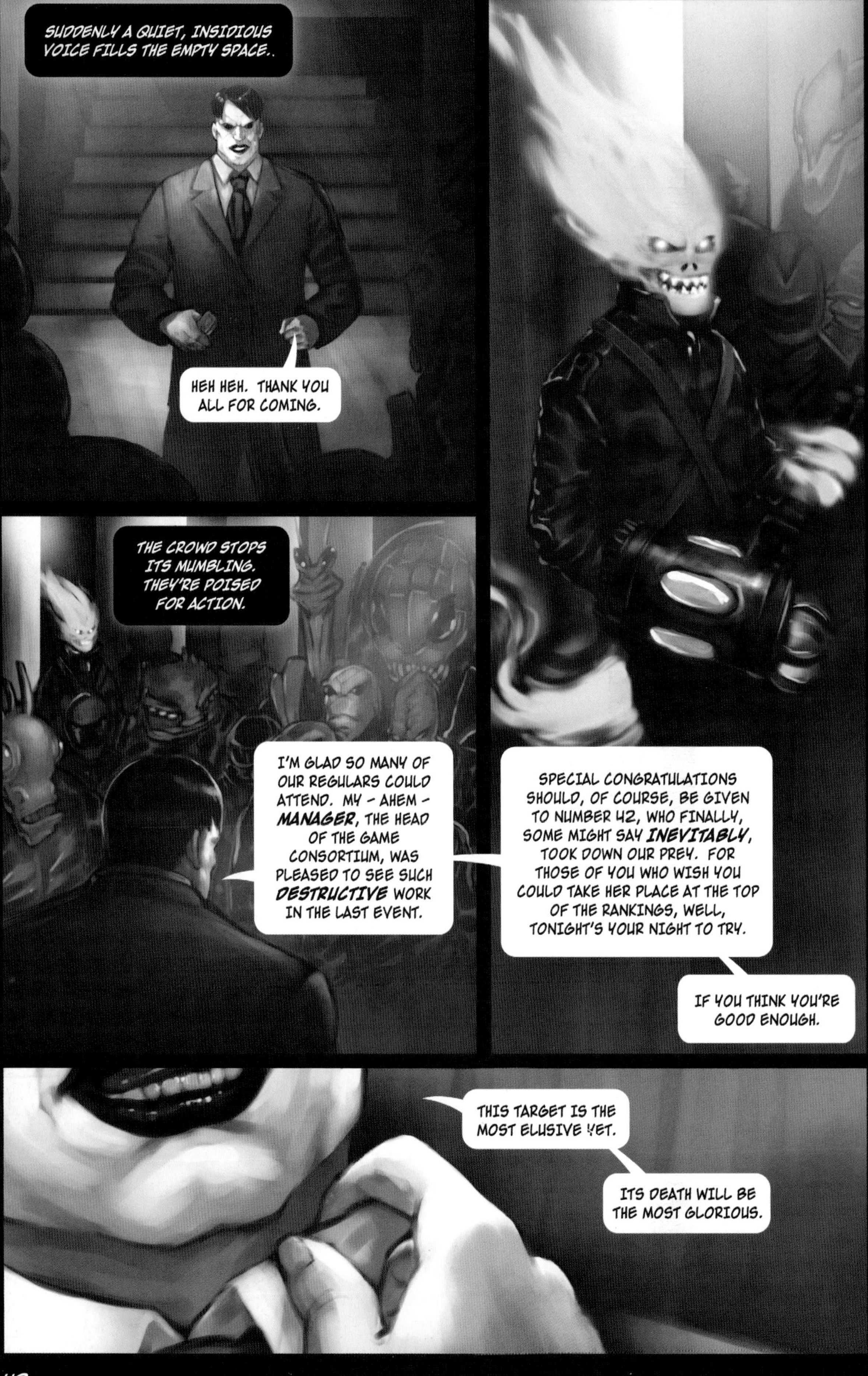
SUDDENLY A QUIET, INSIDIOUS VOICE FILLS THE EMPTY SPACE..
HEH HEH. THANK YOU ALL FOR COMING.
THE CROWD STOPS ITS MUMBLING. THEY'RE POISED FOR ACTION.
I'M GLAD SO MANY OF OUR REGULARS COULD ATTEND. MY - AHEM - MANAGER, THE HEAD OF THE GAME CONSORTIUM, WAS PLEASED TO SEE SUCH DESTRUCTIVE WORK IN THE LAST EVENT.
SPECIAL CONGRATULATIONS SHOULD, OF COURSE, BE GIVEN TO NUMBER 42, WHO FINALLY, SOME MIGHT SAY INEVITABLY, TOOK DOWN OUR PREY. FOR THOSE OF YOU WHO WISH YOU COULD TAKE HER PLACE AT THE TOP OF THE RANKINGS, WELL, TONIGHT'S YOUR NIGHT TO TRY.
IF YOU THINK YOU'RE GOOD ENOUGH.
THIS TARGET IS THE MOST ELUSIVE YET.
ITS DEATH WILL BE THE MOST GLORIOUS.

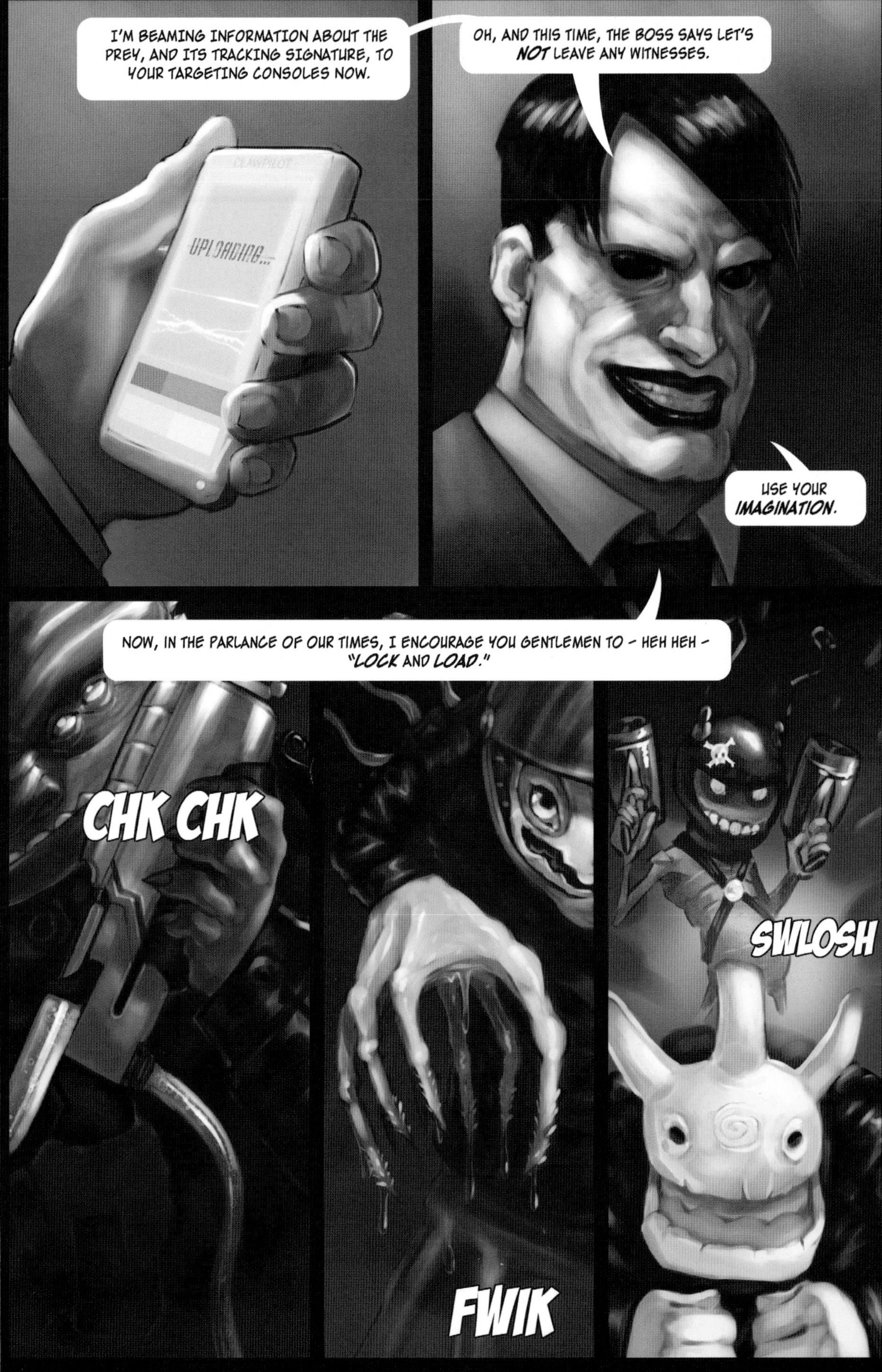
I'M BEAMING INFORMATION ABOUT THE PREY, AND ITS TRACKING SIGNATURE, TO YOUR TARGETING CONSOLES NOW.
CLAWPILOT
UPLOADING...
OH, AND THIS TIME, THE BOSS SAYS LET'S *NOT* LEAVE ANY WITNESSES.
USE YOUR *IMAGINATION*.
NOW, IN THE PARLANCE OF OUR TIMES, I ENCOURAGE YOU GENTLEMEN TO - HEH HEH - "*LOCK* AND *LOAD*."
CHK CHK
FWIK
SWLOSH

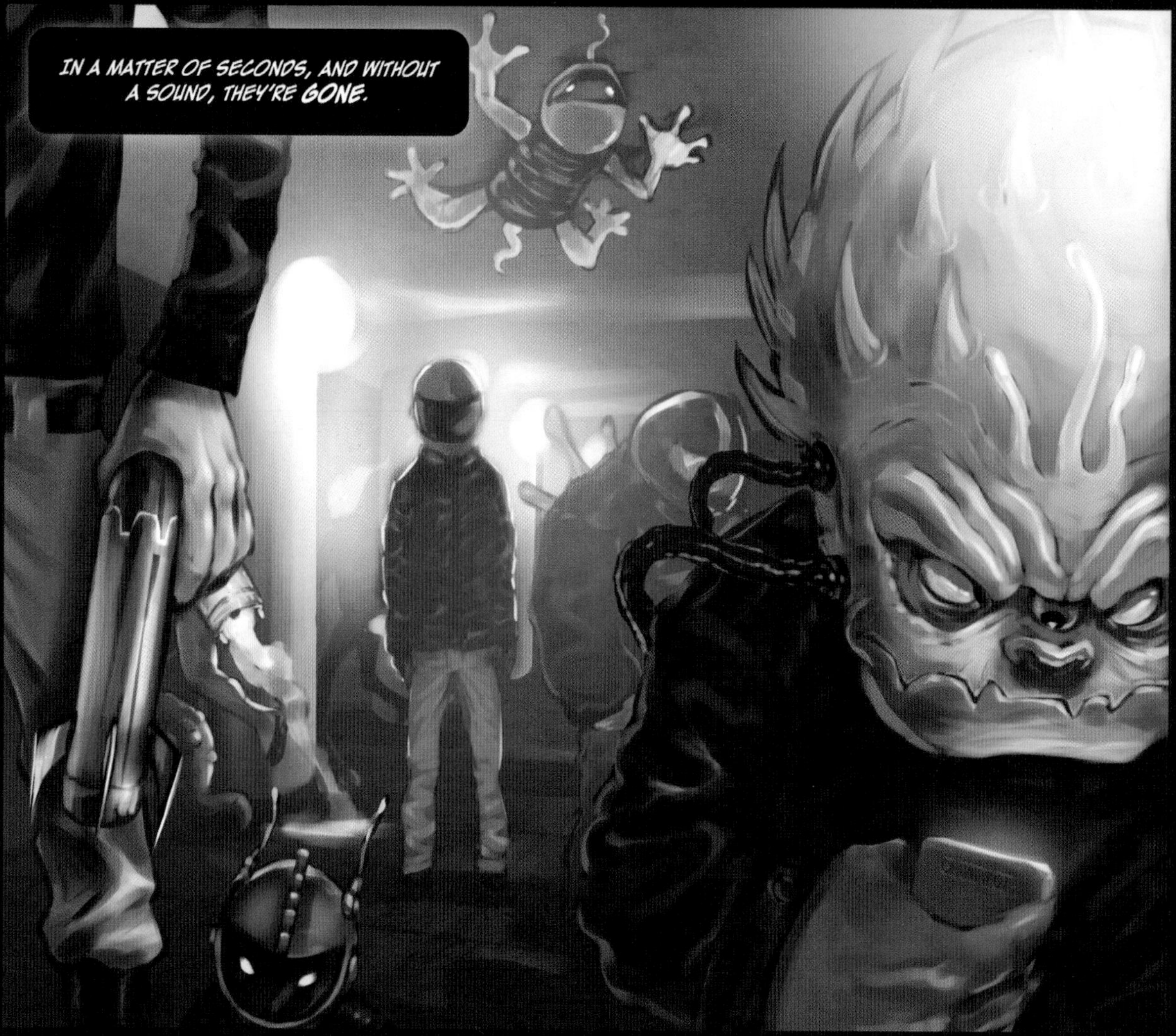
IN A MATTER OF SECONDS, AND WITHOUT A SOUND, THEY'RE GONE.

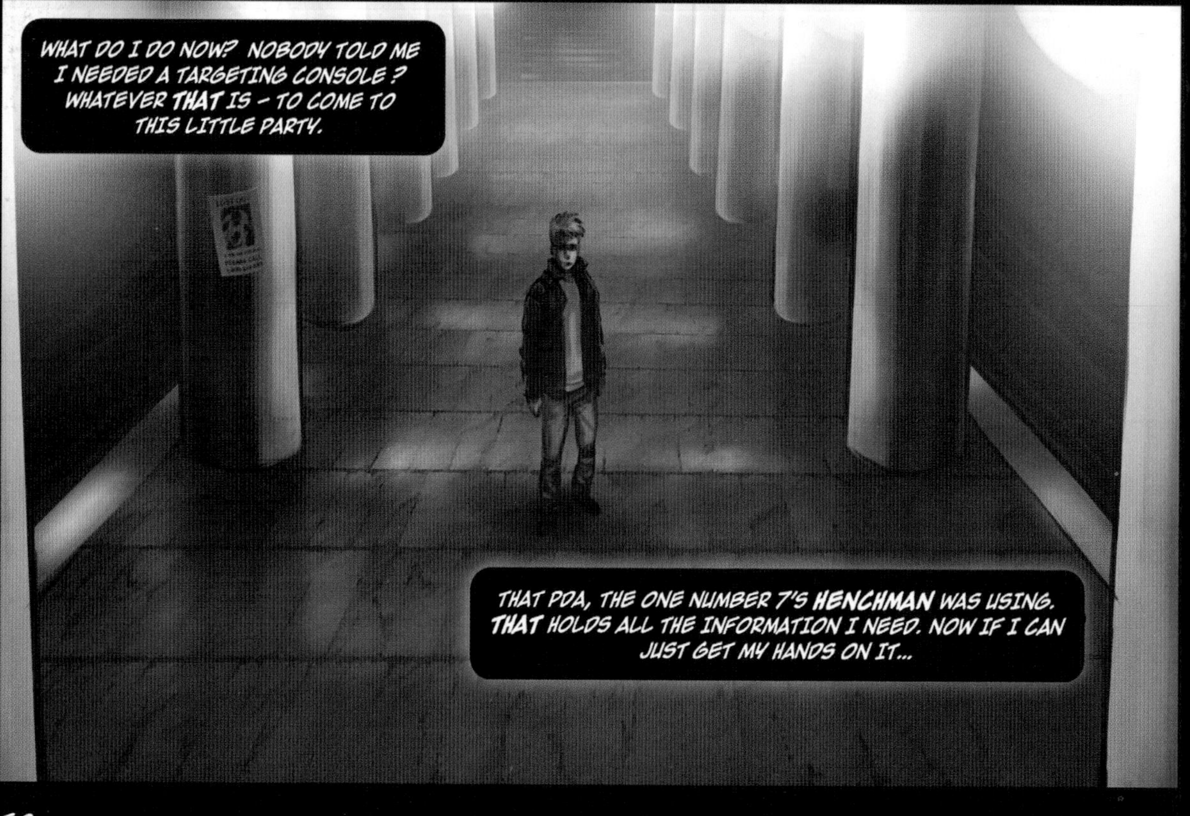
WHAT DO I DO NOW? NOBODY TOLD ME I NEEDED A TARGETING CONSOLE ? WHATEVER THAT IS - TO COME TO THIS LITTLE PARTY.
THAT PDA, THE ONE NUMBER 7'S HENCHMAN WAS USING. THAT HOLDS ALL THE INFORMATION I NEED. NOW IF I CAN JUST GET MY HANDS ON IT...

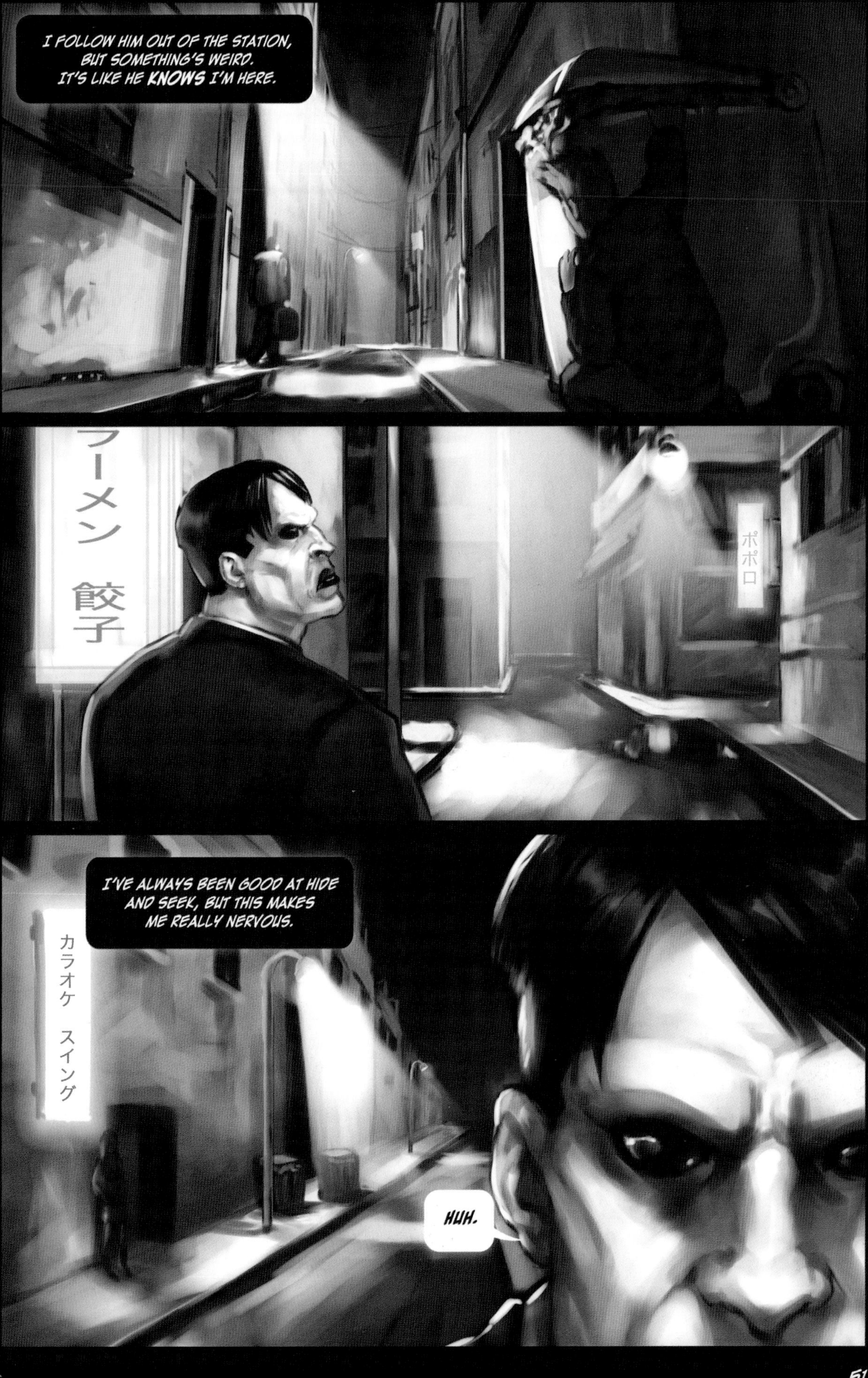
I FOLLOW HIM OUT OF THE STATION, BUT SOMETHING'S WEIRD. IT'S LIKE HE KNOWS I'M HERE.
フーメン 餃子
ポポロ
I'VE ALWAYS BEEN GOOD AT HIDE AND SEEK, BUT THIS MAKES ME REALLY NERVOUS.
カラオケ スイング
HUH.

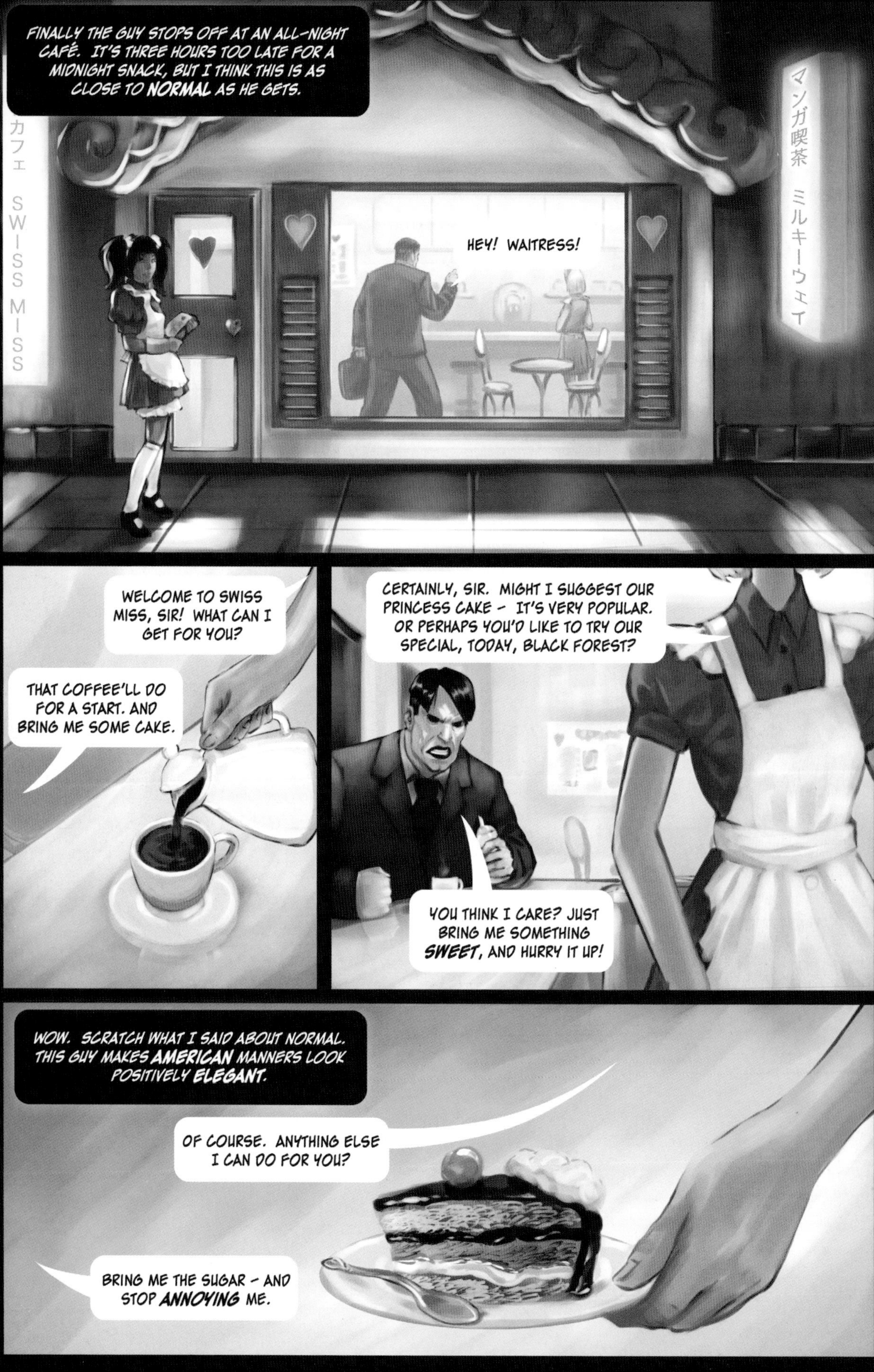
FINALLY THE GUY STOPS OFF AT AN ALL-NIGHT CAFÉ. IT'S THREE HOURS TOO LATE FOR A MIDNIGHT SNACK, BUT I THINK THIS IS AS CLOSE TO NORMAL AS HE GETS.
カフェ SWISS MISS
マンガ喫茶 ミルキーウェイ
HEY! WAITRESS!
WELCOME TO SWISS MISS, SIR! WHAT CAN I GET FOR YOU?
THAT COFFEE'LL DO FOR A START. AND BRING ME SOME CAKE.
CERTAINLY, SIR. MIGHT I SUGGEST OUR PRINCESS CAKE - IT'S VERY POPULAR. OR PERHAPS YOU'D LIKE TO TRY OUR SPECIAL, TODAY, BLACK FOREST?
YOU THINK I CARE? JUST BRING ME SOMETHING SWEET, AND HURRY IT UP!
WOW. SCRATCH WHAT I SAID ABOUT NORMAL. THIS GUY MAKES AMERICAN MANNERS LOOK POSITIVELY ELEGANT.
OF COURSE. ANYTHING ELSE I CAN DO FOR YOU?
BRING ME THE SUGAR - AND STOP ANNOYING ME.

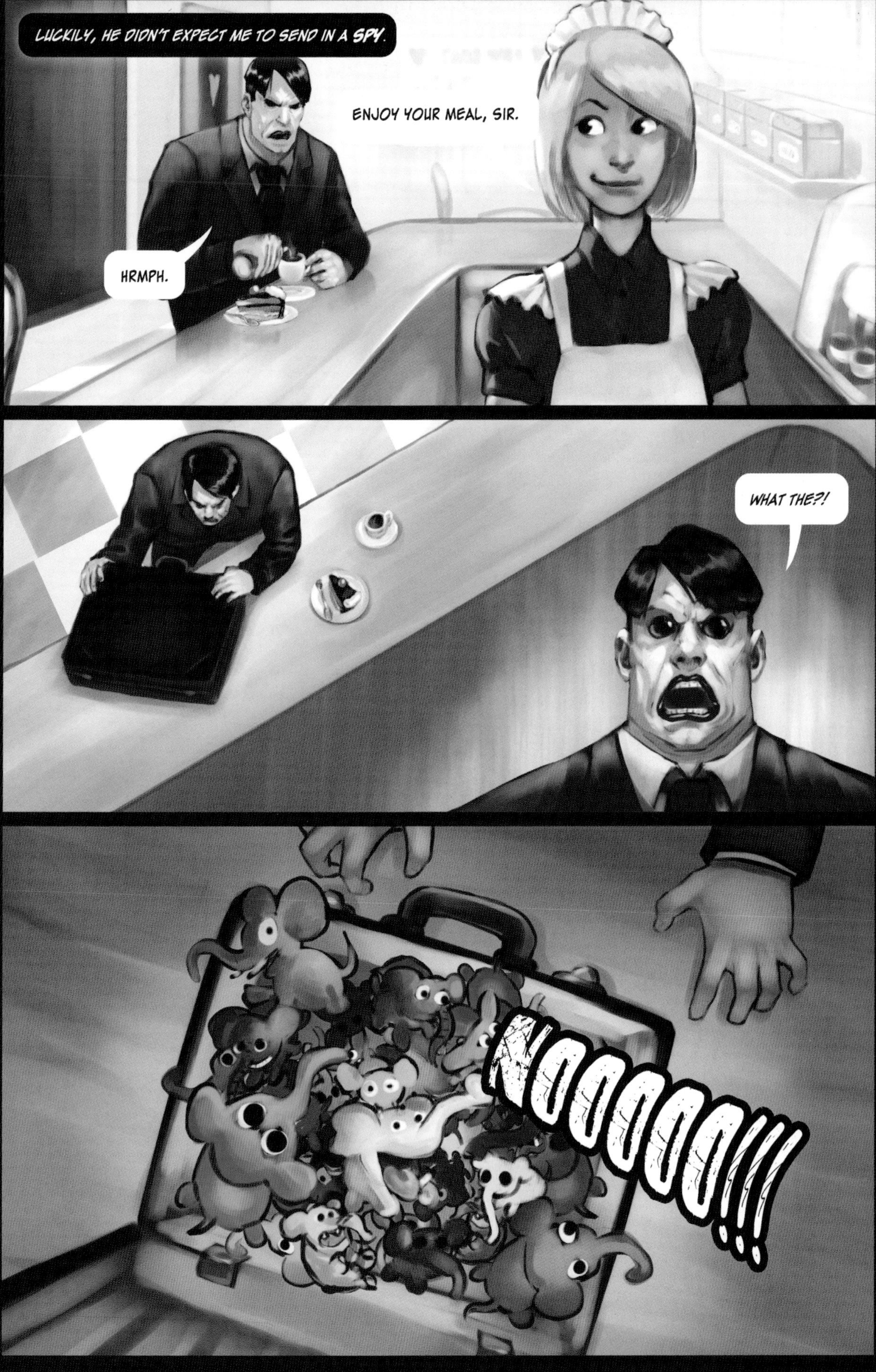
LUCKILY, HE DIDN'T EXPECT ME TO SEND IN A SPY.
ENJOY YOUR MEAL, SIR.
HRMPH.
WHAT THE?!
NOOOOOO!!!

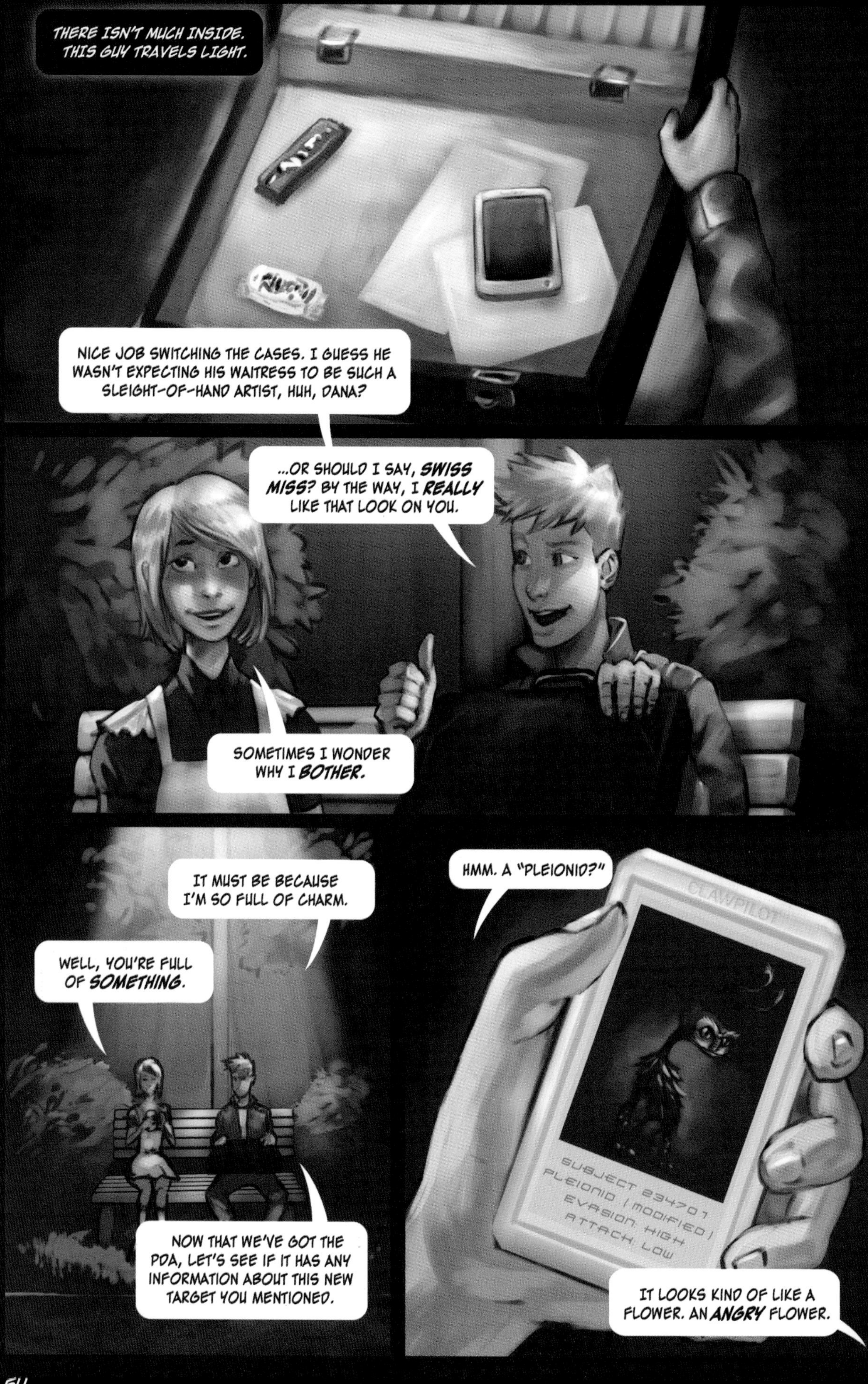
THERE ISN'T MUCH INSIDE. THIS GUY TRAVELS LIGHT.
NICE JOB SWITCHING THE CASES. I GUESS HE WASN'T EXPECTING HIS WAITRESS TO BE SUCH A SLEIGHT-OF-HAND ARTIST, HUH, DANA?
...OR SHOULD I SAY, SWISS MISS? BY THE WAY, I REALLY LIKE THAT LOOK ON YOU.
SOMETIMES I WONDER WHY I BOTHER.
IT MUST BE BECAUSE I'M SO FULL OF CHARM.
WELL, YOU'RE FULL OF SOMETHING.
NOW THAT WE'VE GOT THE PDA, LET'S SEE IF IT HAS ANY INFORMATION ABOUT THIS NEW TARGET YOU MENTIONED.
HMM. A "PLEIONID?"
CLAWPILOT
SUBJECT 234701
PLEIONID (MODIFIED)
EVASION: HIGH
ATTACK: LOW
IT LOOKS KIND OF LIKE A FLOWER. AN ANGRY FLOWER.

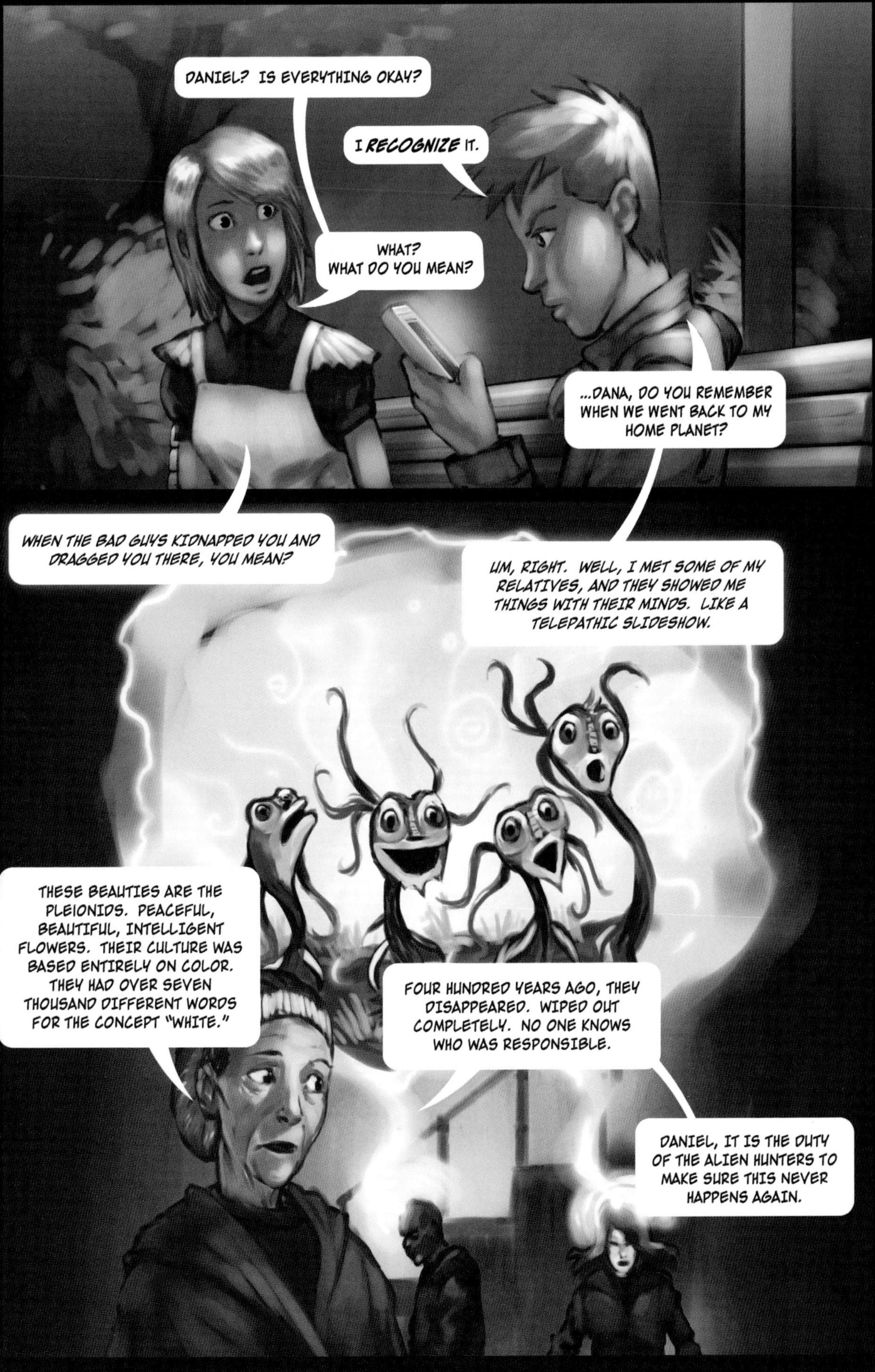
DANIEL? IS EVERYTHING OKAY?
I *RECOGNIZE* IT.
WHAT? WHAT DO YOU MEAN?
...DANA, DO YOU REMEMBER WHEN WE WENT BACK TO MY HOME PLANET?
WHEN THE BAD GUYS KIDNAPPED YOU AND DRAGGED YOU THERE, YOU MEAN?
UM, RIGHT. WELL, I MET SOME OF MY RELATIVES, AND THEY SHOWED ME THINGS WITH THEIR MINDS. LIKE A TELEPATHIC SLIDESHOW.
THESE BEAUTIES ARE THE PLEIONIDS. PEACEFUL, BEAUTIFUL, INTELLIGENT FLOWERS. THEIR CULTURE WAS BASED ENTIRELY ON COLOR. THEY HAD OVER SEVEN THOUSAND DIFFERENT WORDS FOR THE CONCEPT "WHITE."
FOUR HUNDRED YEARS AGO, THEY DISAPPEARED. WIPED OUT COMPLETELY. NO ONE KNOWS WHO WAS RESPONSIBLE.
DANIEL, IT IS THE DUTY OF THE ALIEN HUNTERS TO MAKE SURE THIS NEVER HAPPENS AGAIN.

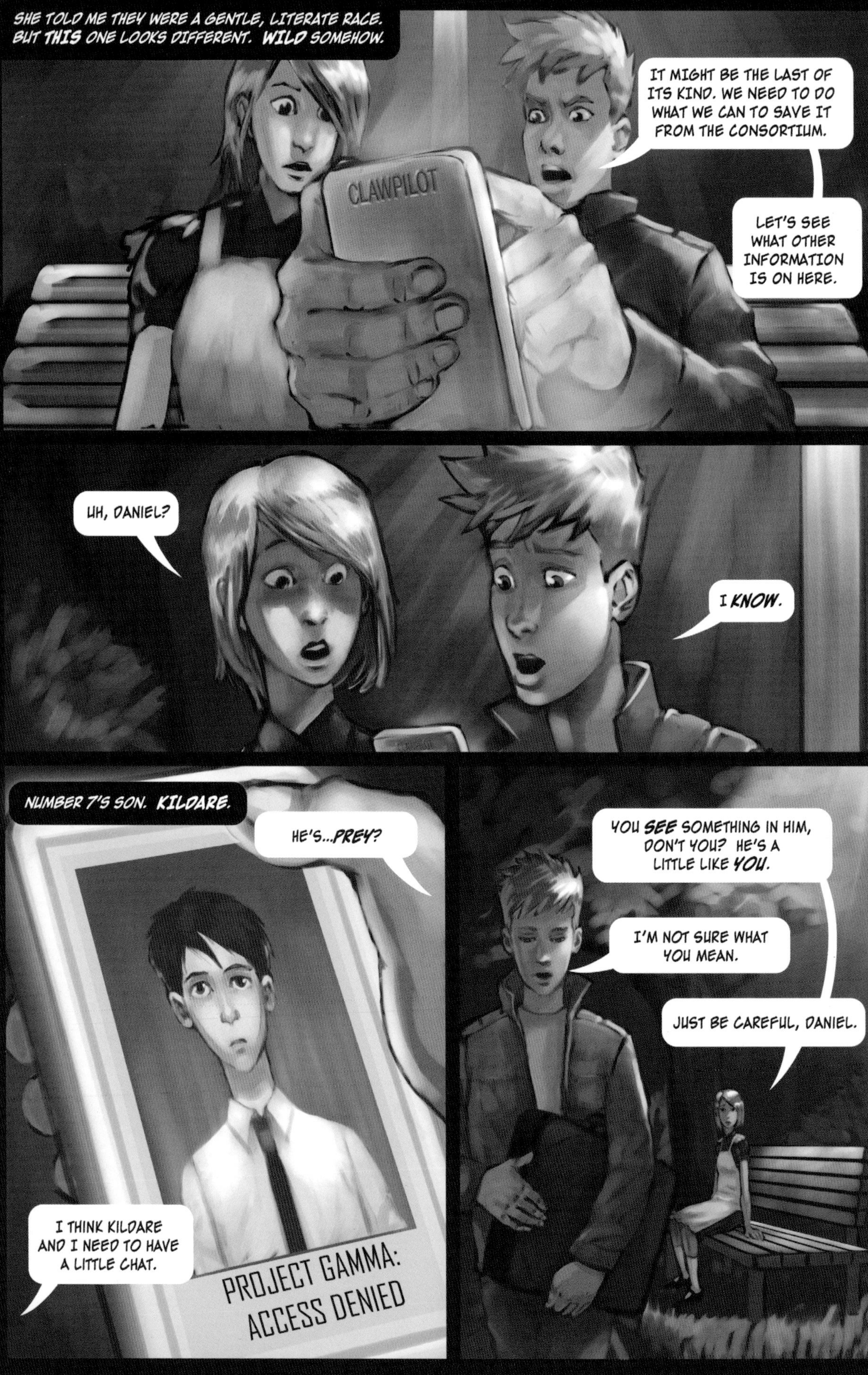
SHE TOLD ME THEY WERE A GENTLE, LITERATE RACE. BUT THIS ONE LOOKS DIFFERENT. WILD SOMEHOW.
IT MIGHT BE THE LAST OF ITS KIND. WE NEED TO DO WHAT WE CAN TO SAVE IT FROM THE CONSORTIUM.
CLAWPILOT
LET'S SEE WHAT OTHER INFORMATION IS ON HERE.
UH, DANIEL?
I KNOW.
NUMBER 7'S SON. KILDARE.
HE'S...PREY?
I THINK KILDARE AND I NEED TO HAVE A LITTLE CHAT.
PROJECT GAMMA: ACCESS DENIED
YOU SEE SOMETHING IN HIM, DON'T YOU? HE'S A LITTLE LIKE YOU.
I'M NOT SURE WHAT YOU MEAN.
JUST BE CAREFUL, DANIEL.

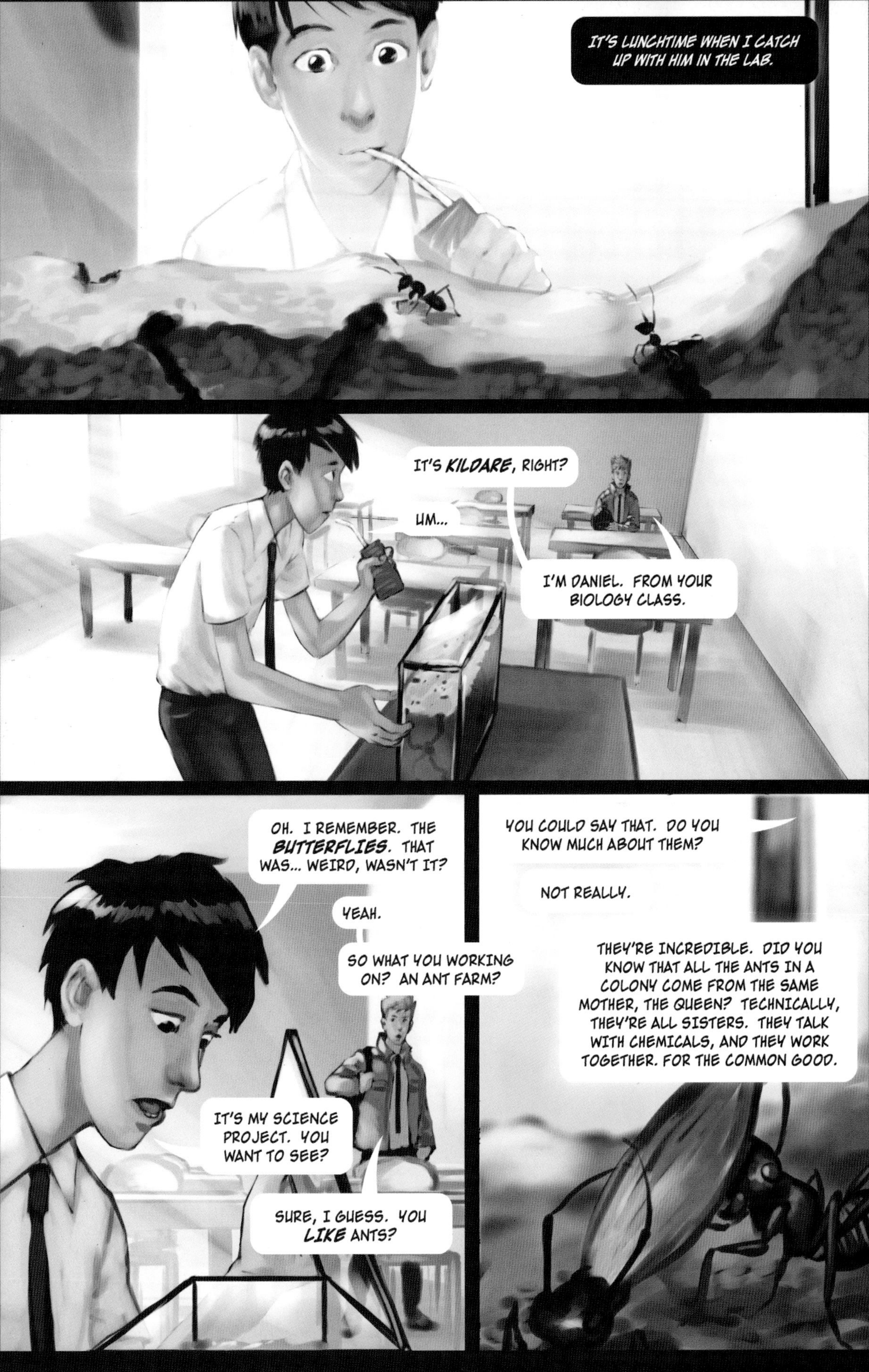
IT'S LUNCHTIME WHEN I CATCH UP WITH HIM IN THE LAB.
IT'S KILDARE, RIGHT?
UM...
I'M DANIEL. FROM YOUR BIOLOGY CLASS.
OH. I REMEMBER. THE BUTTERFLIES. THAT WAS... WEIRD, WASN'T IT?
YEAH.
SO WHAT YOU WORKING ON? AN ANT FARM?
IT'S MY SCIENCE PROJECT. YOU WANT TO SEE?
SURE, I GUESS. YOU LIKE ANTS?
YOU COULD SAY THAT. DO YOU KNOW MUCH ABOUT THEM?
NOT REALLY.
THEY'RE INCREDIBLE. DID YOU KNOW THAT ALL THE ANTS IN A COLONY COME FROM THE SAME MOTHER, THE QUEEN? TECHNICALLY, THEY'RE ALL SISTERS. THEY TALK WITH CHEMICALS, AND THEY WORK TOGETHER. FOR THE COMMON GOOD.

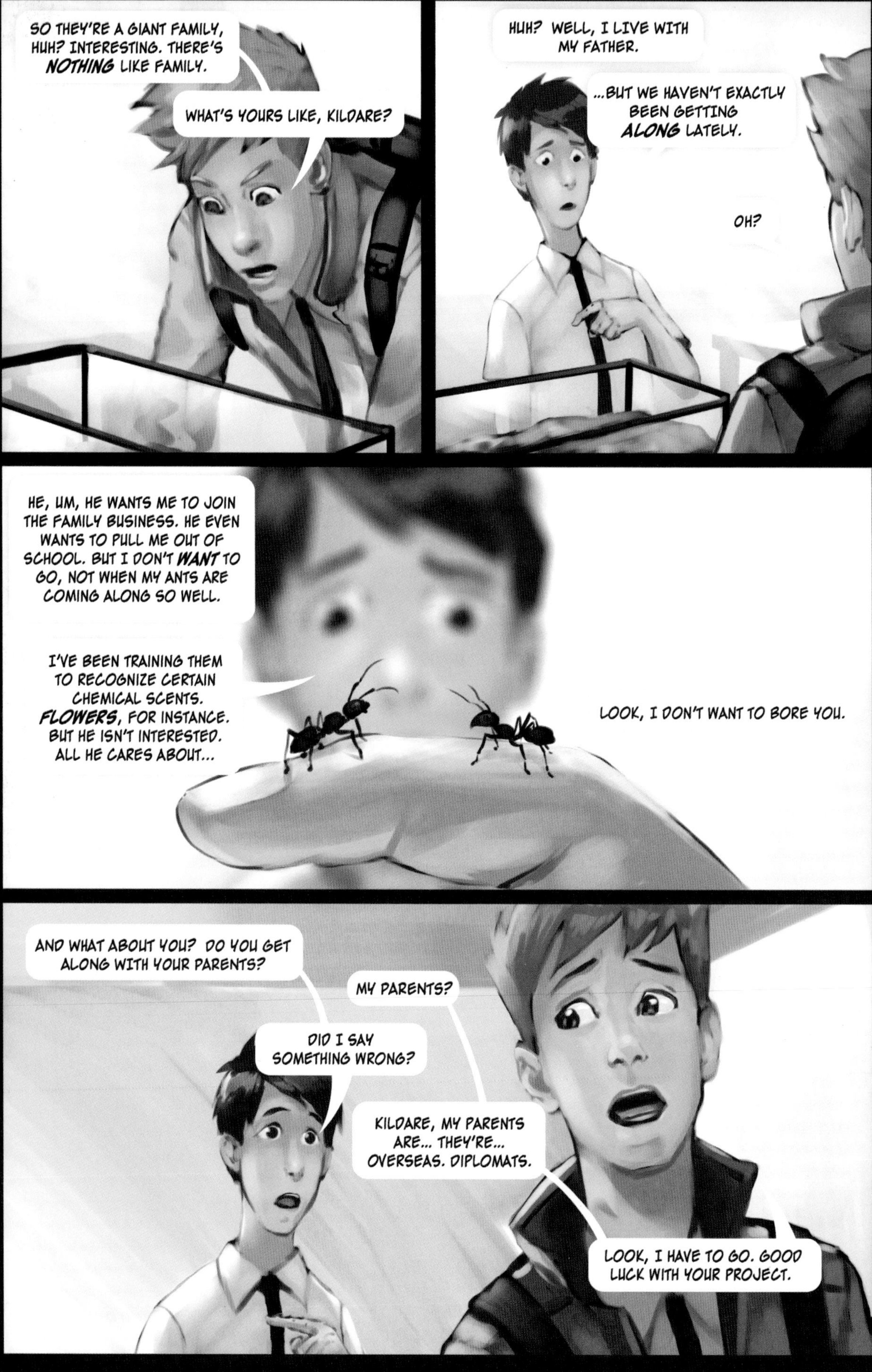
SO THEY'RE A GIANT FAMILY, HUH? INTERESTING. THERE'S NOTHING LIKE FAMILY.
WHAT'S YOURS LIKE, KILDARE?
HUH? WELL, I LIVE WITH MY FATHER.
...BUT WE HAVEN'T EXACTLY BEEN GETTING ALONG LATELY.
OH?
HE, UM, HE WANTS ME TO JOIN THE FAMILY BUSINESS. HE EVEN WANTS TO PULL ME OUT OF SCHOOL. BUT I DON'T WANT TO GO, NOT WHEN MY ANTS ARE COMING ALONG SO WELL.
I'VE BEEN TRAINING THEM TO RECOGNIZE CERTAIN CHEMICAL SCENTS. FLOWERS, FOR INSTANCE. BUT HE ISN'T INTERESTED. ALL HE CARES ABOUT...
LOOK, I DON'T WANT TO BORE YOU.
AND WHAT ABOUT YOU? DO YOU GET ALONG WITH YOUR PARENTS?
MY PARENTS?
DID I SAY SOMETHING WRONG?
KILDARE, MY PARENTS ARE... THEY'RE... OVERSEAS. DIPLOMATS.
LOOK, I HAVE TO GO. GOOD LUCK WITH YOUR PROJECT.

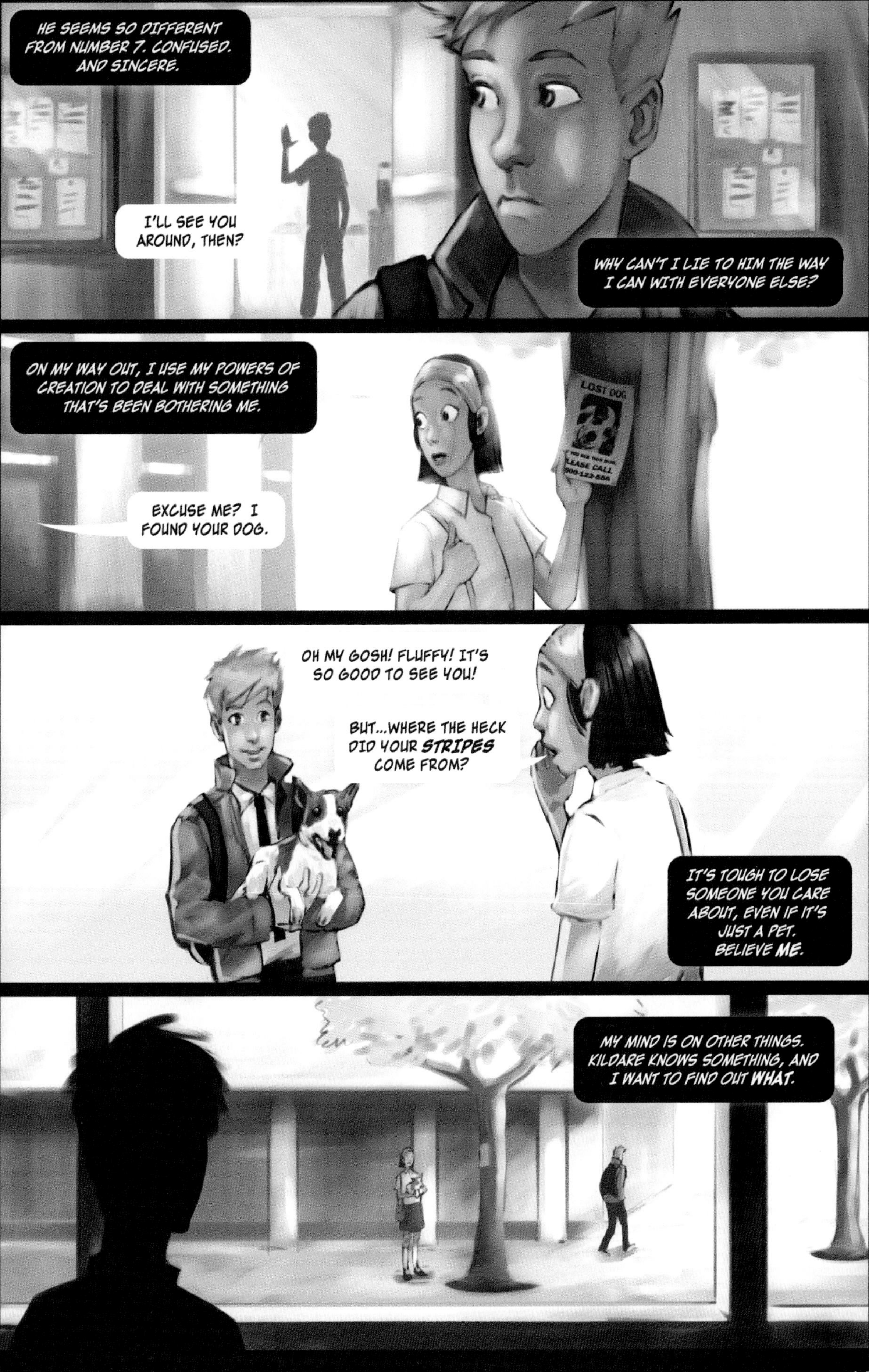

HE SEEMS SO DIFFERENT FROM NUMBER 7. CONFUSED. AND SINCERE.
I'LL SEE YOU AROUND, THEN?
WHY CAN'T I LIE TO HIM THE WAY I CAN WITH EVERYONE ELSE?
ON MY WAY OUT, I USE MY POWERS OF CREATION TO DEAL WITH SOMETHING THAT'S BEEN BOTHERING ME.
LOST DOG
EXCUSE ME? I FOUND YOUR DOG.
OH MY GOSH! FLUFFY! IT'S SO GOOD TO SEE YOU!
BUT...WHERE THE HECK DID YOUR **STRIPES** COME FROM?
IT'S TOUGH TO LOSE SOMEONE YOU CARE ABOUT, EVEN IF IT'S JUST A PET. BELIEVE **ME**.
MY MIND IS ON OTHER THINGS. KILDARE KNOWS SOMETHING, AND I WANT TO FIND OUT **WHAT**.

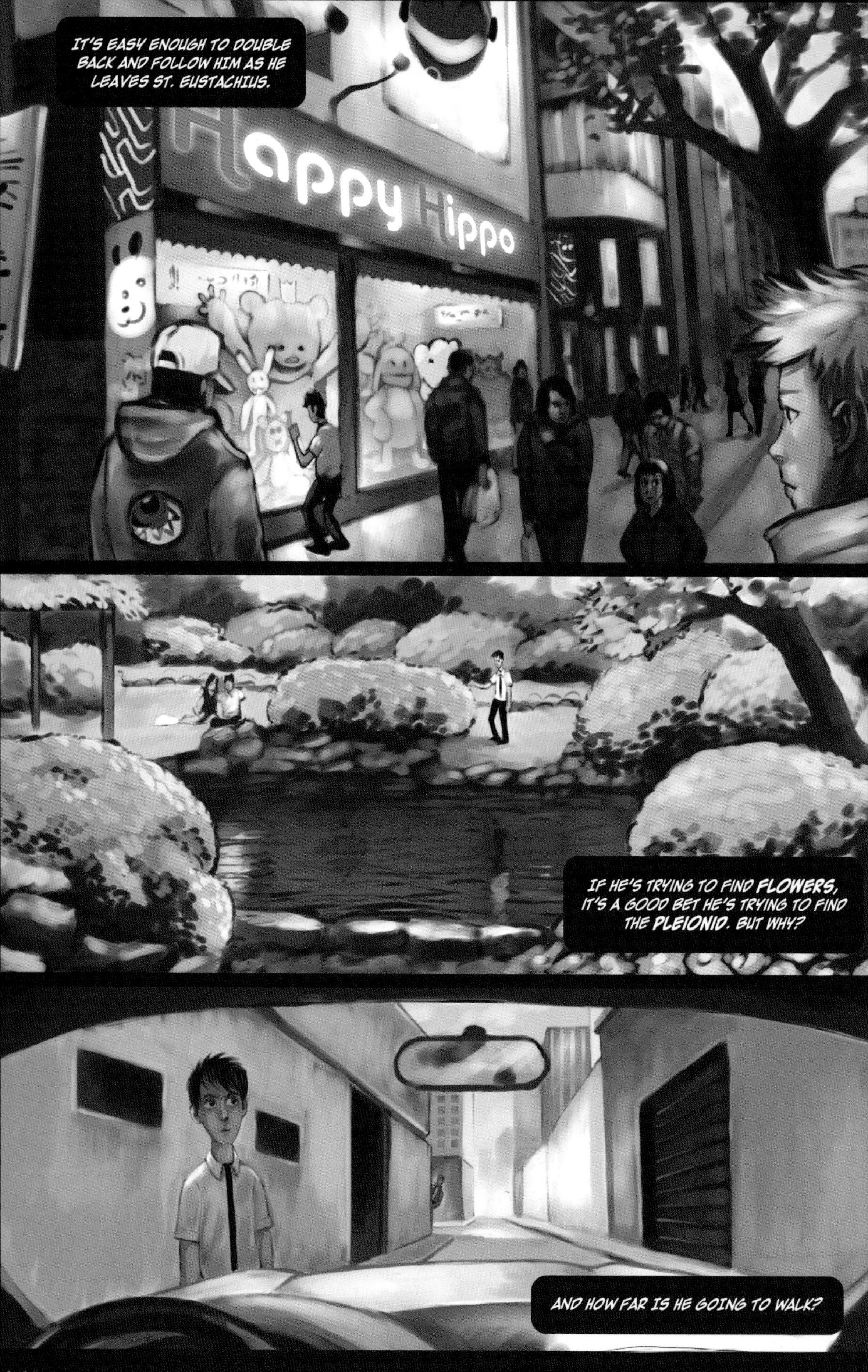
IT'S EASY ENOUGH TO DOUBLE BACK AND FOLLOW HIM AS HE LEAVES ST. EUSTACHIUS.
Happy Hippo
IF HE'S TRYING TO FIND FLOWERS, IT'S A GOOD BET HE'S TRYING TO FIND THE PLEIONID. BUT WHY?
AND HOW FAR IS HE GOING TO WALK?

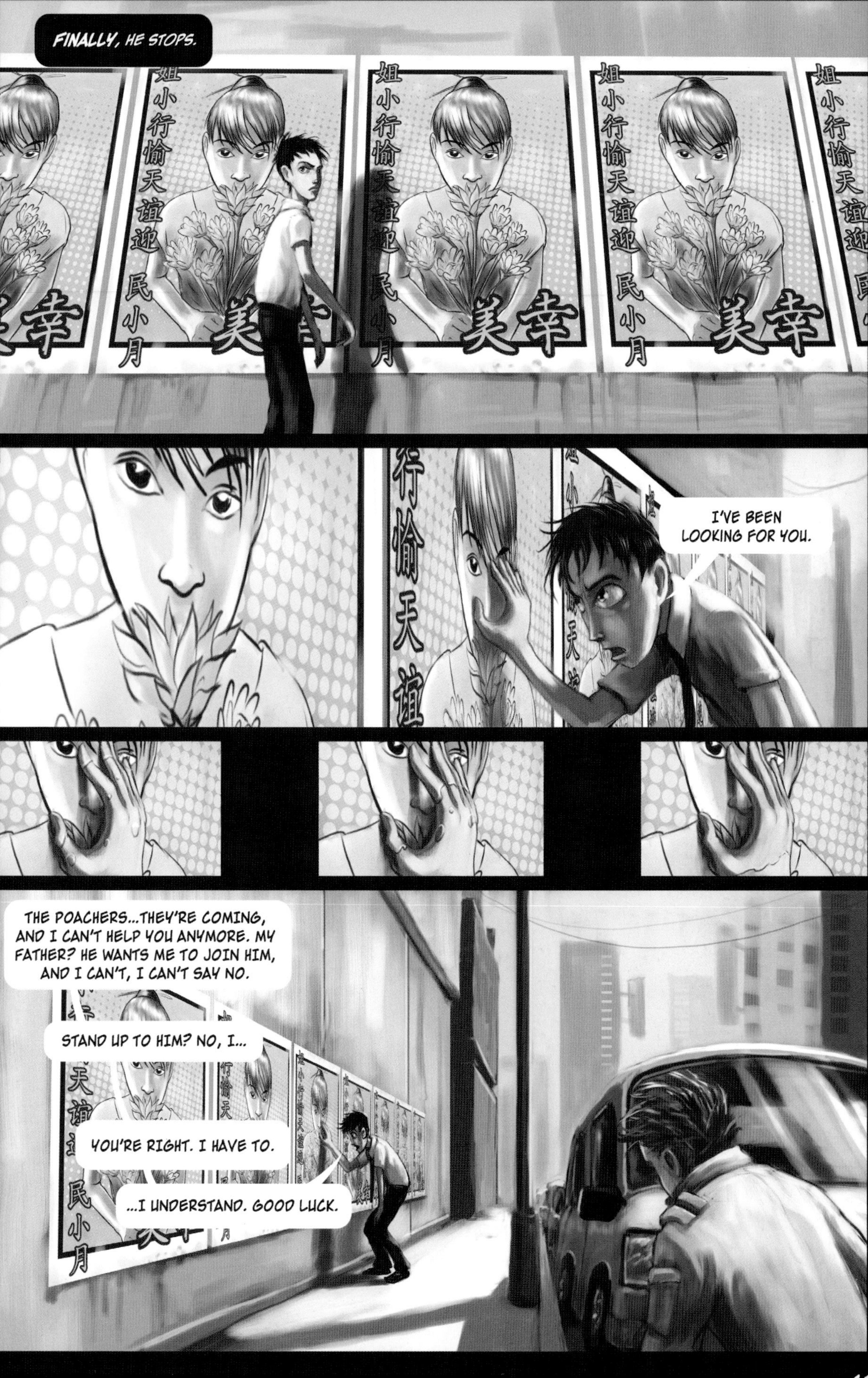
FINALLY, HE STOPS.
姐小行愉天谊迎
民小月
美幸
I'VE BEEN LOOKING FOR YOU.
THE POACHERS...THEY'RE COMING, AND I CAN'T HELP YOU ANYMORE. MY FATHER? HE WANTS ME TO JOIN HIM, AND I CAN'T, I CAN'T SAY NO.
STAND UP TO HIM? NO, I...
YOU'RE RIGHT. I HAVE TO.
...I UNDERSTAND. GOOD LUCK.

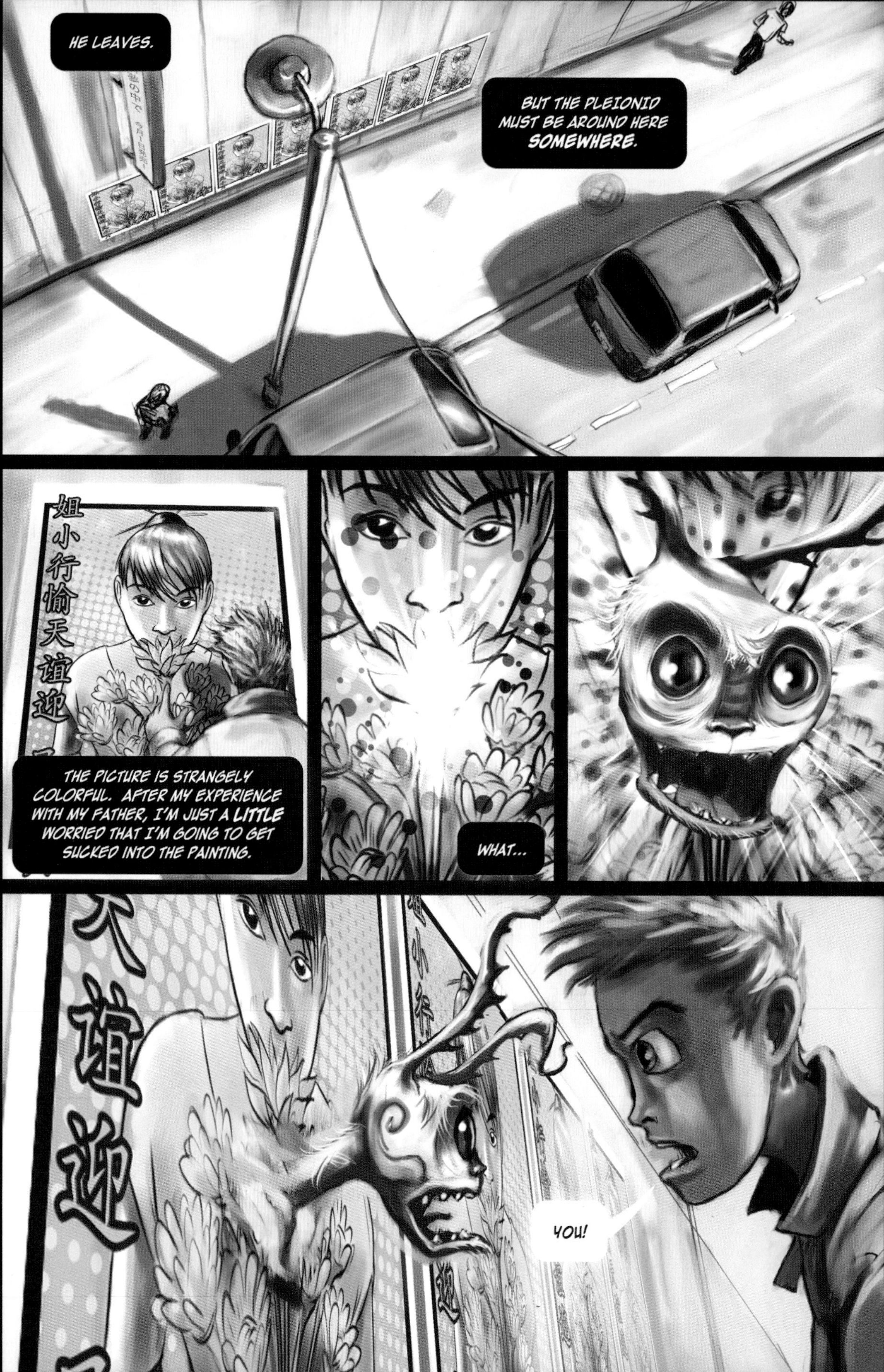
HE LEAVES.
BUT THE PLEIONID MUST BE AROUND HERE SOMEWHERE.
姐小行愉天誼迎
THE PICTURE IS STRANGELY COLORFUL. AFTER MY EXPERIENCE WITH MY FATHER, I'M JUST A LITTLE WORRIED THAT I'M GOING TO GET SUCKED INTO THE PAINTING.
WHAT...
YOU!

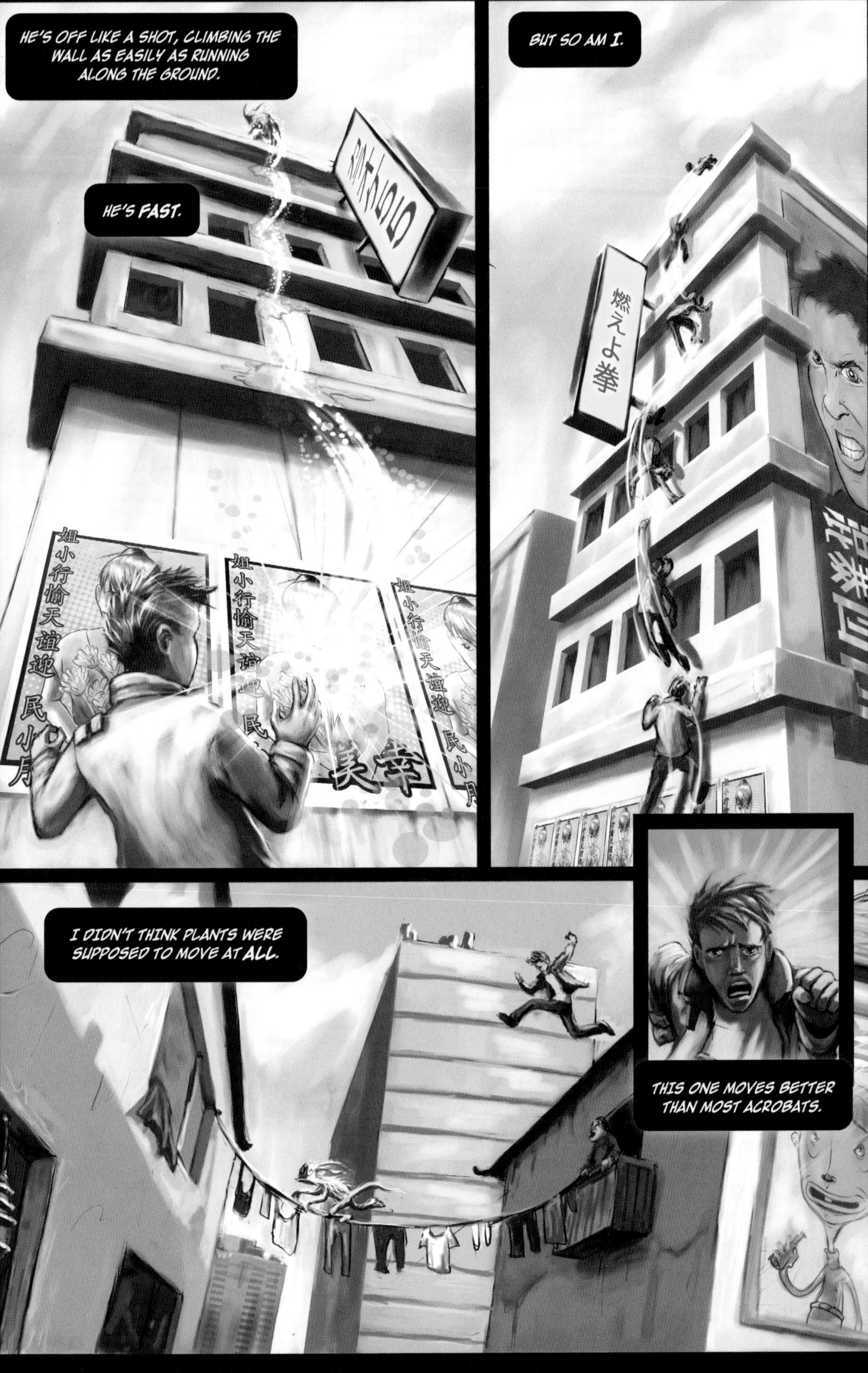
HE'S OFF LIKE A SHOT, CLIMBING THE WALL AS EASILY AS RUNNING ALONG THE GROUND.
HE'S FAST.
BUT SO AM I.
燃えよ拳
I DIDN'T THINK PLANTS WERE SUPPOSED TO MOVE AT ALL.
THIS ONE MOVES BETTER THAN MOST ACROBATS.

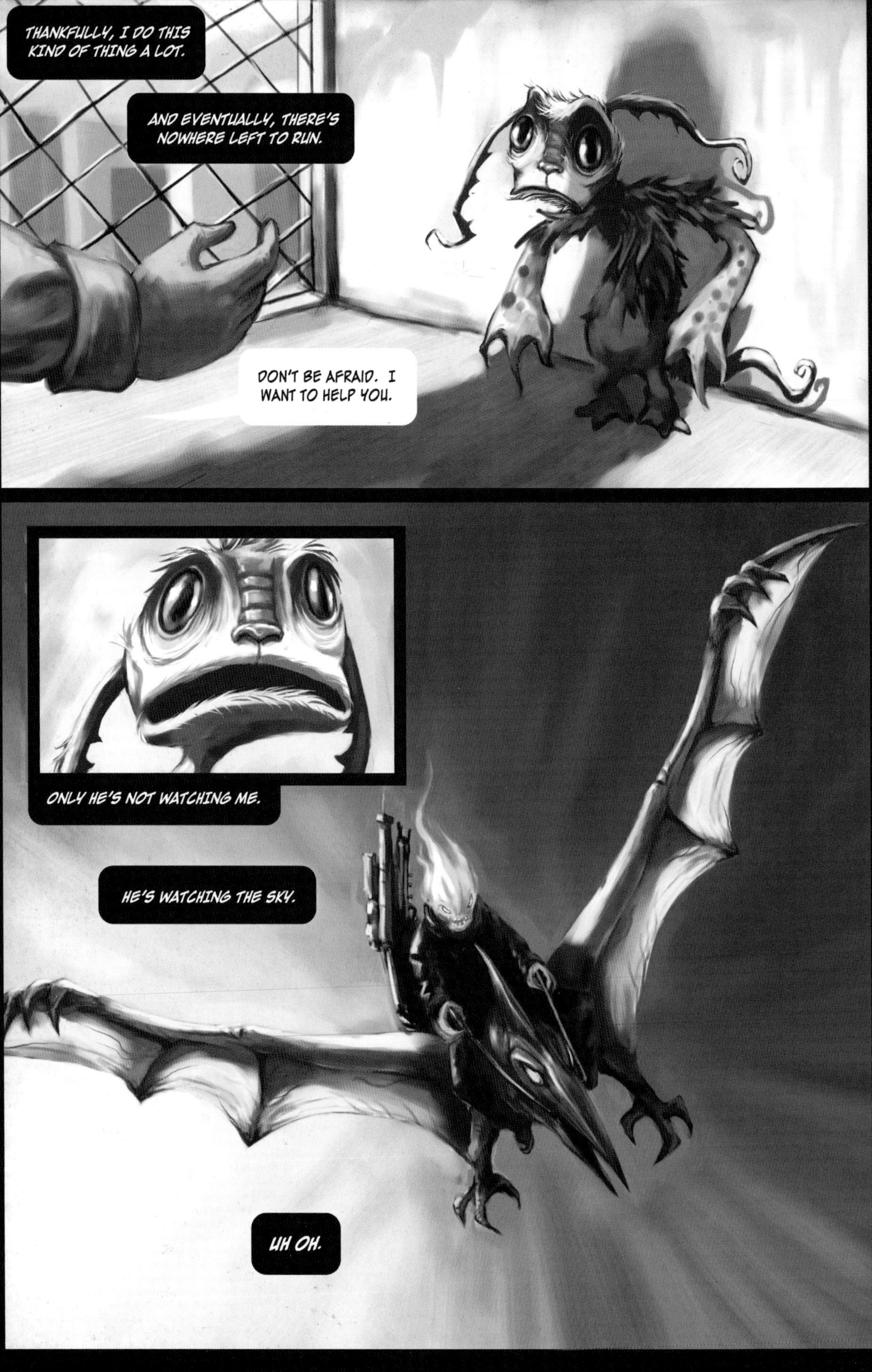
THANKFULLY, I DO THIS KIND OF THING A LOT.
AND EVENTUALLY, THERE'S NOWHERE LEFT TO RUN.
DON'T BE AFRAID. I WANT TO HELP YOU.
ONLY HE'S NOT WATCHING ME.
HE'S WATCHING THE SKY.
UH OH.

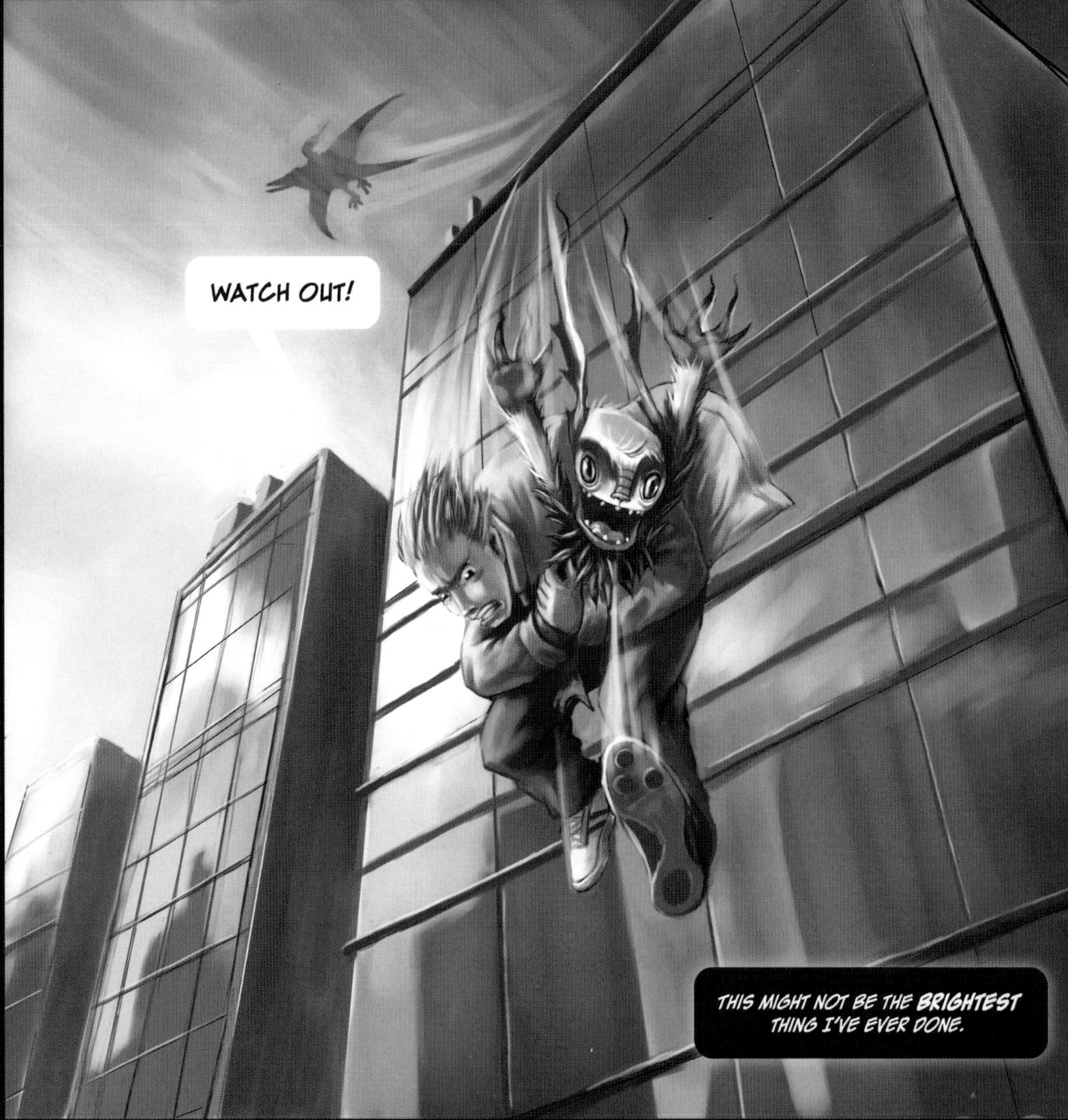
WATCH OUT!
THIS MIGHT NOT BE THE BRIGHTEST THING I'VE EVER DONE.

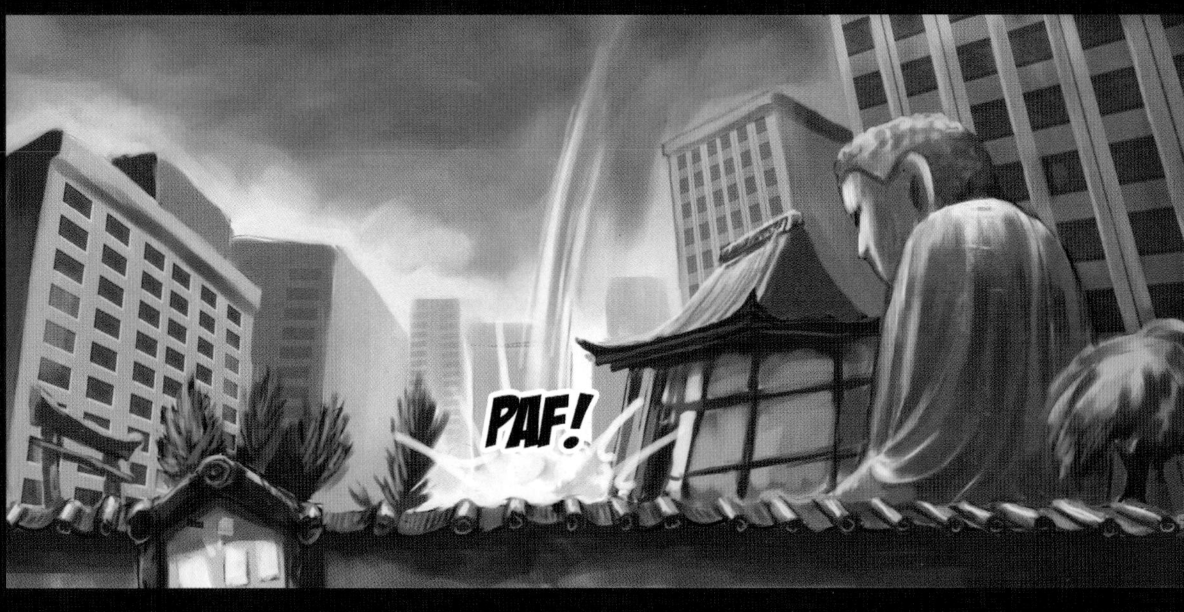
PAF!

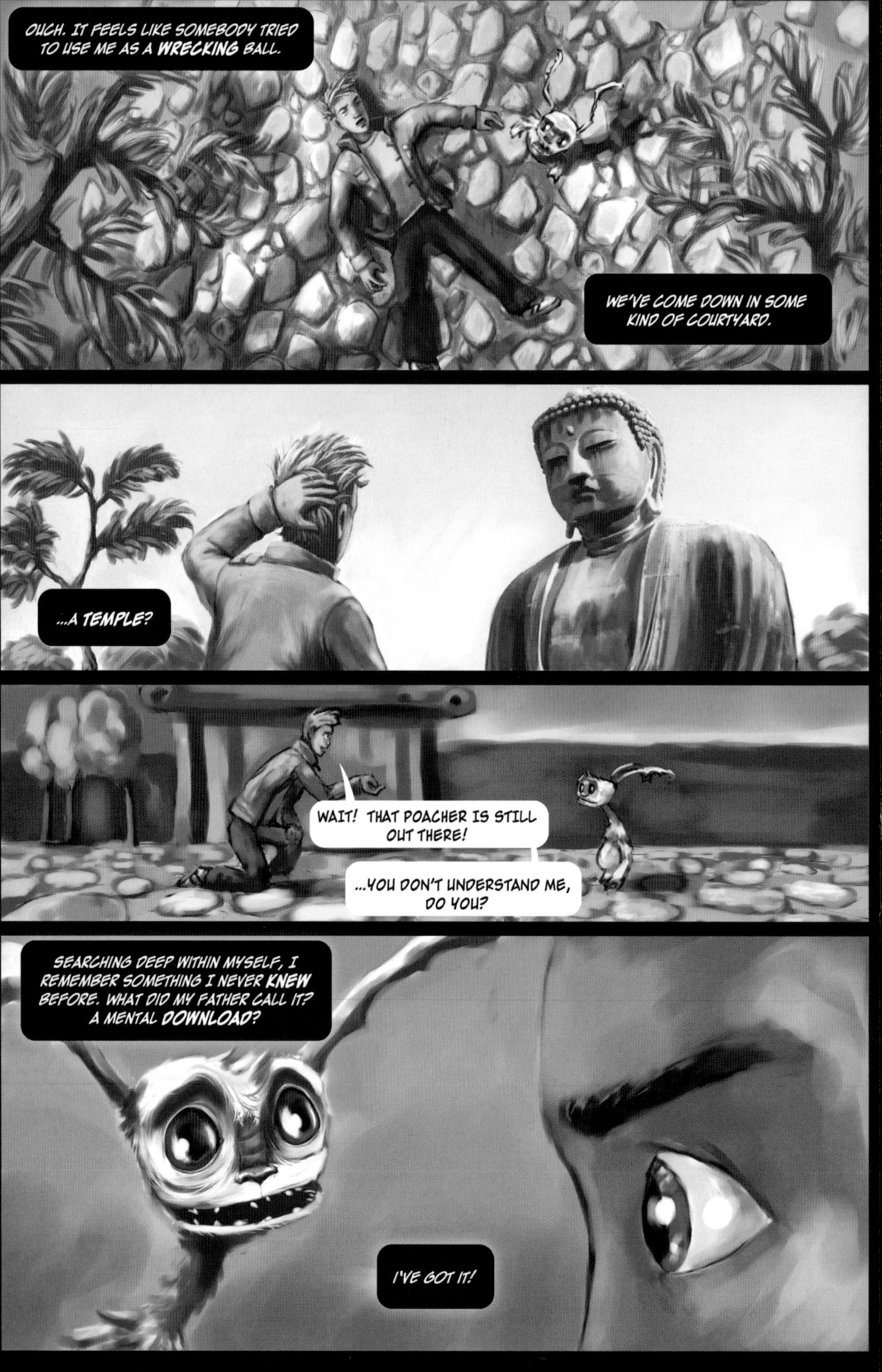
OUCH. IT FEELS LIKE SOMEBODY TRIED TO USE ME AS A WRECKING BALL.
WE'VE COME DOWN IN SOME KIND OF COURTYARD.
...A TEMPLE?
WAIT! THAT POACHER IS STILL OUT THERE!
...YOU DON'T UNDERSTAND ME, DO YOU?
SEARCHING DEEP WITHIN MYSELF, I REMEMBER SOMETHING I NEVER KNEW BEFORE. WHAT DID MY FATHER CALL IT? A MENTAL DOWNLOAD?
I'VE GOT IT!

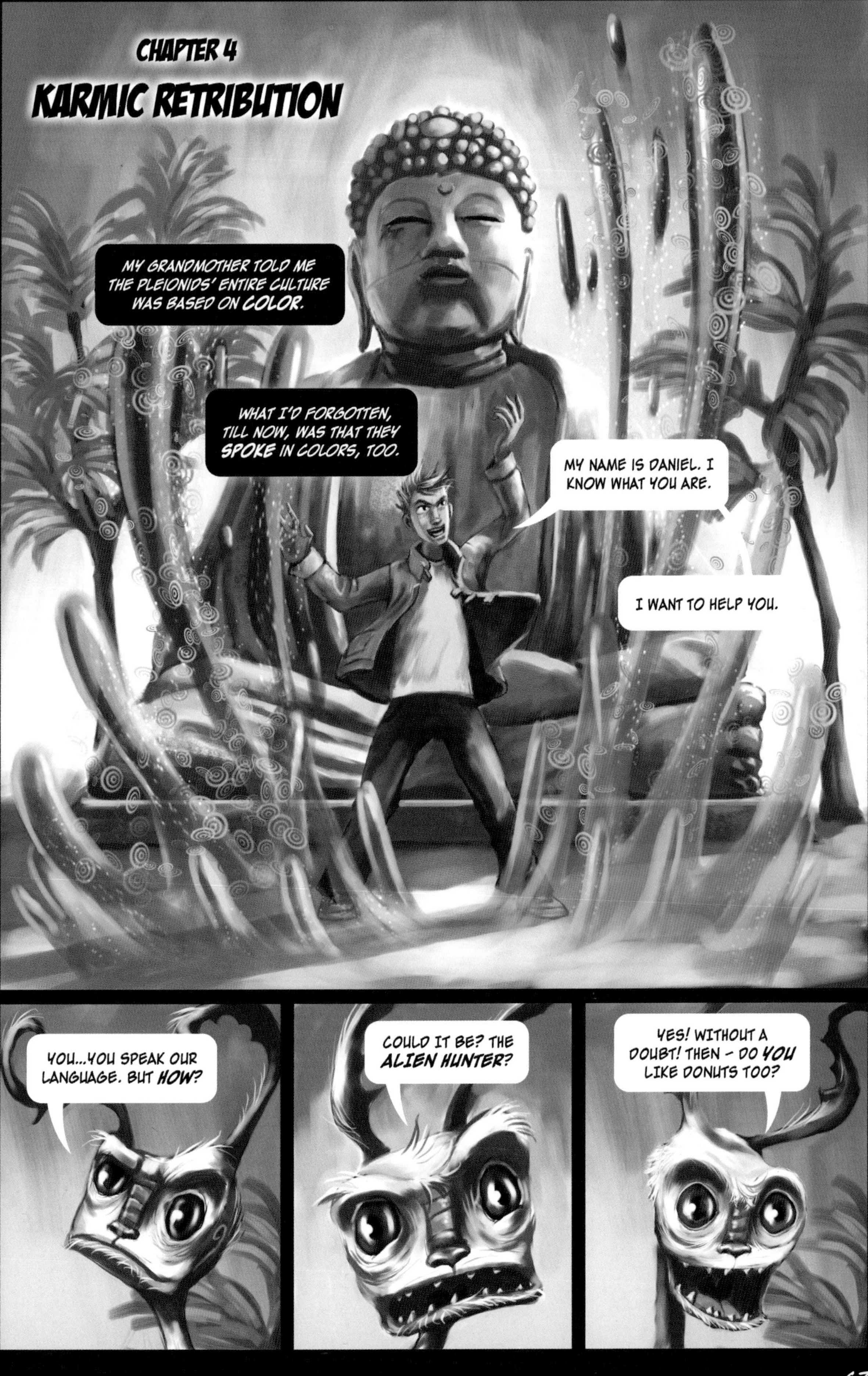
CHAPTER 4
KARMIC RETRIBUTION
MY GRANDMOTHER TOLD ME THE PLEIONIDS' ENTIRE CULTURE WAS BASED ON COLOR.
WHAT I'D FORGOTTEN, TILL NOW, WAS THAT THEY SPOKE IN COLORS, TOO.
MY NAME IS DANIEL. I KNOW WHAT YOU ARE.
I WANT TO HELP YOU.
YOU...YOU SPEAK OUR LANGUAGE. BUT HOW?
COULD IT BE? THE ALIEN HUNTER?
YES! WITHOUT A DOUBT! THEN - DO YOU LIKE DONUTS TOO?

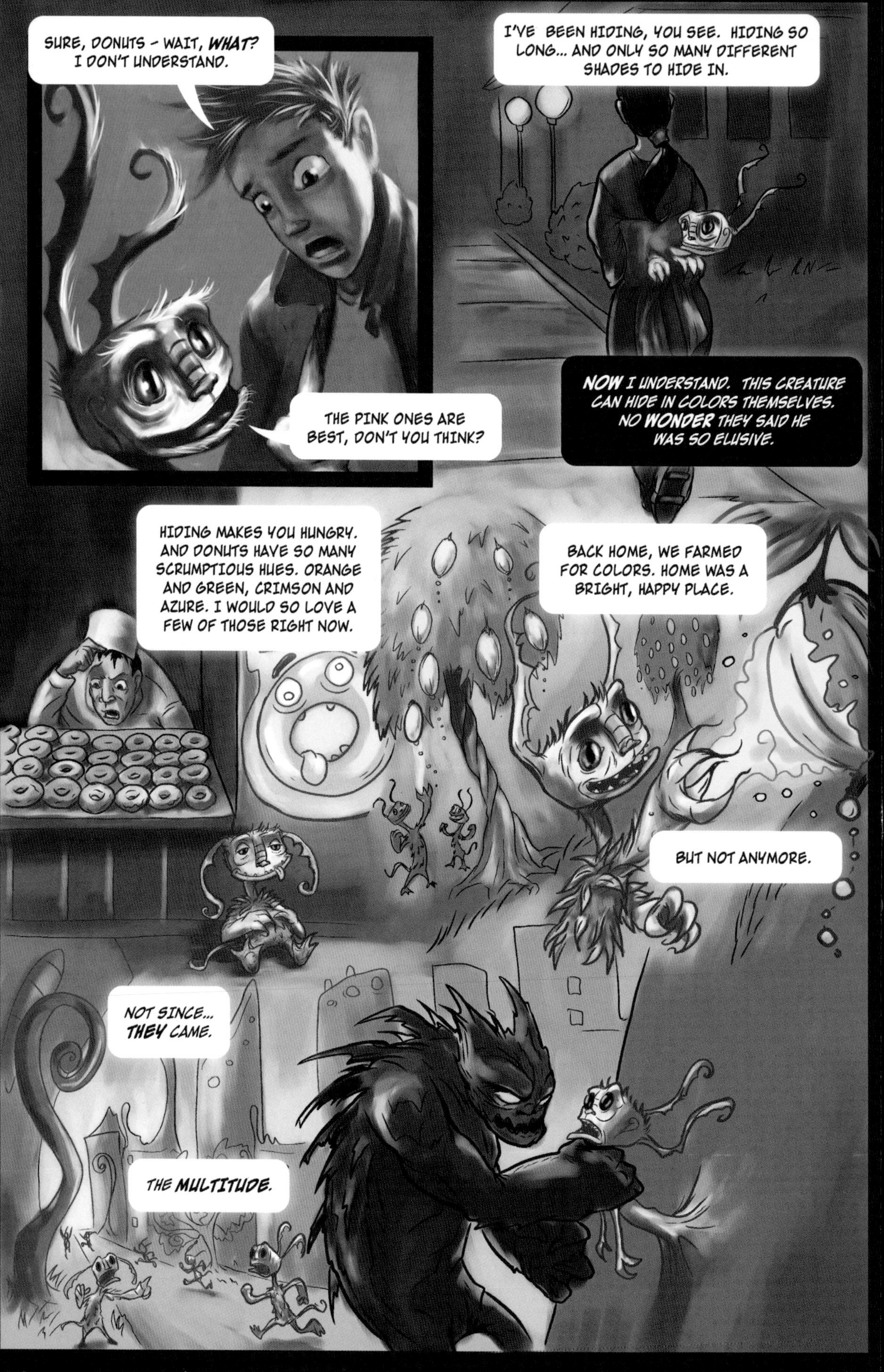
SURE, DONUTS - WAIT, WHAT? I DON'T UNDERSTAND.
THE PINK ONES ARE BEST, DON'T YOU THINK?
I'VE BEEN HIDING, YOU SEE. HIDING SO LONG... AND ONLY SO MANY DIFFERENT SHADES TO HIDE IN.
NOW I UNDERSTAND. THIS CREATURE CAN HIDE IN COLORS THEMSELVES. NO WONDER THEY SAID HE WAS SO ELUSIVE.
HIDING MAKES YOU HUNGRY. AND DONUTS HAVE SO MANY SCRUMPTIOUS HUES. ORANGE AND GREEN, CRIMSON AND AZURE. I WOULD SO LOVE A FEW OF THOSE RIGHT NOW.
BACK HOME, WE FARMED FOR COLORS. HOME WAS A BRIGHT, HAPPY PLACE.
BUT NOT ANYMORE.
NOT SINCE... THEY CAME.
THE MULTITUDE.

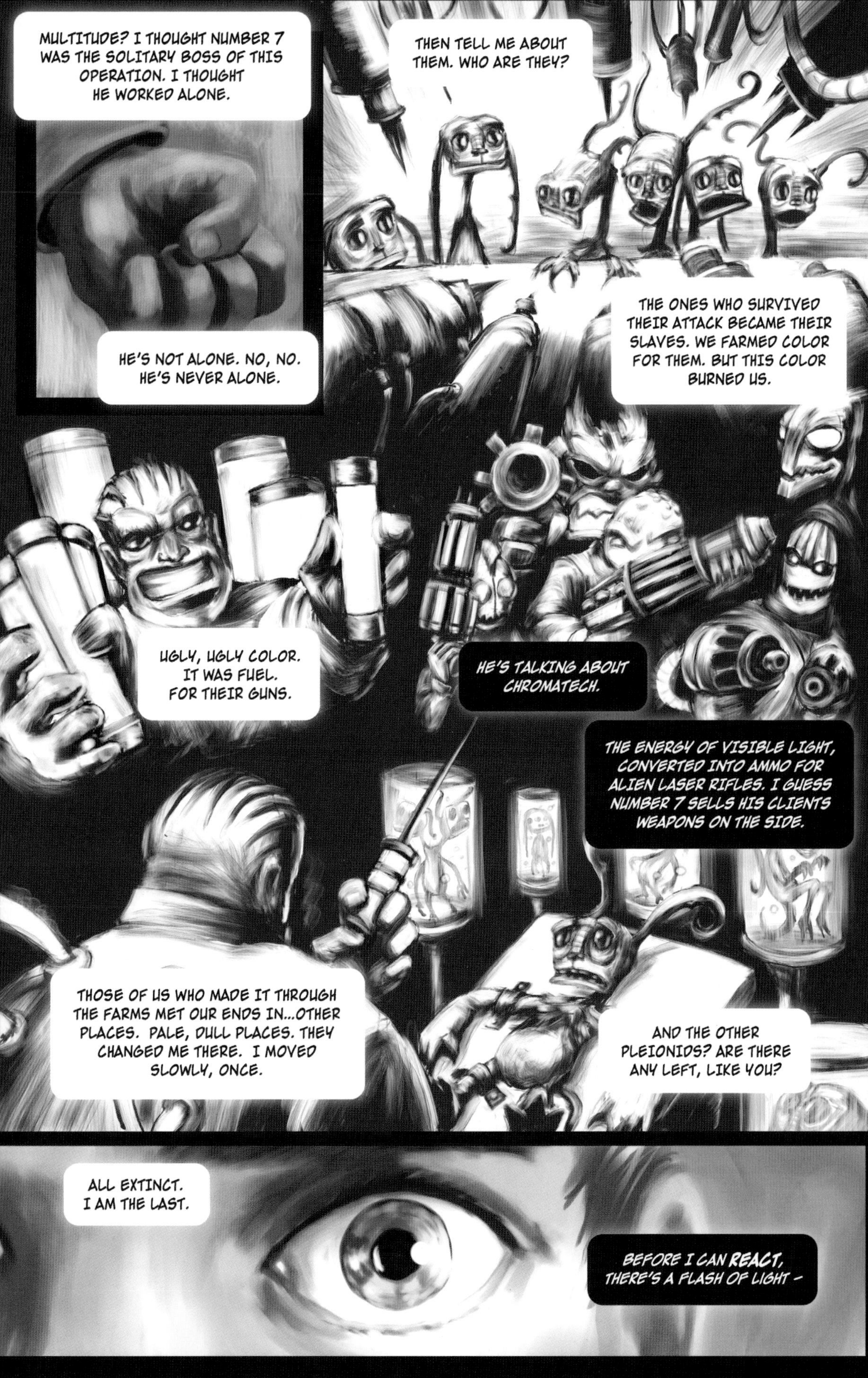
MULTITUDE? I THOUGHT NUMBER 7 WAS THE SOLITARY BOSS OF THIS OPERATION. I THOUGHT HE WORKED ALONE.
THEN TELL ME ABOUT THEM. WHO ARE THEY?
HE'S NOT ALONE. NO, NO. HE'S NEVER ALONE.
THE ONES WHO SURVIVED THEIR ATTACK BECAME THEIR SLAVES. WE FARMED COLOR FOR THEM. BUT THIS COLOR BURNED US.
UGLY, UGLY COLOR. IT WAS FUEL. FOR THEIR GUNS.
HE'S TALKING ABOUT CHROMATECH.
THE ENERGY OF VISIBLE LIGHT, CONVERTED INTO AMMO FOR ALIEN LASER RIFLES. I GUESS NUMBER 7 SELLS HIS CLIENTS WEAPONS ON THE SIDE.
THOSE OF US WHO MADE IT THROUGH THE FARMS MET OUR ENDS IN...OTHER PLACES. PALE, DULL PLACES. THEY CHANGED ME THERE. I MOVED SLOWLY, ONCE.
AND THE OTHER PLEIONIDS? ARE THERE ANY LEFT, LIKE YOU?
ALL EXTINCT. I AM THE LAST.
BEFORE I CAN **REACT**, THERE'S A FLASH OF LIGHT -

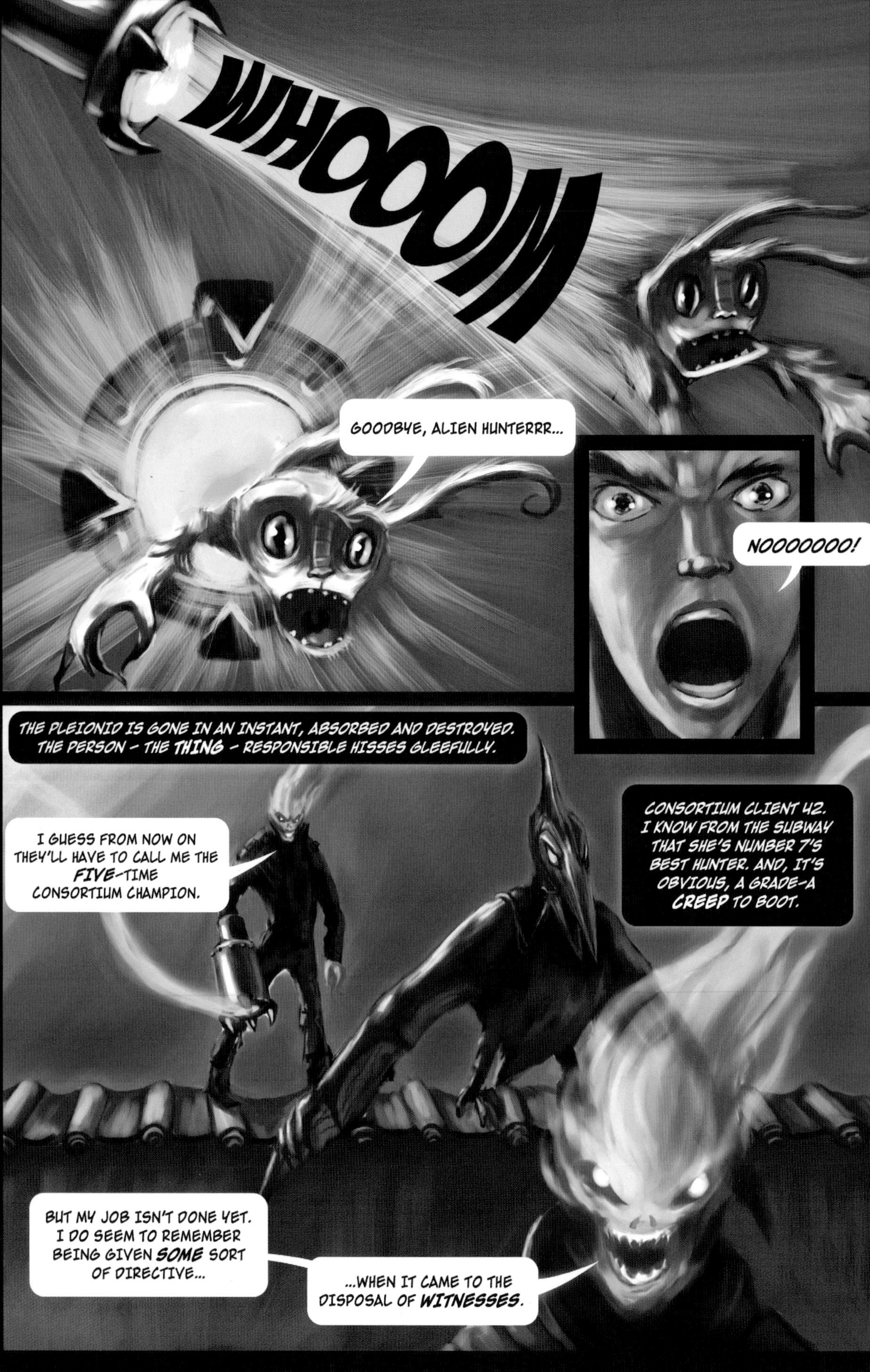
WHOOOM
GOODBYE, ALIEN HUNTERRR...
NOOOOOOO!
THE PLEIONID IS GONE IN AN INSTANT, ABSORBED AND DESTROYED. THE PERSON - THE THING - RESPONSIBLE HISSES GLEEFULLY.
I GUESS FROM NOW ON THEY'LL HAVE TO CALL ME THE FIVE-TIME CONSORTIUM CHAMPION.
CONSORTIUM CLIENT 42. I KNOW FROM THE SUBWAY THAT SHE'S NUMBER 7'S BEST HUNTER. AND, IT'S OBVIOUS, A GRADE-A CREEP TO BOOT.
BUT MY JOB ISN'T DONE YET. I DO SEEM TO REMEMBER BEING GIVEN SOME SORT OF DIRECTIVE...
...WHEN IT CAME TO THE DISPOSAL OF WITNESSES.

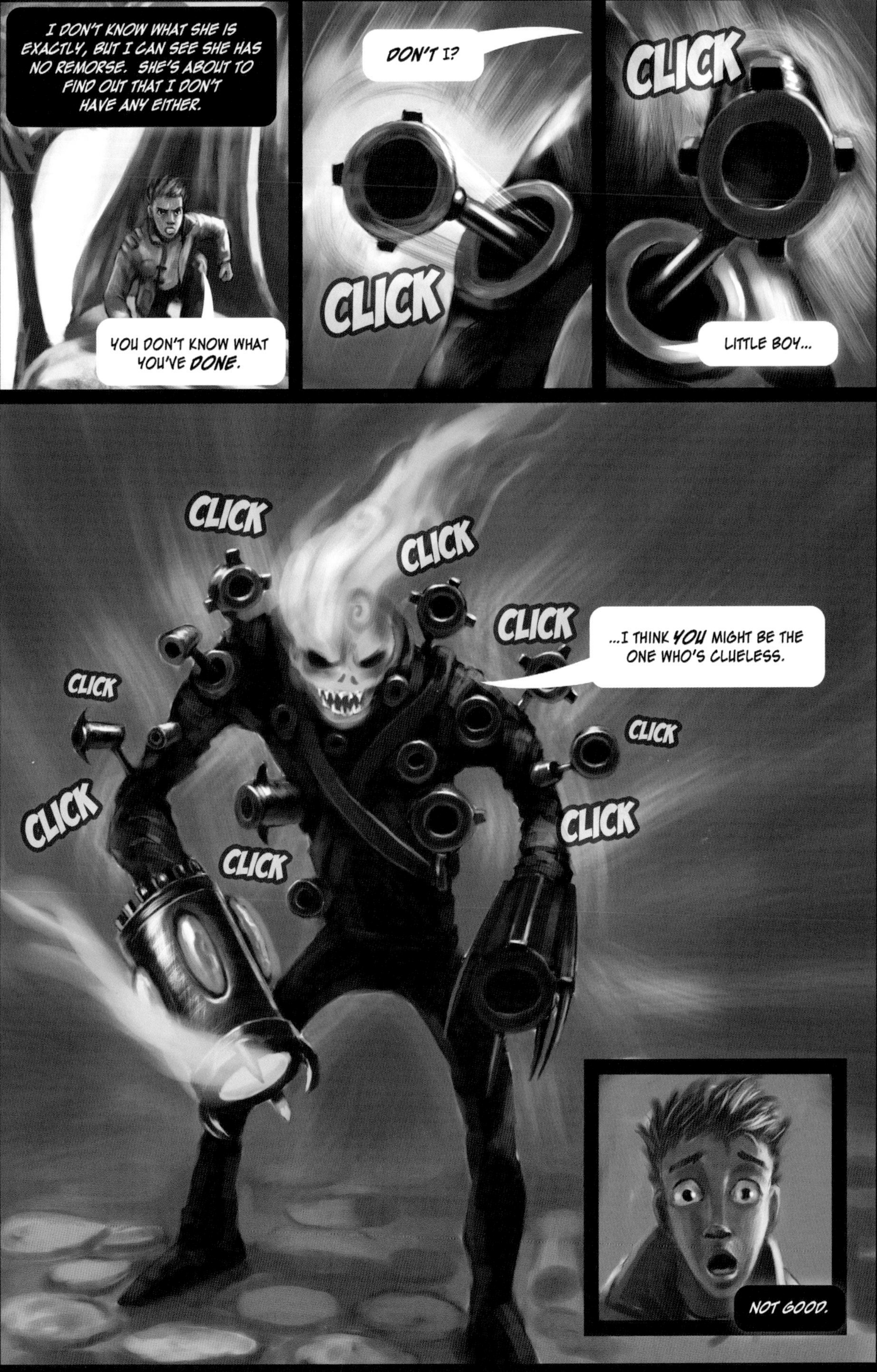
I DON'T KNOW WHAT SHE IS EXACTLY, BUT I CAN SEE SHE HAS NO REMORSE. SHE'S ABOUT TO FIND OUT THAT I DON'T HAVE ANY EITHER.
YOU DON'T KNOW WHAT YOU'VE DONE.
DON'T I?
CLICK
CLICK
LITTLE BOY...
CLICK
CLICK
CLICK
...I THINK YOU MIGHT BE THE ONE WHO'S CLUELESS.
CLICK
CLICK
CLICK
CLICK
CLICK
NOT GOOD.

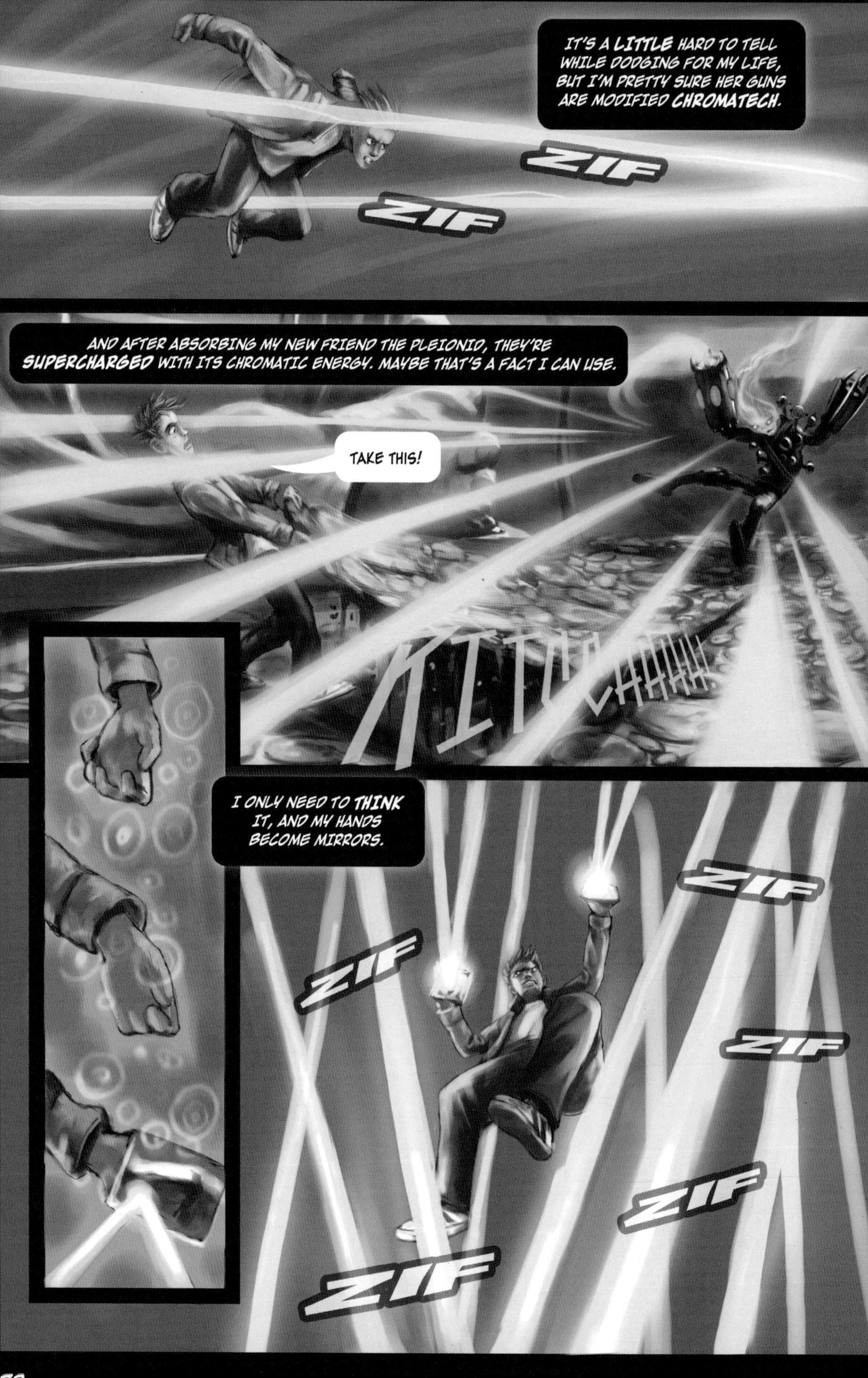
IT'S A LITTLE HARD TO TELL WHILE DODGING FOR MY LIFE, BUT I'M PRETTY SURE HER GUNS ARE MODIFIED CHROMATECH.
ZIF
ZIF
AND AFTER ABSORBING MY NEW FRIEND THE PLEIONID, THEY'RE SUPERCHARGED WITH ITS CHROMATIC ENERGY. MAYBE THAT'S A FACT I CAN USE.
TAKE THIS!
I ONLY NEED TO THINK IT, AND MY HANDS BECOME MIRRORS.
ZIF
ZIF
ZIF
ZIF
ZIF

ZWAAAAAAK

WHAT...WHAT HAVE YOU DONE?

WHAT'S **HAPPENING** TO ME?

SHE SHOULD KNOW. THE PLEIONID COULD HIDE INSIDE COLORS, AND HER GUN **ABSORBED** IT. NOW **SHE'S** DOING THE SAME THING.

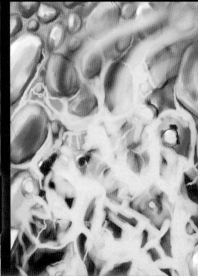

MAYBE SPENDING THE NEXT COUPLE HUNDRED YEARS AS PART OF THE TEMPLE COURTYARD WILL TEACH THIS HUNTER THE VIRTUES OF LIVING **PEACEFULLY**.

IT'S ONLY AFTER SHE'S DISAPPEARED THAT I REALIZE WE WEREN'T **ALONE** HERE.

GREETINGS, YOUNG MAN.

A BUDDHIST MONK...AND HE ACTS LIKE HE DIDN'T EVEN **NOTICE** THE FIGHT.

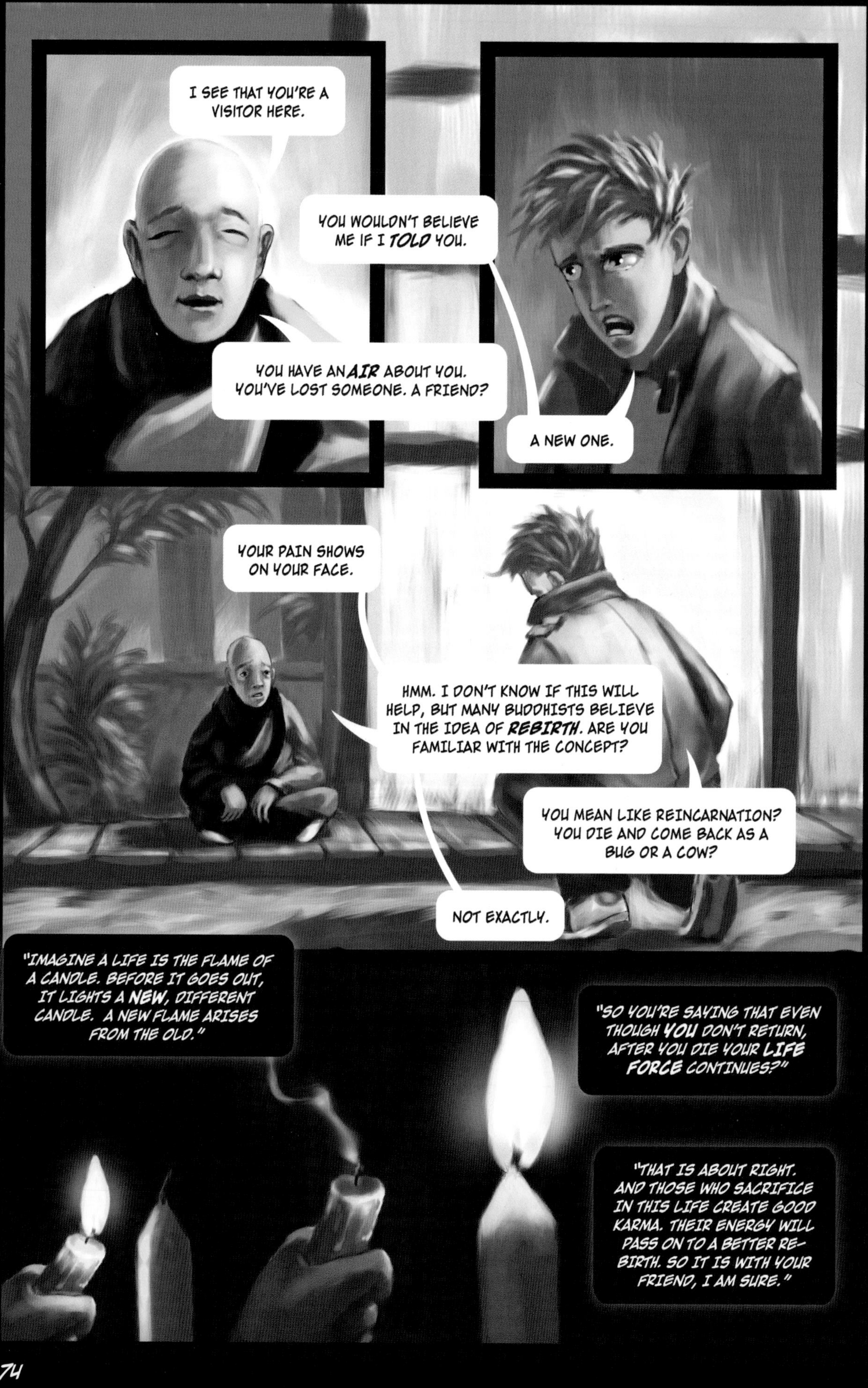
I SEE THAT YOU'RE A VISITOR HERE.
YOU WOULDN'T BELIEVE ME IF I TOLD YOU.
YOU HAVE AN AIR ABOUT YOU. YOU'VE LOST SOMEONE. A FRIEND?
A NEW ONE.
YOUR PAIN SHOWS ON YOUR FACE.
HMM. I DON'T KNOW IF THIS WILL HELP, BUT MANY BUDDHISTS BELIEVE IN THE IDEA OF REBIRTH. ARE YOU FAMILIAR WITH THE CONCEPT?
YOU MEAN LIKE REINCARNATION? YOU DIE AND COME BACK AS A BUG OR A COW?
NOT EXACTLY.
"IMAGINE A LIFE IS THE FLAME OF A CANDLE. BEFORE IT GOES OUT, IT LIGHTS A NEW, DIFFERENT CANDLE. A NEW FLAME ARISES FROM THE OLD."
"SO YOU'RE SAYING THAT EVEN THOUGH YOU DON'T RETURN, AFTER YOU DIE YOUR LIFE FORCE CONTINUES?"
"THAT IS ABOUT RIGHT. AND THOSE WHO SACRIFICE IN THIS LIFE CREATE GOOD KARMA. THEIR ENERGY WILL PASS ON TO A BETTER RE-BIRTH. SO IT IS WITH YOUR FRIEND, I AM SURE."

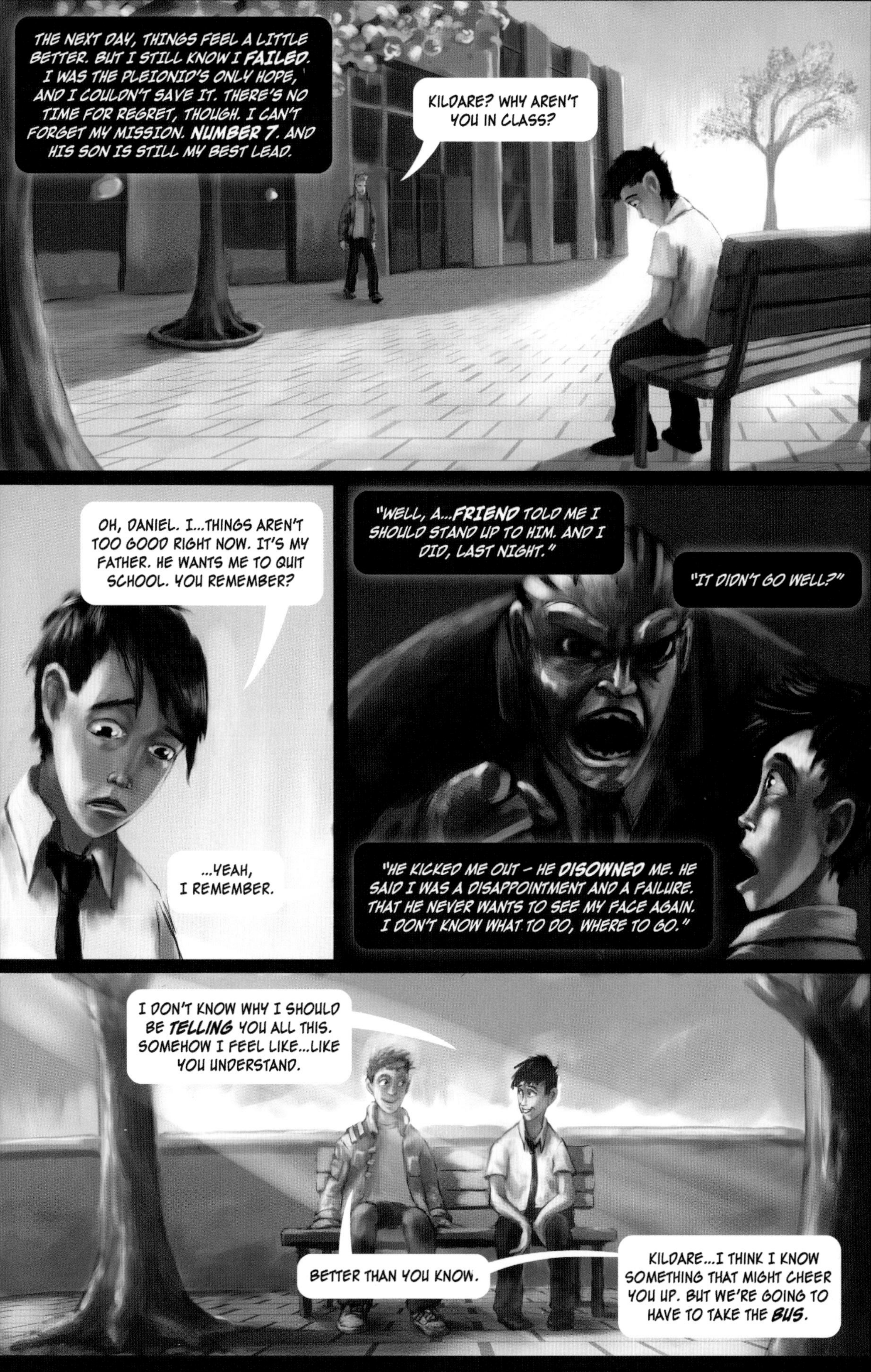
THE NEXT DAY, THINGS FEEL A LITTLE BETTER. BUT I STILL KNOW I FAILED. I WAS THE PLEIONID'S ONLY HOPE, AND I COULDN'T SAVE IT. THERE'S NO TIME FOR REGRET, THOUGH. I CAN'T FORGET MY MISSION. NUMBER 7. AND HIS SON IS STILL MY BEST LEAD.
KILDARE? WHY AREN'T YOU IN CLASS?
OH, DANIEL. I...THINGS AREN'T TOO GOOD RIGHT NOW. IT'S MY FATHER. HE WANTS ME TO QUIT SCHOOL. YOU REMEMBER?
...YEAH, I REMEMBER.
"WELL, A...FRIEND TOLD ME I SHOULD STAND UP TO HIM. AND I DID, LAST NIGHT."
"IT DIDN'T GO WELL?"
"HE KICKED ME OUT - HE DISOWNED ME. HE SAID I WAS A DISAPPOINTMENT AND A FAILURE. THAT HE NEVER WANTS TO SEE MY FACE AGAIN. I DON'T KNOW WHAT TO DO, WHERE TO GO."
I DON'T KNOW WHY I SHOULD BE TELLING YOU ALL THIS. SOMEHOW I FEEL LIKE...LIKE YOU UNDERSTAND.
BETTER THAN YOU KNOW.
KILDARE...I THINK I KNOW SOMETHING THAT MIGHT CHEER YOU UP. BUT WE'RE GOING TO HAVE TO TAKE THE BUS.

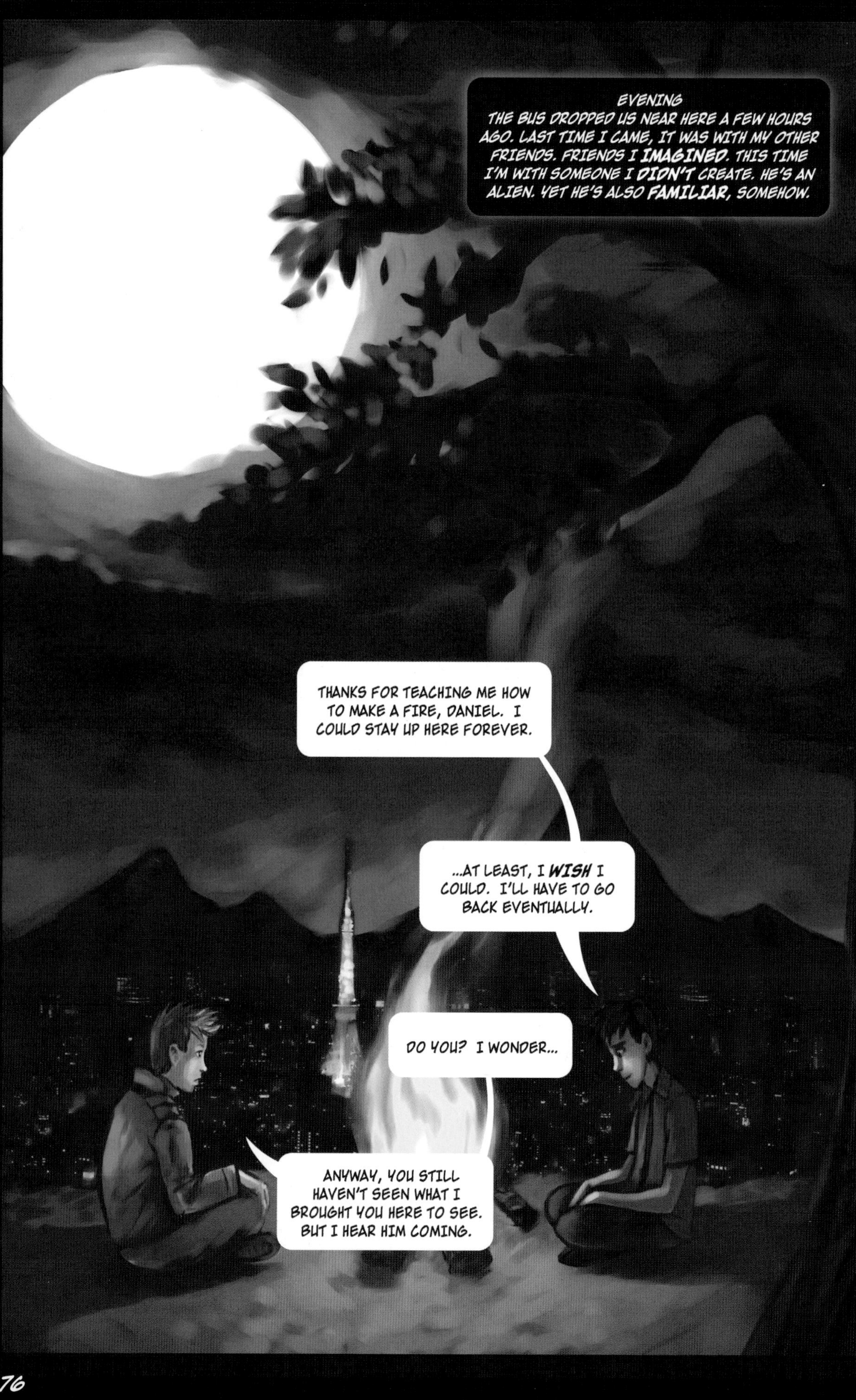
EVENING
THE BUS DROPPED US NEAR HERE A FEW HOURS AGO. LAST TIME I CAME, IT WAS WITH MY OTHER FRIENDS. FRIENDS I IMAGINED. THIS TIME I'M WITH SOMEONE I DIDN'T CREATE. HE'S AN ALIEN. YET HE'S ALSO FAMILIAR, SOMEHOW.
THANKS FOR TEACHING ME HOW TO MAKE A FIRE, DANIEL. I COULD STAY UP HERE FOREVER.
...AT LEAST, I WISH I COULD. I'LL HAVE TO GO BACK EVENTUALLY.
DO YOU? I WONDER...
ANYWAY, YOU STILL HAVEN'T SEEN WHAT I BROUGHT YOU HERE TO SEE. BUT I HEAR HIM COMING.

OH MY GOSH... A GOLDEN EAGLE? THEY'RE SO RARE!
HE'S MAGNIFICENT, ISN'T HE?
AS THE BIRD DRINKS FROM MY HAND, I CAN FEEL HIM RADIATING INDEPENDENCE, FREEDOM. THE STRENGTH OF A SURVIVOR.
I, WELL, TO BE HONEST, DANIEL, I - I DON'T MUCH CARE FOR BIRDS.
IT - OH, BUT HE REALLY IS INCREDIBLE, ISN'T HE?

ALL TOO SOON, THE EAGLE FLIES AWAY, FRIGHTENED. HE WAS GRIPPING SO TIGHT THAT THERE'S BLOOD ON MY ARM. I'M AFRAID TO TURN AROUND.
WELL, WELL, WELL. IT SEEMS YOU'VE FOUND NOTHING BETTER TO DO THAN BABYSIT OUR WORTHLESS OFFSPRING. IT'S A TASK UNWORTHY OF YOUR TALENTS...
...ALIEN HUNTER.
GOD, NO. HE'S FOUND ME. HE'S –
WAIT, DANIEL? ALIEN HUNTER? WHAT DOES HE MEAN?
I WISH I COULD SAY THIS IS A PLEASANT SURPRISE, CHAIRMAN. BUT THE ONLY UNWORTHY ONE HERE IS YOU.
YOU AND YOUR COHORTS ARE INSANE, GENOCIDAL MONSTERS.
KILDARE'S NOT LIKE YOU. HE'S A GOOD PERSON. HE'S MY FRIEND.

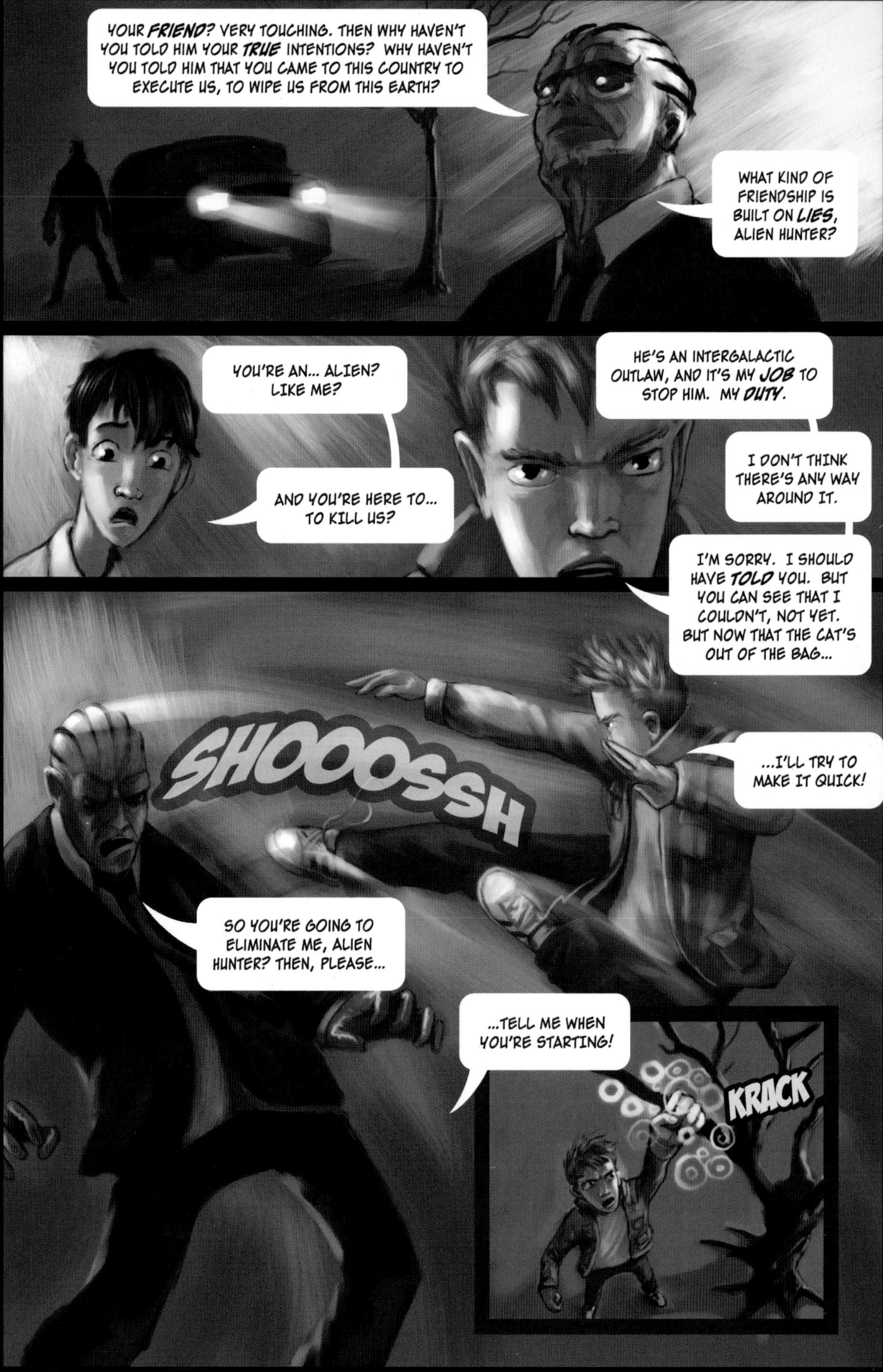
YOUR FRIEND? VERY TOUCHING. THEN WHY HAVEN'T YOU TOLD HIM YOUR TRUE INTENTIONS? WHY HAVEN'T YOU TOLD HIM THAT YOU CAME TO THIS COUNTRY TO EXECUTE US, TO WIPE US FROM THIS EARTH?
WHAT KIND OF FRIENDSHIP IS BUILT ON LIES, ALIEN HUNTER?
YOU'RE AN... ALIEN? LIKE ME?
AND YOU'RE HERE TO... TO KILL US?
HE'S AN INTERGALACTIC OUTLAW, AND IT'S MY JOB TO STOP HIM. MY DUTY.
I DON'T THINK THERE'S ANY WAY AROUND IT.
I'M SORRY. I SHOULD HAVE TOLD YOU. BUT YOU CAN SEE THAT I COULDN'T, NOT YET. BUT NOW THAT THE CAT'S OUT OF THE BAG...
SHOOOSSH
...I'LL TRY TO MAKE IT QUICK!
SO YOU'RE GOING TO ELIMINATE ME, ALIEN HUNTER? THEN, PLEASE...
...TELL ME WHEN YOU'RE STARTING!
KRACK

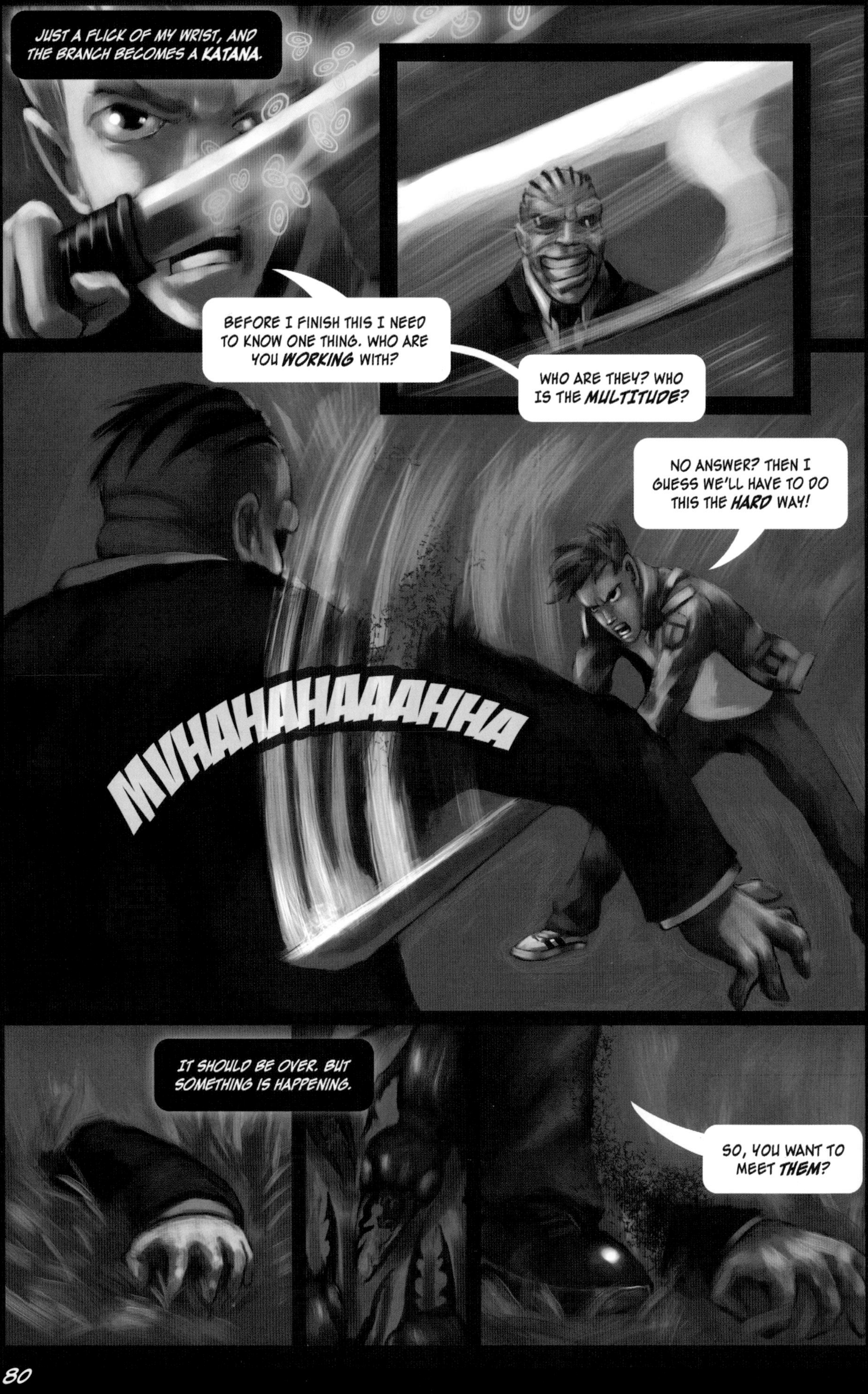
JUST A FLICK OF MY WRIST, AND THE BRANCH BECOMES A KATANA.
BEFORE I FINISH THIS I NEED TO KNOW ONE THING. WHO ARE YOU WORKING WITH?
WHO ARE THEY? WHO IS THE MULTITUDE?
NO ANSWER? THEN I GUESS WE'LL HAVE TO DO THIS THE HARD WAY!
MVHAHAHAAAHHA
IT SHOULD BE OVER. BUT SOMETHING IS HAPPENING.
SO, YOU WANT TO MEET THEM?

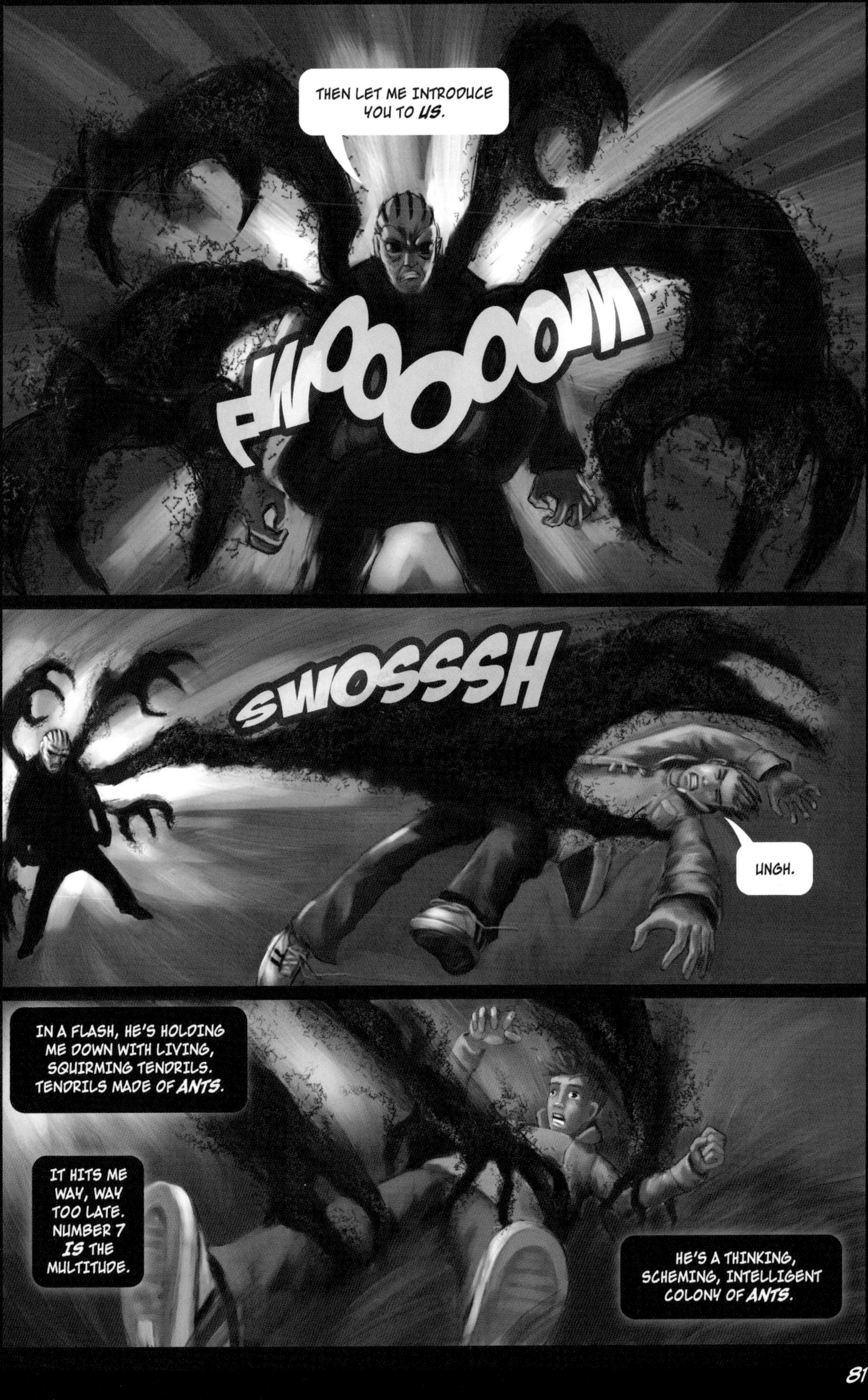
THEN LET ME INTRODUCE YOU TO US.
FWOOOOOM
SWOSSSH
UNGH.
IN A FLASH, HE'S HOLDING ME DOWN WITH LIVING, SQUIRMING TENDRILS. TENDRILS MADE OF ANTS.
IT HITS ME WAY, WAY TOO LATE. NUMBER 7 IS THE MULTITUDE.
HE'S A THINKING, SCHEMING, INTELLIGENT COLONY OF ANTS.

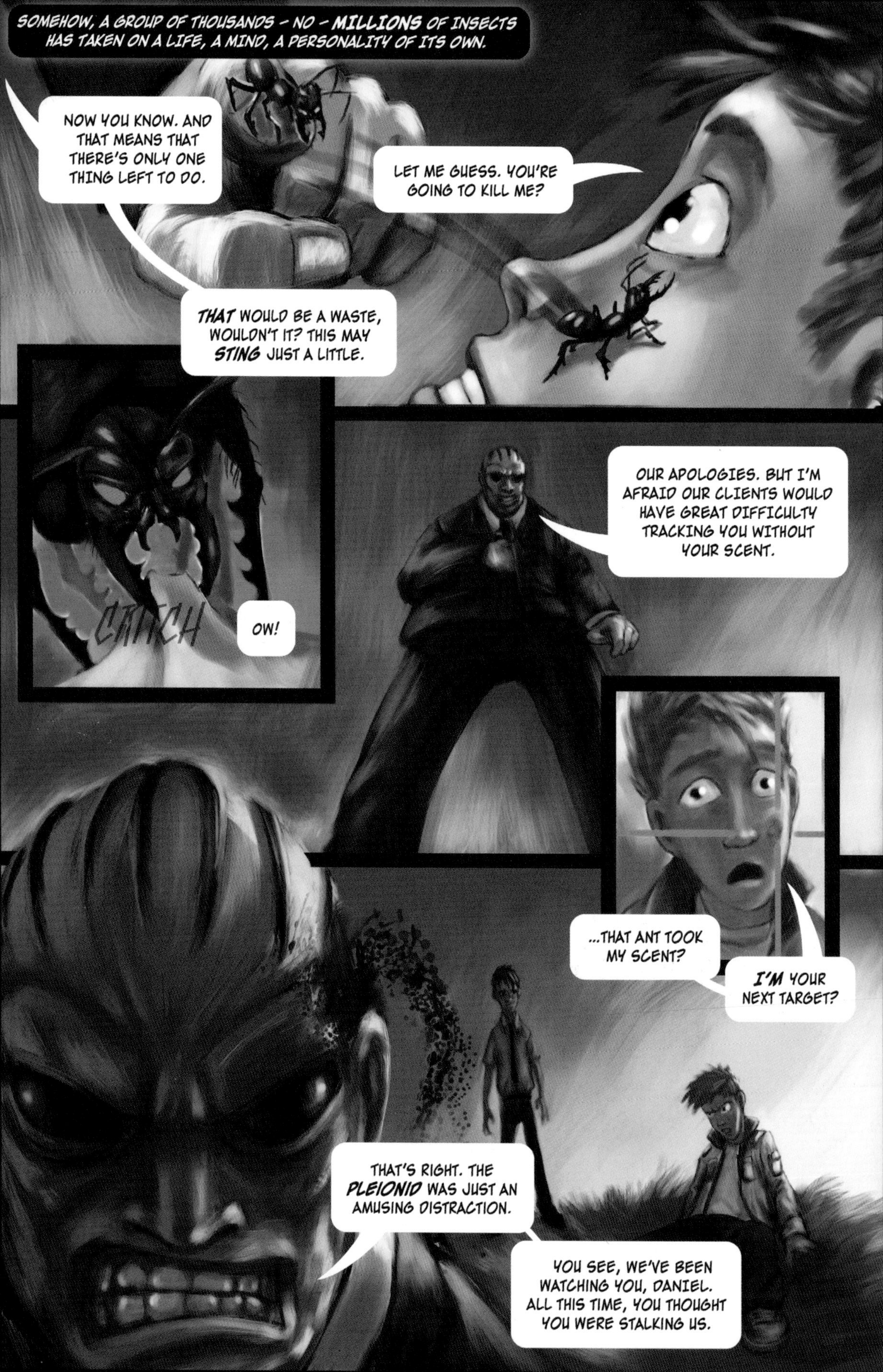
SOMEHOW, A GROUP OF THOUSANDS – NO – MILLIONS OF INSECTS HAS TAKEN ON A LIFE, A MIND, A PERSONALITY OF ITS OWN.
NOW YOU KNOW. AND THAT MEANS THAT THERE'S ONLY ONE THING LEFT TO DO.
LET ME GUESS. YOU'RE GOING TO KILL ME?
THAT WOULD BE A WASTE, WOULDN'T IT? THIS MAY STING JUST A LITTLE.
CRTCH
OW!
OUR APOLOGIES. BUT I'M AFRAID OUR CLIENTS WOULD HAVE GREAT DIFFICULTY TRACKING YOU WITHOUT YOUR SCENT.
...THAT ANT TOOK MY SCENT?
I'M YOUR NEXT TARGET?
THAT'S RIGHT. THE PLEIONID WAS JUST AN AMUSING DISTRACTION.
YOU SEE, WE'VE BEEN WATCHING YOU, DANIEL. ALL THIS TIME, YOU THOUGHT YOU WERE STALKING US.

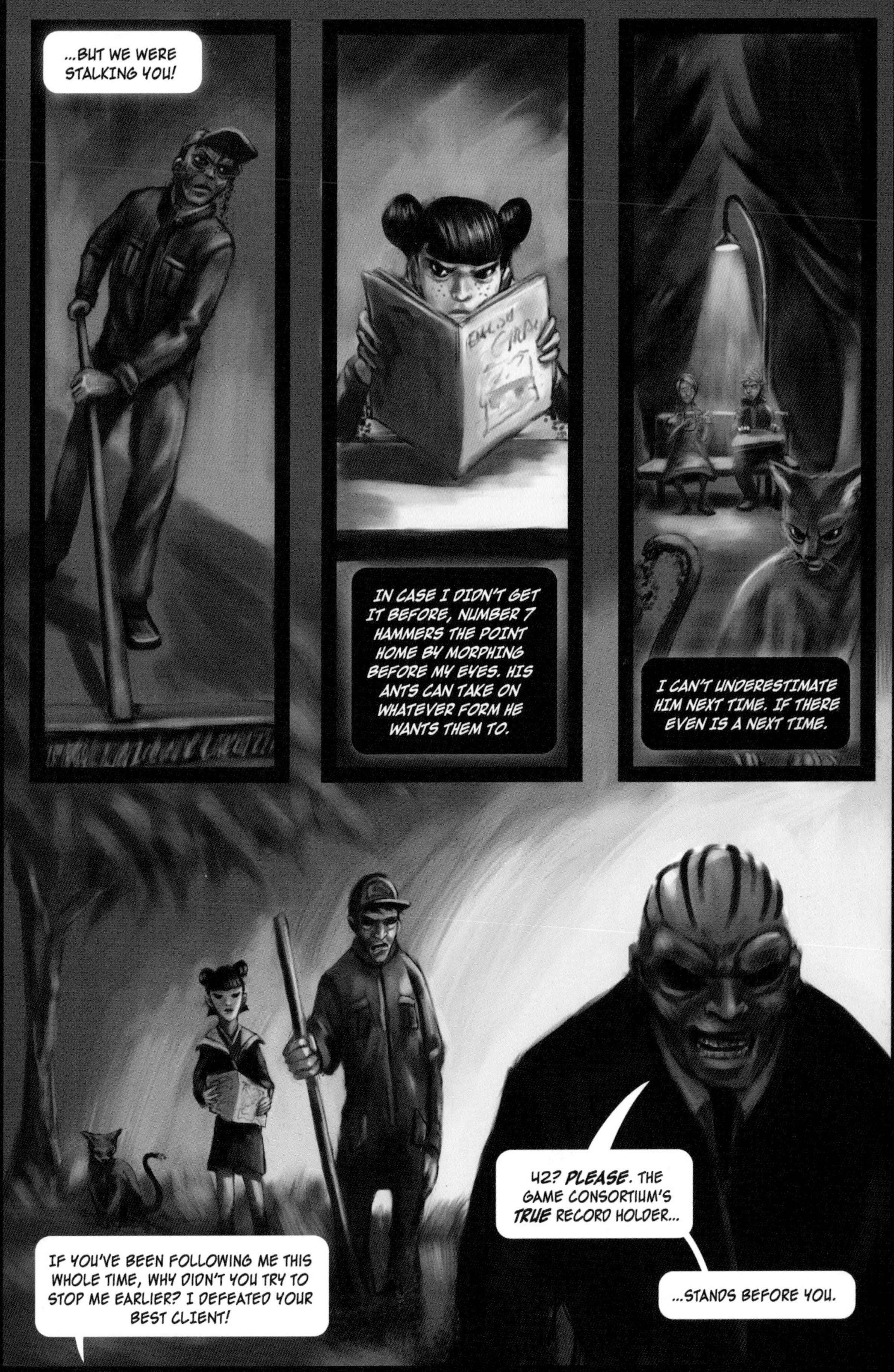
...BUT WE WERE STALKING YOU!
IN CASE I DIDN'T GET IT BEFORE, NUMBER 7 HAMMERS THE POINT HOME BY MORPHING BEFORE MY EYES. HIS ANTS CAN TAKE ON WHATEVER FORM HE WANTS THEM TO.
I CAN'T UNDERESTIMATE HIM NEXT TIME. IF THERE EVEN IS A NEXT TIME.
IF YOU'VE BEEN FOLLOWING ME THIS WHOLE TIME, WHY DIDN'T YOU TRY TO STOP ME EARLIER? I DEFEATED YOUR BEST CLIENT!
42? PLEASE. THE GAME CONSORTIUM'S TRUE RECORD HOLDER...
...STANDS BEFORE YOU.

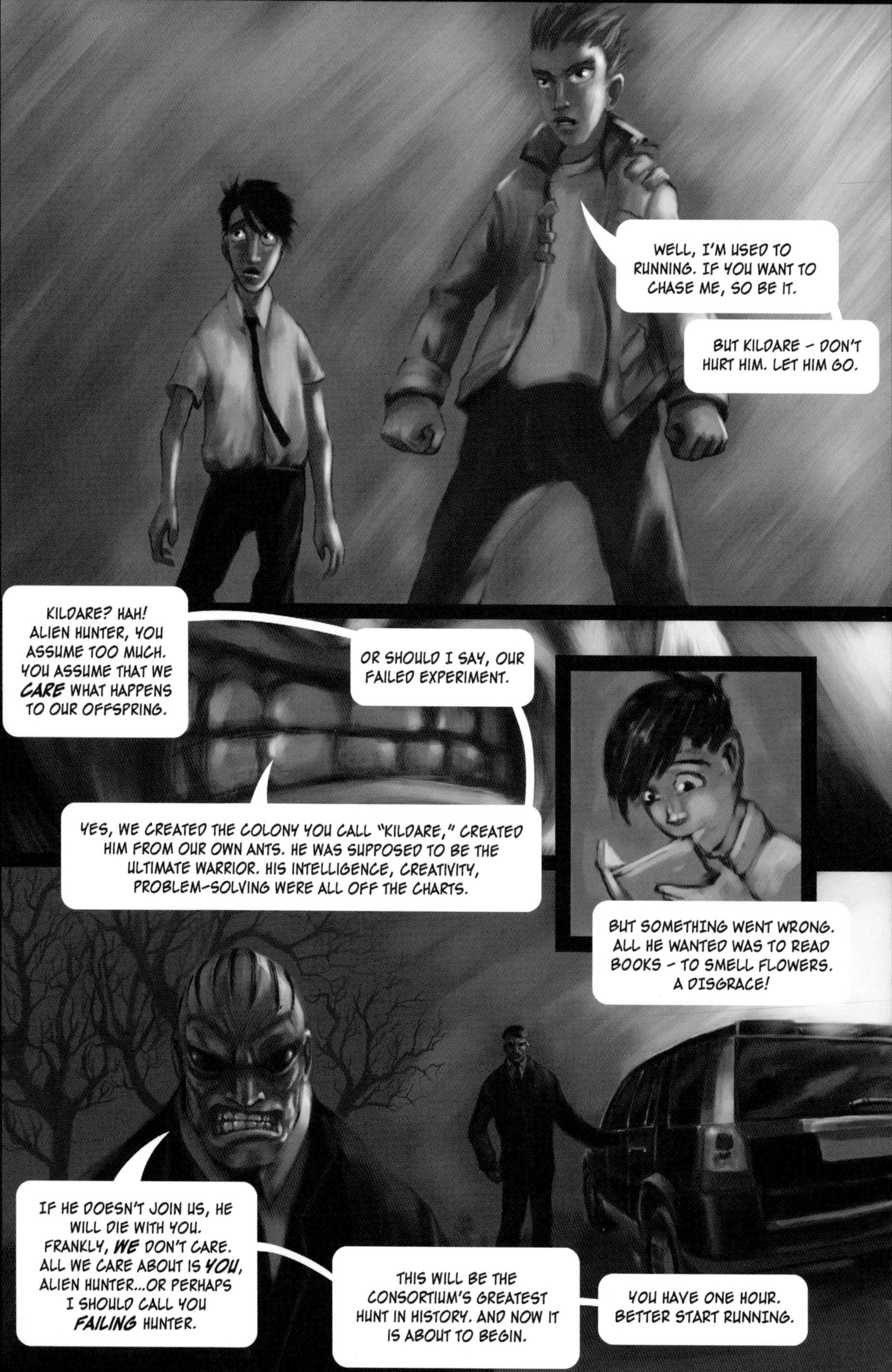
WELL, I'M USED TO RUNNING. IF YOU WANT TO CHASE ME, SO BE IT.
BUT KILDARE – DON'T HURT HIM. LET HIM GO.
KILDARE? HAH! ALIEN HUNTER, YOU ASSUME TOO MUCH. YOU ASSUME THAT WE CARE WHAT HAPPENS TO OUR OFFSPRING.
OR SHOULD I SAY, OUR FAILED EXPERIMENT.
YES, WE CREATED THE COLONY YOU CALL "KILDARE," CREATED HIM FROM OUR OWN ANTS. HE WAS SUPPOSED TO BE THE ULTIMATE WARRIOR. HIS INTELLIGENCE, CREATIVITY, PROBLEM-SOLVING WERE ALL OFF THE CHARTS.
BUT SOMETHING WENT WRONG. ALL HE WANTED WAS TO READ BOOKS – TO SMELL FLOWERS. A DISGRACE!
IF HE DOESN'T JOIN US, HE WILL DIE WITH YOU. FRANKLY, WE DON'T CARE. ALL WE CARE ABOUT IS YOU, ALIEN HUNTER...OR PERHAPS I SHOULD CALL YOU FAILING HUNTER.
THIS WILL BE THE CONSORTIUM'S GREATEST HUNT IN HISTORY. AND NOW IT IS ABOUT TO BEGIN.
YOU HAVE ONE HOUR. BETTER START RUNNING.

HE AND HIS HENCHMAN TEAR AWAY DOWN THE ROAD. KILDARE AND I ARE ON OUR OWN. FOR AN HOUR, AT LEAST.
YOU OKAY?
I THINK SO.
WE HAVE TO GET OUT OF HERE. I THINK HALF THE GALAXY IS ABOUT TO COME DOWN ON US.
I DON'T KNOW...MAYBE THERE'S NO POINT IN RUNNING. YOU DON'T KNOW HIM LIKE I DO. BESIDES, WE'RE MILES AWAY FROM THE CITY.
DON'T GIVE UP JUST YET.
UM, I KNOW WE'RE DESPERATE, DANIEL. BUT THOSE DON'T EVEN LOOK LIKE THEY WORK.
THEY DO NOW!
WE NEED TO MOVE FAST AND WE NEED TO LEARN ABOUT ANTS!

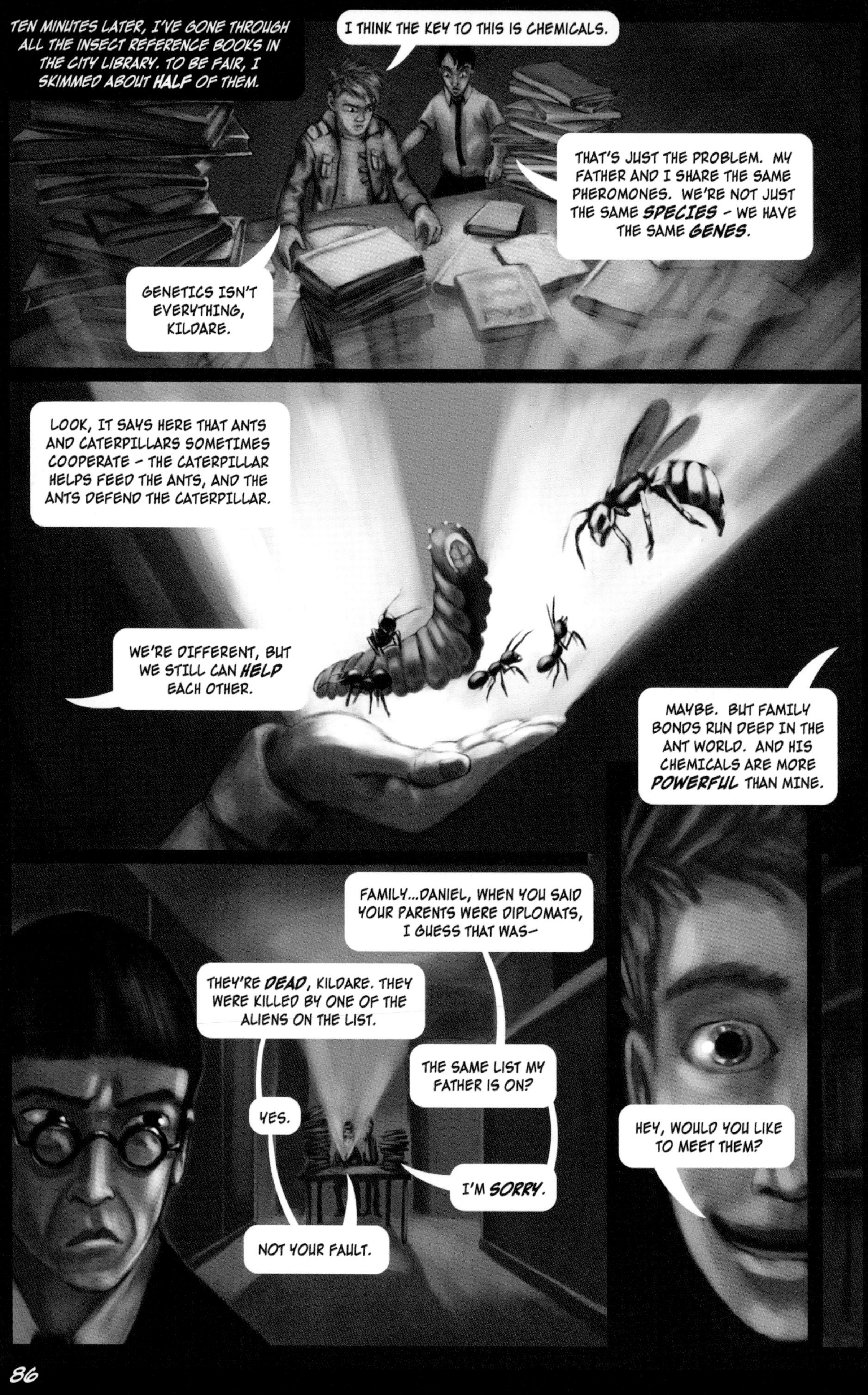
TEN MINUTES LATER, I'VE GONE THROUGH ALL THE INSECT REFERENCE BOOKS IN THE CITY LIBRARY. TO BE FAIR, I SKIMMED ABOUT HALF OF THEM.
I THINK THE KEY TO THIS IS CHEMICALS.
THAT'S JUST THE PROBLEM. MY FATHER AND I SHARE THE SAME PHEROMONES. WE'RE NOT JUST THE SAME SPECIES - WE HAVE THE SAME GENES.
GENETICS ISN'T EVERYTHING, KILDARE.
LOOK, IT SAYS HERE THAT ANTS AND CATERPILLARS SOMETIMES COOPERATE - THE CATERPILLAR HELPS FEED THE ANTS, AND THE ANTS DEFEND THE CATERPILLAR.
WE'RE DIFFERENT, BUT WE STILL CAN HELP EACH OTHER.
MAYBE. BUT FAMILY BONDS RUN DEEP IN THE ANT WORLD. AND HIS CHEMICALS ARE MORE POWERFUL THAN MINE.
FAMILY...DANIEL, WHEN YOU SAID YOUR PARENTS WERE DIPLOMATS, I GUESS THAT WAS-
THEY'RE DEAD, KILDARE. THEY WERE KILLED BY ONE OF THE ALIENS ON THE LIST.
THE SAME LIST MY FATHER IS ON?
YES.
I'M SORRY.
NOT YOUR FAULT.
HEY, WOULD YOU LIKE TO MEET THEM?

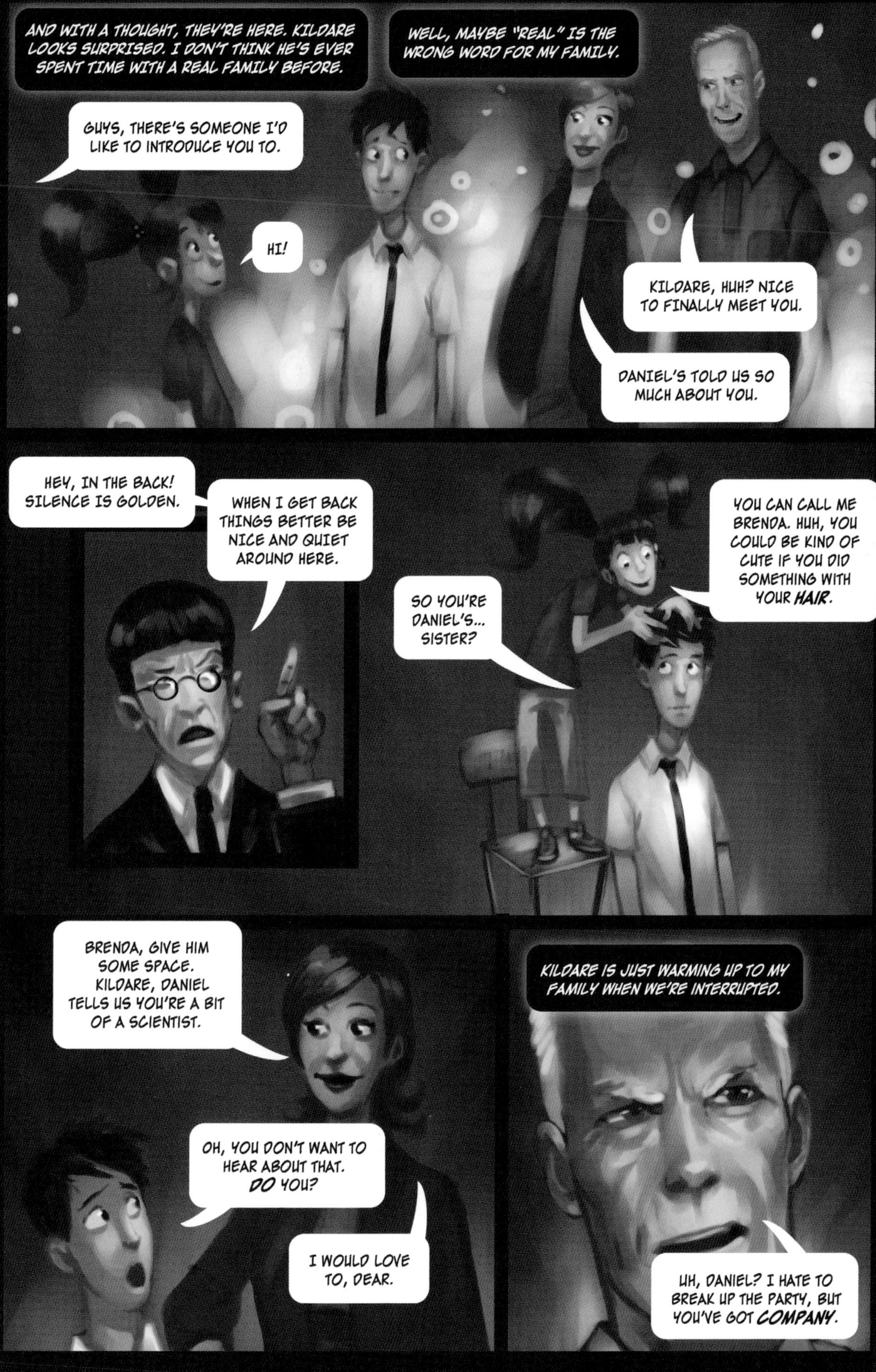

AND WITH A THOUGHT, THEY'RE HERE. KILDARE LOOKS SURPRISED. I DON'T THINK HE'S EVER SPENT TIME WITH A REAL FAMILY BEFORE.
WELL, MAYBE "REAL" IS THE WRONG WORD FOR MY FAMILY.
GUYS, THERE'S SOMEONE I'D LIKE TO INTRODUCE YOU TO.
HI!
KILDARE, HUH? NICE TO FINALLY MEET YOU.
DANIEL'S TOLD US SO MUCH ABOUT YOU.
HEY, IN THE BACK! SILENCE IS GOLDEN.
WHEN I GET BACK THINGS BETTER BE NICE AND QUIET AROUND HERE.
SO YOU'RE DANIEL'S... SISTER?
YOU CAN CALL ME BRENDA. HUH, YOU COULD BE KIND OF CUTE IF YOU DID SOMETHING WITH YOUR HAIR.
BRENDA, GIVE HIM SOME SPACE. KILDARE, DANIEL TELLS US YOU'RE A BIT OF A SCIENTIST.
OH, YOU DON'T WANT TO HEAR ABOUT THAT. DO YOU?
I WOULD LOVE TO, DEAR.
KILDARE IS JUST WARMING UP TO MY FAMILY WHEN WE'RE INTERRUPTED.
UH, DANIEL? I HATE TO BREAK UP THE PARTY, BUT YOU'VE GOT COMPANY.

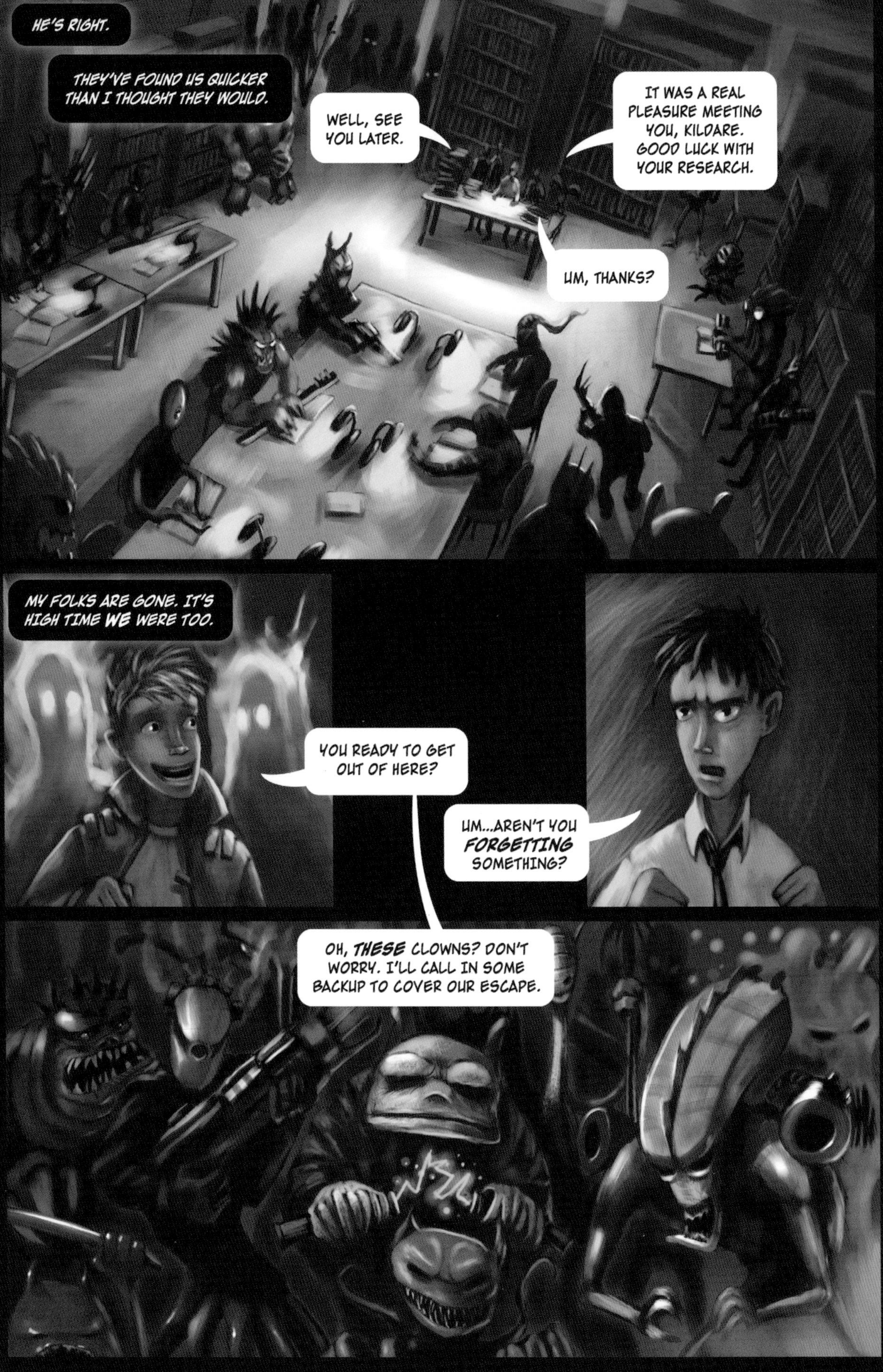
HE'S RIGHT.
THEY'VE FOUND US QUICKER THAN I THOUGHT THEY WOULD.
WELL, SEE YOU LATER.
IT WAS A REAL PLEASURE MEETING YOU, KILDARE. GOOD LUCK WITH YOUR RESEARCH.
UM, THANKS?
MY FOLKS ARE GONE. IT'S HIGH TIME WE WERE TOO.
YOU READY TO GET OUT OF HERE?
UM...AREN'T YOU FORGETTING SOMETHING?
OH, THESE CLOWNS? DON'T WORRY. I'LL CALL IN SOME BACKUP TO COVER OUR ESCAPE.

THESE THUGS DON'T STRIKE ME AS THE TYPE THAT DO MUCH READING.
WELL, I'M ABOUT TO UNLOCK THE WORLD OF BOOKS FOR THEM.
BOOOOOK!
THIS IS OUR BACK-UP?
KIND OF A NOVEL IDEA, WOULDN'T YOU SAY?
I THINK YOU NEED TO WORK ON YOUR PUNS.
I DON'T THINK WE'RE GOING TO HAVE TO WORRY ABOUT THESE GUYS FOR A WHILE.
TOO BAD THEY'RE JUST THE TIP OF THE ICEBERG. THOUSANDS OF CONSORTIUM POACHERS ARE ALREADY COMBING THE CITY, LOOKING FOR US.
RUN FOR IT!!
BWWAARGH!!

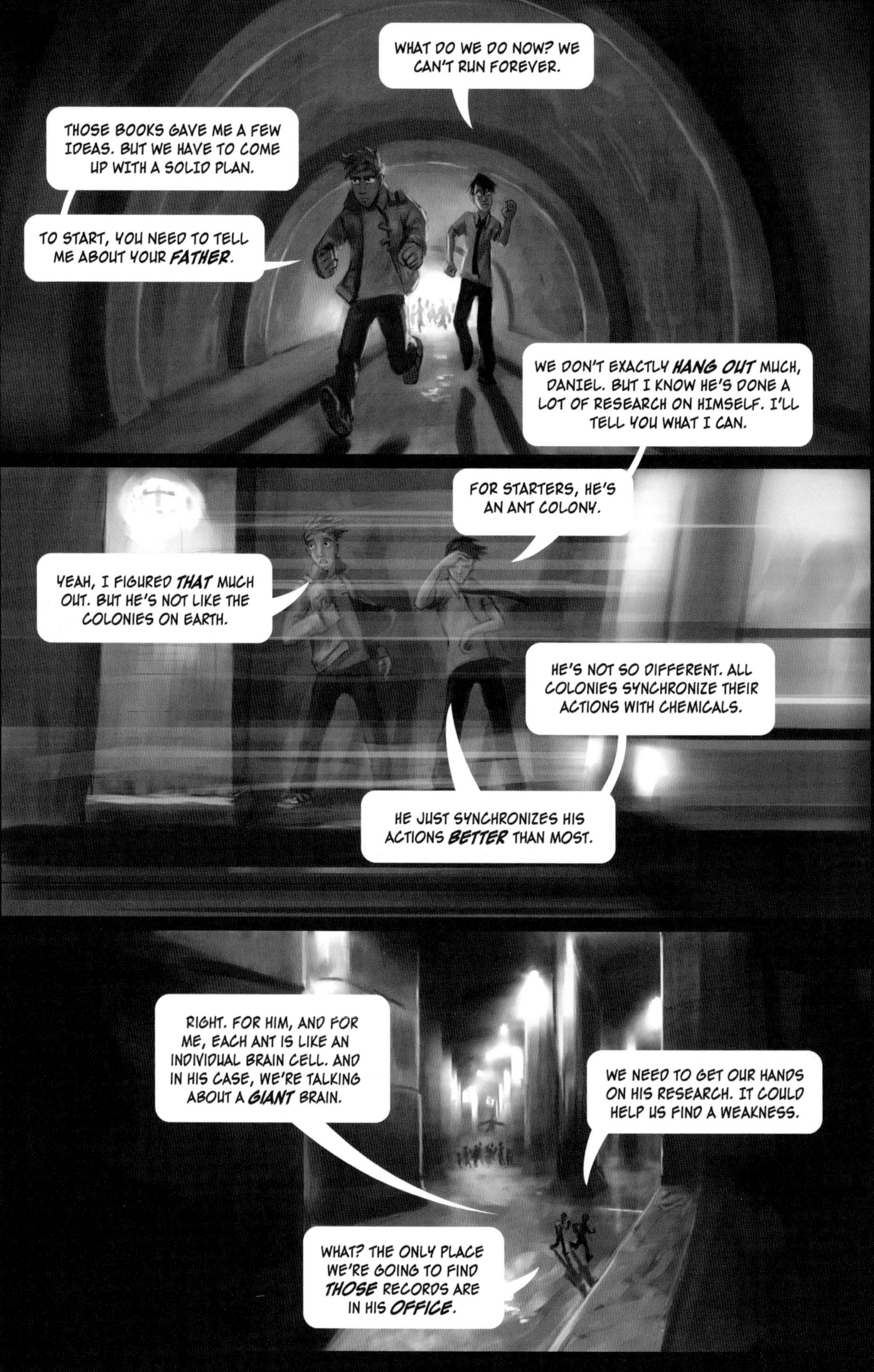
WHAT DO WE DO NOW? WE CAN'T RUN FOREVER.
THOSE BOOKS GAVE ME A FEW IDEAS. BUT WE HAVE TO COME UP WITH A SOLID PLAN.
TO START, YOU NEED TO TELL ME ABOUT YOUR *FATHER*.
WE DON'T EXACTLY *HANG OUT* MUCH, DANIEL. BUT I KNOW HE'S DONE A LOT OF RESEARCH ON HIMSELF. I'LL TELL YOU WHAT I CAN.
FOR STARTERS, HE'S AN ANT COLONY.
YEAH, I FIGURED *THAT* MUCH OUT. BUT HE'S NOT LIKE THE COLONIES ON EARTH.
HE'S NOT SO DIFFERENT. ALL COLONIES SYNCHRONIZE THEIR ACTIONS WITH CHEMICALS.
HE JUST SYNCHRONIZES HIS ACTIONS *BETTER* THAN MOST.
RIGHT. FOR HIM, AND FOR ME, EACH ANT IS LIKE AN INDIVIDUAL BRAIN CELL. AND IN HIS CASE, WE'RE TALKING ABOUT A *GIANT* BRAIN.
WE NEED TO GET OUR HANDS ON HIS RESEARCH. IT COULD HELP US FIND A WEAKNESS.
WHAT? THE ONLY PLACE WE'RE GOING TO FIND *THOSE* RECORDS ARE IN HIS *OFFICE*.

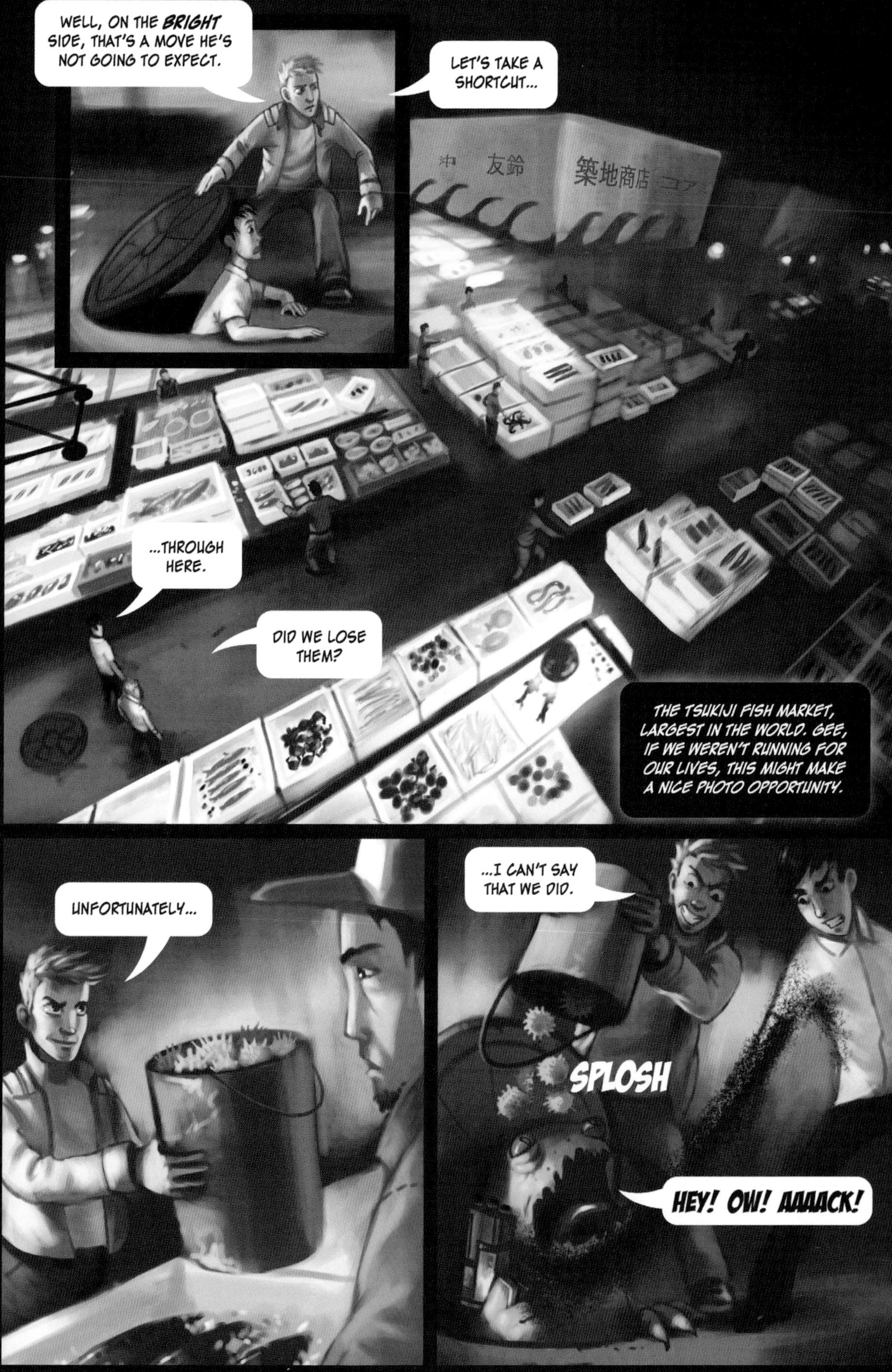
WELL, ON THE **BRIGHT** SIDE, THAT'S A MOVE HE'S NOT GOING TO EXPECT.
LET'S TAKE A SHORTCUT...
友鈴
築地商店
...THROUGH HERE.
DID WE LOSE THEM?
THE TSUKIJI FISH MARKET, LARGEST IN THE WORLD. GEE, IF WE WEREN'T RUNNING FOR OUR LIVES, THIS MIGHT MAKE A NICE PHOTO OPPORTUNITY.
UNFORTUNATELY...
...I CAN'T SAY THAT WE DID.
SPLOSH
HEY! OW! AAAACK!

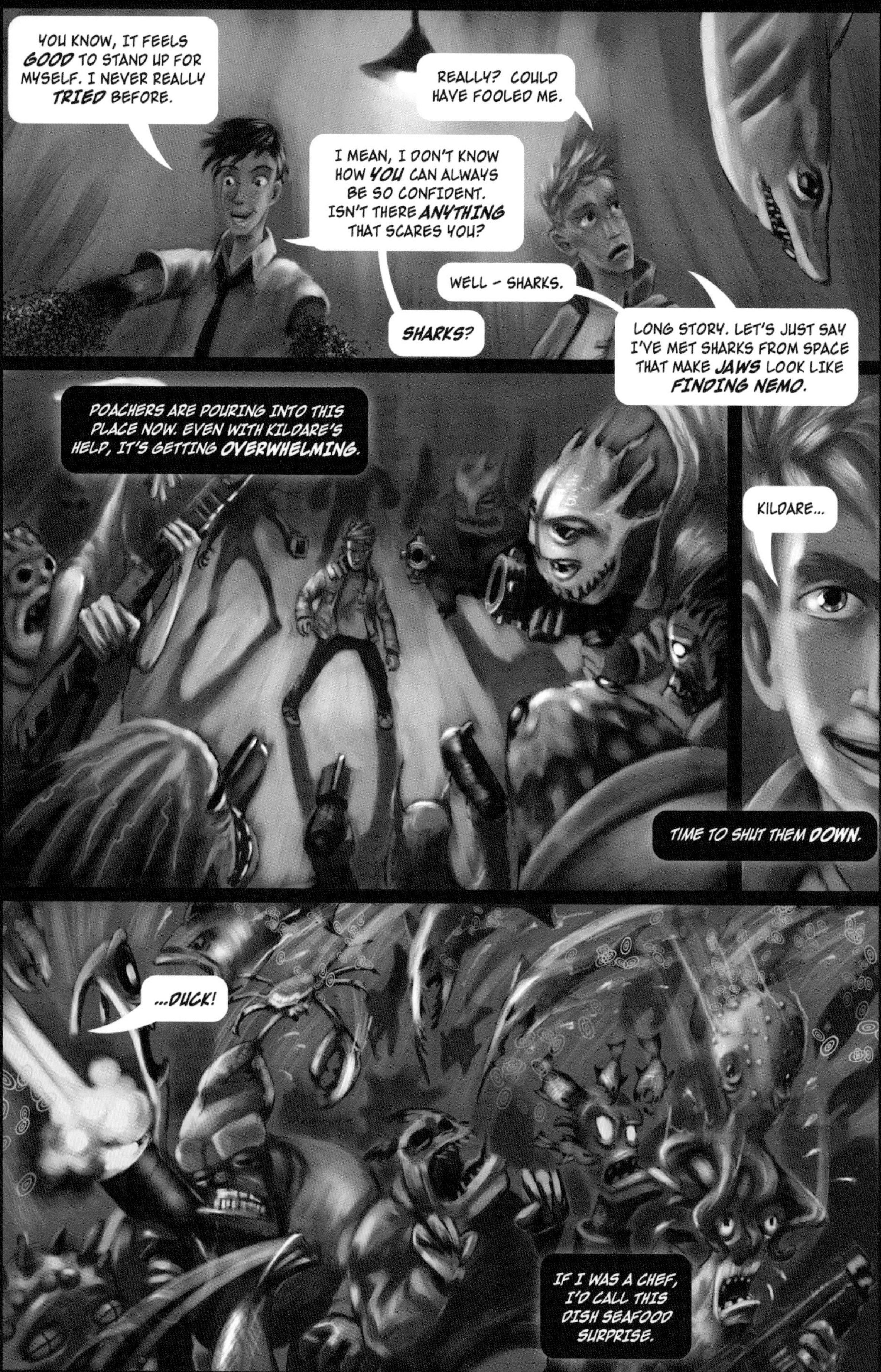
YOU KNOW, IT FEELS GOOD TO STAND UP FOR MYSELF. I NEVER REALLY TRIED BEFORE.
REALLY? COULD HAVE FOOLED ME.
I MEAN, I DON'T KNOW HOW YOU CAN ALWAYS BE SO CONFIDENT. ISN'T THERE ANYTHING THAT SCARES YOU?
WELL - SHARKS.
SHARKS?
LONG STORY. LET'S JUST SAY I'VE MET SHARKS FROM SPACE THAT MAKE JAWS LOOK LIKE FINDING NEMO.
POACHERS ARE POURING INTO THIS PLACE NOW. EVEN WITH KILDARE'S HELP, IT'S GETTING OVERWHELMING.
KILDARE...
TIME TO SHUT THEM DOWN.
...DUCK!
IF I WAS A CHEF, I'D CALL THIS DISH SEAFOOD SURPRISE.

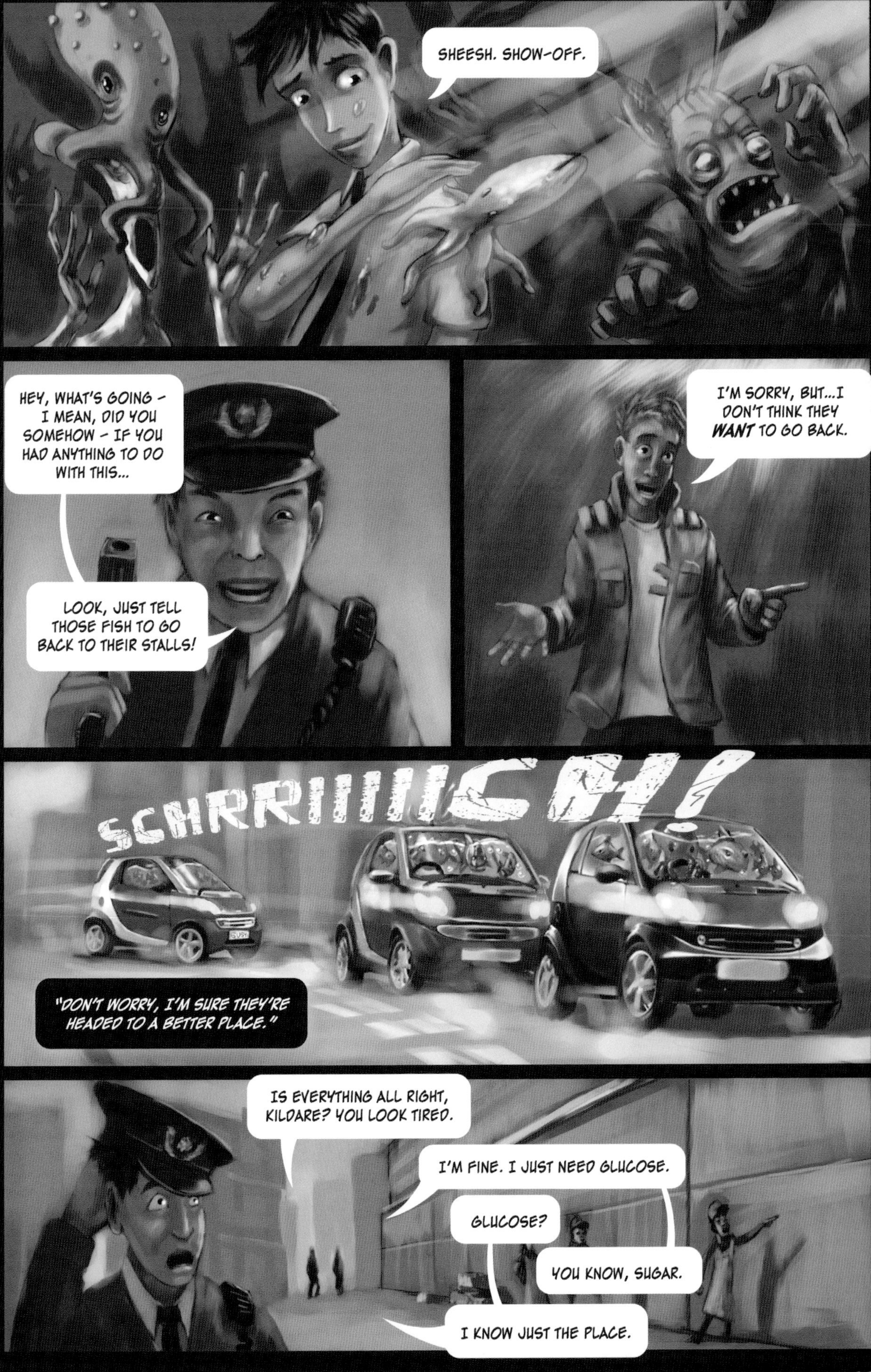
SHEESH. SHOW-OFF.
HEY, WHAT'S GOING - I MEAN, DID YOU SOMEHOW - IF YOU HAD ANYTHING TO DO WITH THIS...
LOOK, JUST TELL THOSE FISH TO GO BACK TO THEIR STALLS!
I'M SORRY, BUT...I DON'T THINK THEY *WANT* TO GO BACK.
SCHRRIIIIGH!
"DON'T WORRY, I'M SURE THEY'RE HEADED TO A BETTER PLACE."
IS EVERYTHING ALL RIGHT, KILDARE? YOU LOOK TIRED.
I'M FINE. I JUST NEED GLUCOSE.
GLUCOSE?
YOU KNOW, SUGAR.
I KNOW JUST THE PLACE.

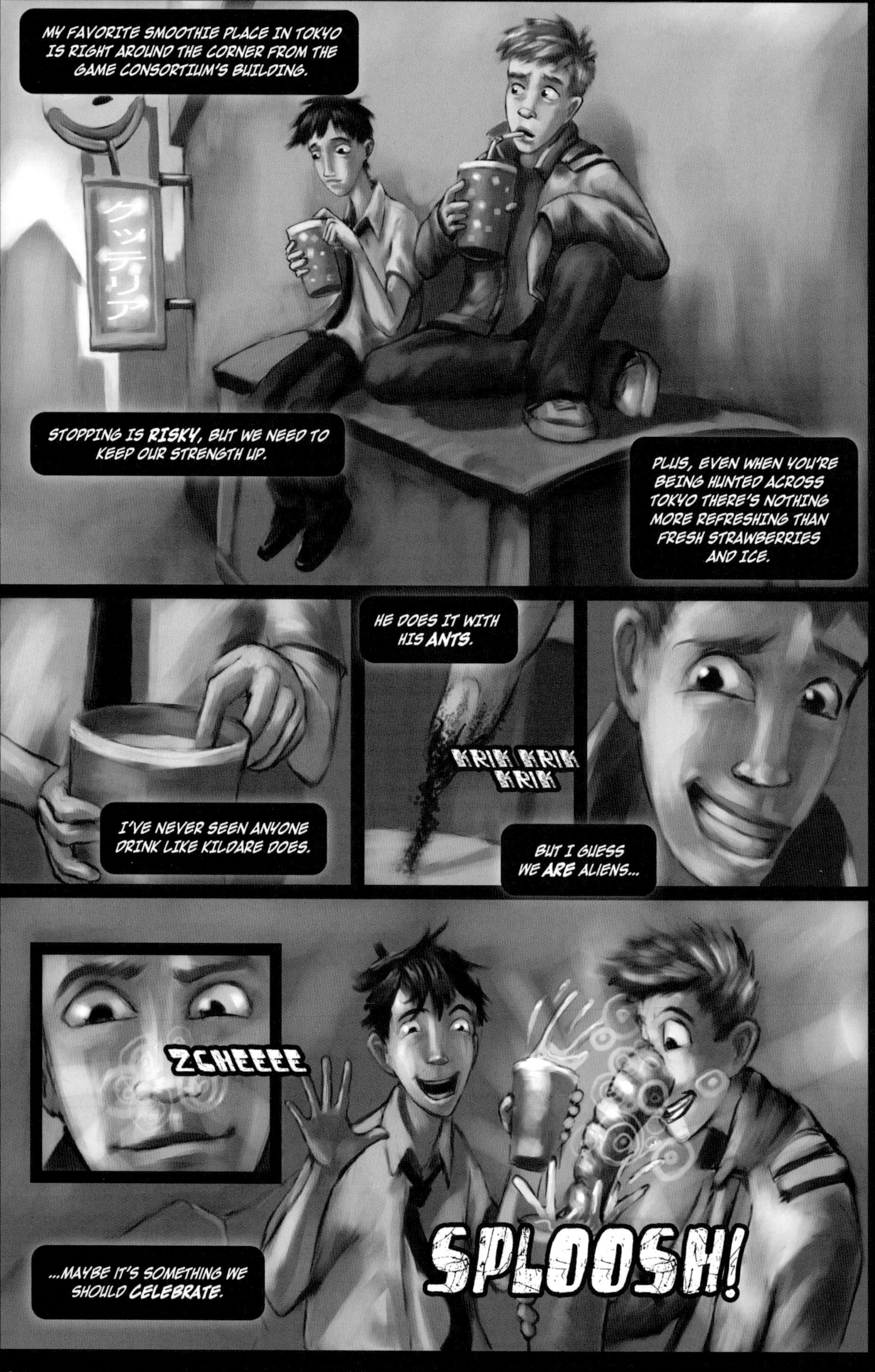
MY FAVORITE SMOOTHIE PLACE IN TOKYO IS RIGHT AROUND THE CORNER FROM THE GAME CONSORTIUM'S BUILDING.
クッテリア
STOPPING IS RISKY, BUT WE NEED TO KEEP OUR STRENGTH UP.
PLUS, EVEN WHEN YOU'RE BEING HUNTED ACROSS TOKYO THERE'S NOTHING MORE REFRESHING THAN FRESH STRAWBERRIES AND ICE.
I'VE NEVER SEEN ANYONE DRINK LIKE KILDARE DOES.
HE DOES IT WITH HIS ANTS.
KRIK KRIK KRIK
BUT I GUESS WE ARE ALIENS...
ZCHEEEE
...MAYBE IT'S SOMETHING WE SHOULD CELEBRATE.
SPLOOSH!

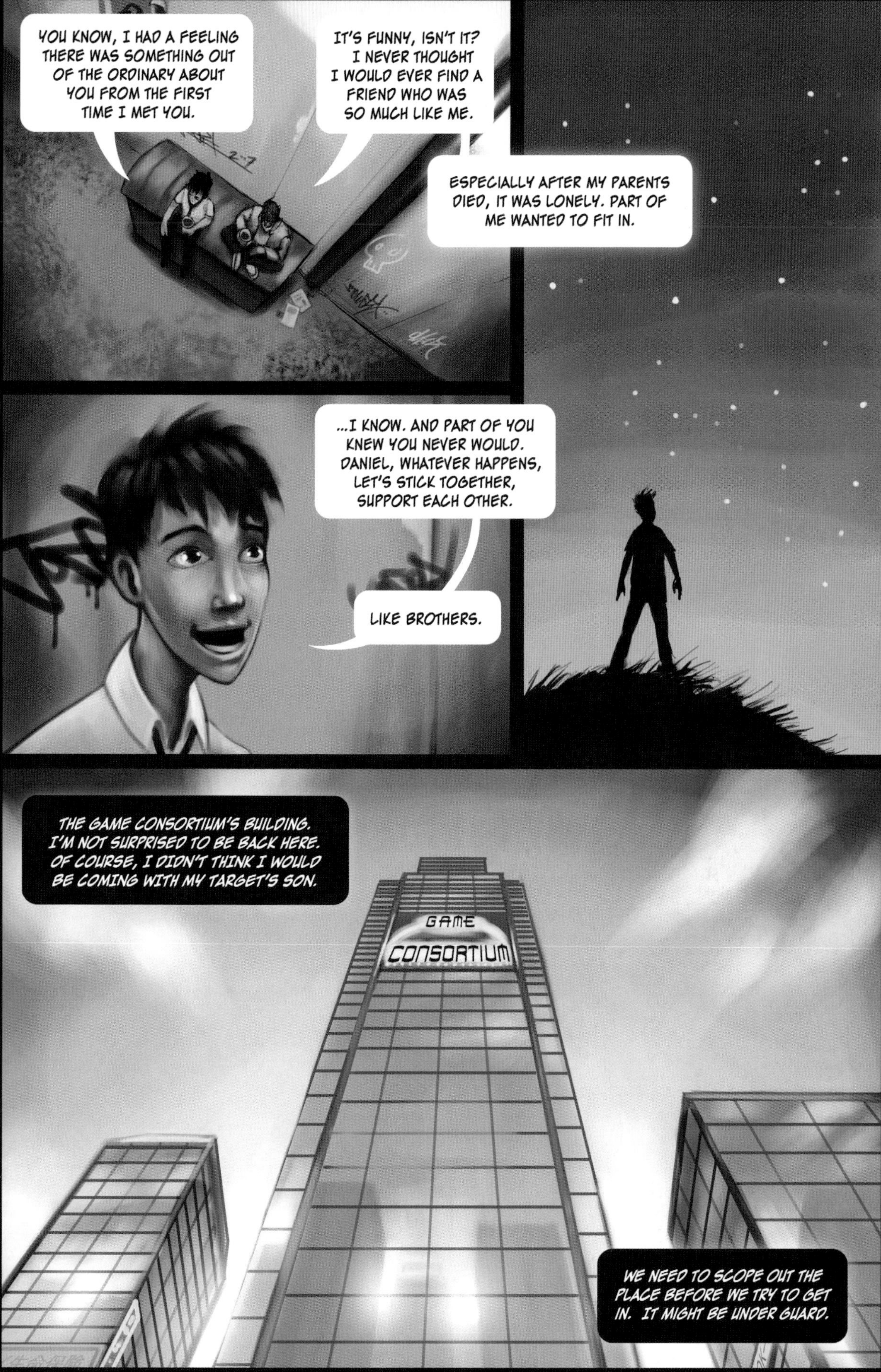
YOU KNOW, I HAD A FEELING THERE WAS SOMETHING OUT OF THE ORDINARY ABOUT YOU FROM THE FIRST TIME I MET YOU.
IT'S FUNNY, ISN'T IT? I NEVER THOUGHT I WOULD EVER FIND A FRIEND WHO WAS SO MUCH LIKE ME.
ESPECIALLY AFTER MY PARENTS DIED, IT WAS LONELY. PART OF ME WANTED TO FIT IN.
...I KNOW. AND PART OF YOU KNEW YOU NEVER WOULD. DANIEL, WHATEVER HAPPENS, LET'S STICK TOGETHER, SUPPORT EACH OTHER.
LIKE BROTHERS.
THE GAME CONSORTIUM'S BUILDING. I'M NOT SURPRISED TO BE BACK HERE. OF COURSE, I DIDN'T THINK I WOULD BE COMING WITH MY TARGET'S SON.
GAME CONSORTIUM
WE NEED TO SCOPE OUT THE PLACE BEFORE WE TRY TO GET IN. IT MIGHT BE UNDER GUARD.

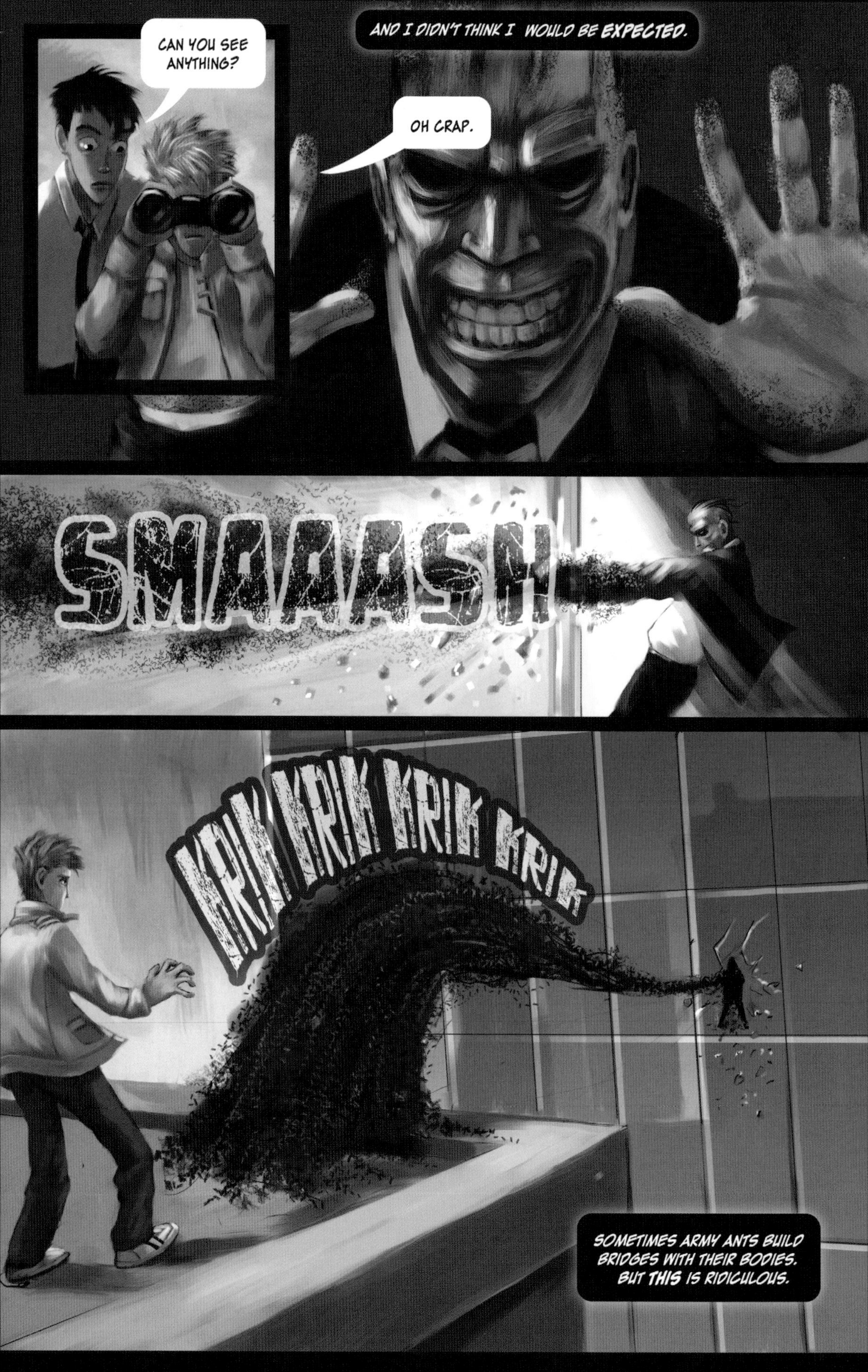
CAN YOU SEE ANYTHING?
AND I DIDN'T THINK I WOULD BE EXPECTED.
OH CRAP.
SMAAASH!
KRIK KRIK KRIK KRIK
SOMETIMES ARMY ANTS BUILD BRIDGES WITH THEIR BODIES. BUT THIS IS RIDICULOUS.

NUMBER 7 RE-FORMS RIGHT NEXT TO US...AND GRINS.
AH, RIGHT ON TIME. YOU KNOW, THE HUNT IS MUCH LESS INTERESTING WHEN THE PREY IS SO PREDICTABLE.
I'LL ADMIT IT. YOU SURPRISED ME BEFORE. BUT NOW THAT I KNOW WHAT YOU ARE I'M NOT GOING TO HOLD BACK.
AND MAYBE YOU DIDN'T NOTICE, BUT THERE ARE TWO OF US, AND ONLY ONE OF YOU.
DANIEL... ABOUT THAT...I KNOW WHAT I SAID ABOUT STICKING TOGETHER, BUT YOU - YOU CAN'T ASK ME TO FIGHT HIM! YOU DON'T SEE HIM THE WAY I DO!
HE'S RIGHT, ALIEN HUNTER. WE ARE THE MASTER COLONY. WE CREATED YOUR "FRIEND." HE BELONGS TO US.
YOU CANNOT DEFEAT ME. AND LOOK AT HIM - HE CANNOT EVEN FIGHT ME.
THERE ARE CHEMICALS IN THE AIR. I CAN SENSE IT. NUMBER 7 IS SWIMMING IN THEM, HE'S COMMUNICATING WITH KILDARE SOMEHOW.

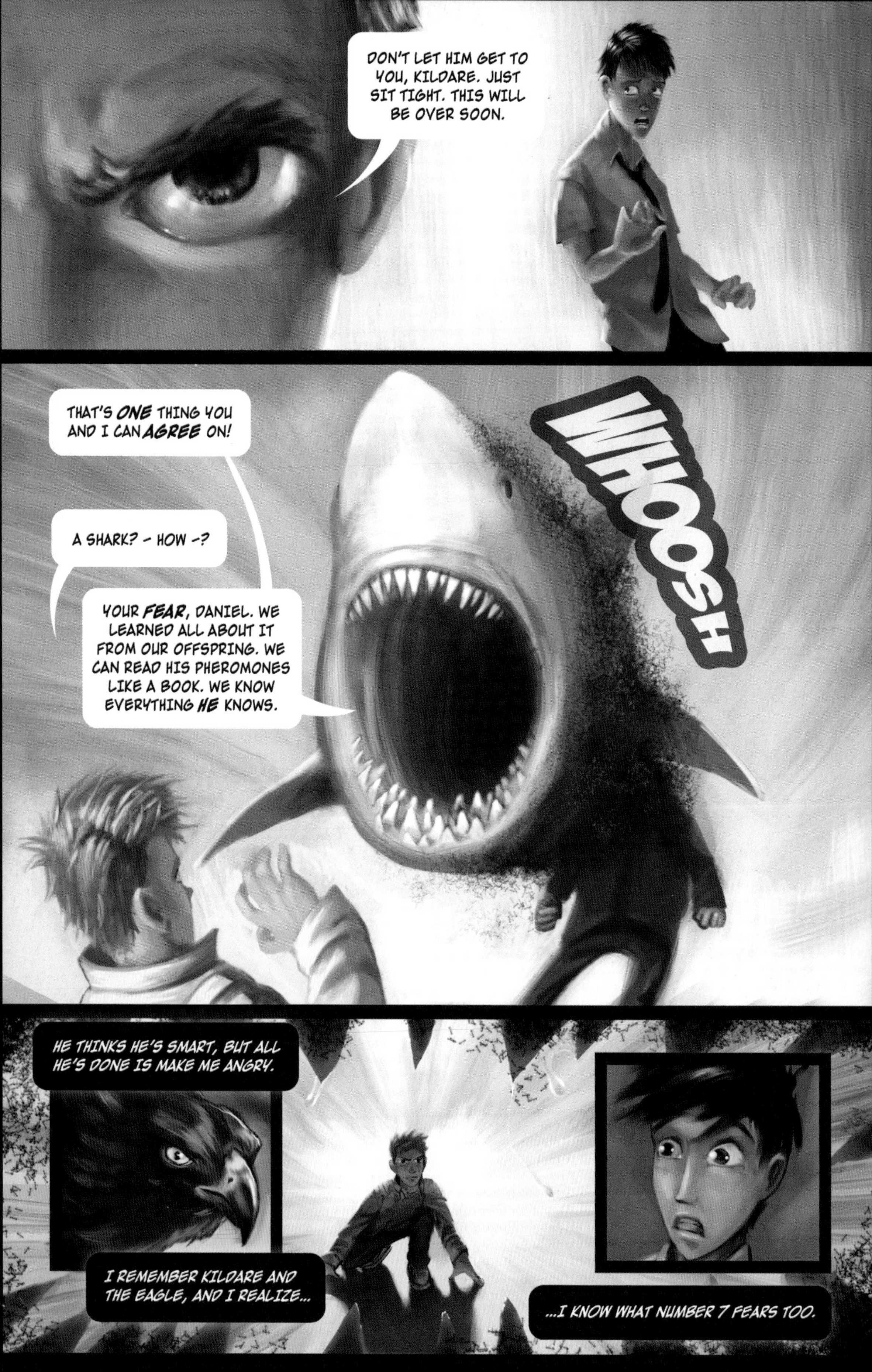
DON'T LET HIM GET TO YOU, KILDARE. JUST SIT TIGHT. THIS WILL BE OVER SOON.
THAT'S ONE THING YOU AND I CAN AGREE ON!
WHOOSH
A SHARK? - HOW -?
YOUR FEAR, DANIEL. WE LEARNED ALL ABOUT IT FROM OUR OFFSPRING. WE CAN READ HIS PHEROMONES LIKE A BOOK. WE KNOW EVERYTHING HE KNOWS.
HE THINKS HE'S SMART, BUT ALL HE'S DONE IS MAKE ME ANGRY.
I REMEMBER KILDARE AND THE EAGLE, AND I REALIZE...
...I KNOW WHAT NUMBER 7 FEARS TOO.

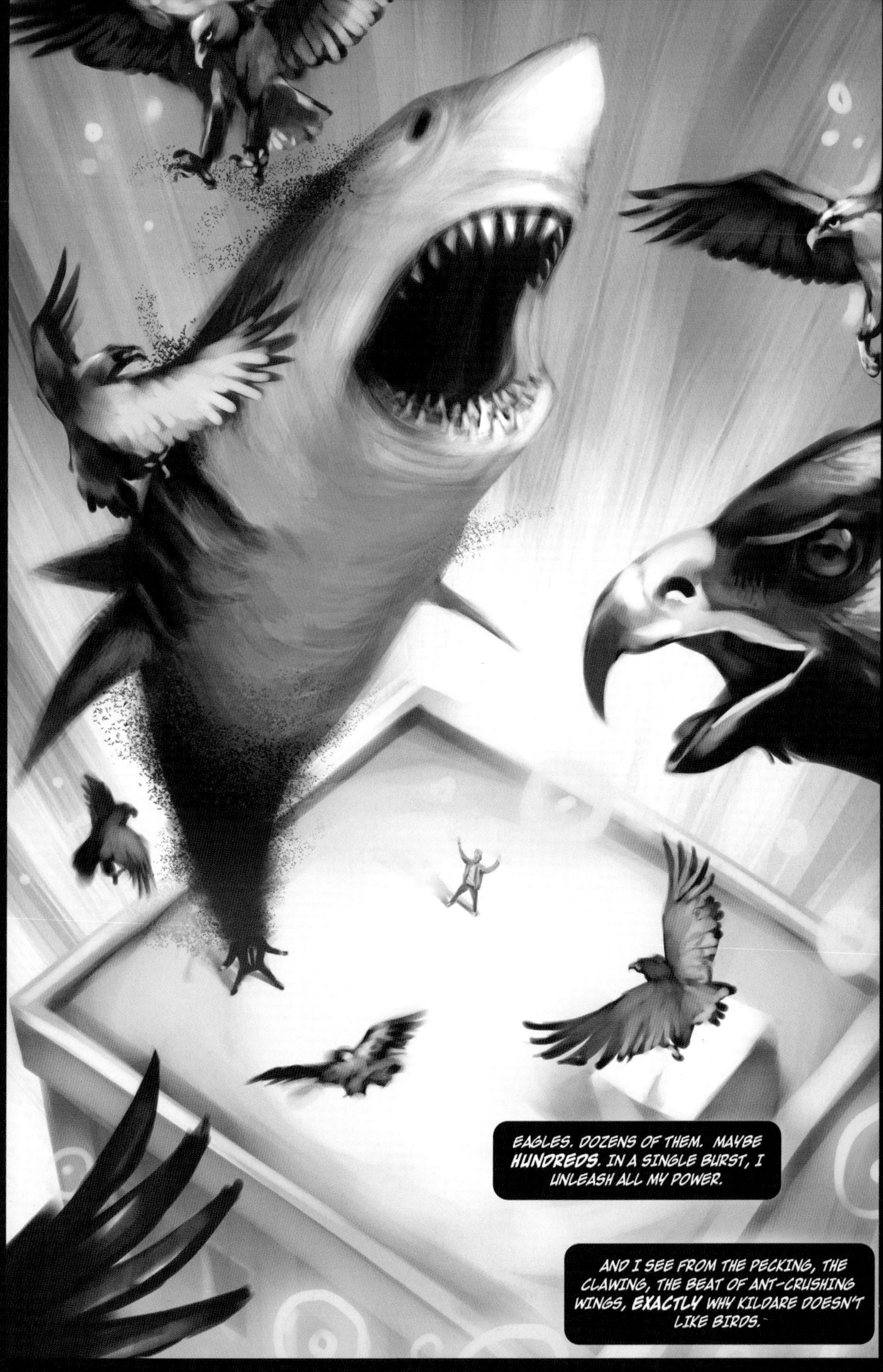
EAGLES. DOZENS OF THEM. MAYBE **HUNDREDS**. IN A SINGLE BURST, I UNLEASH ALL MY POWER.
AND I SEE FROM THE PECKING, THE CLAWING, THE BEAT OF ANT-CRUSHING WINGS, **EXACTLY** WHY KILDARE DOESN'T LIKE BIRDS.

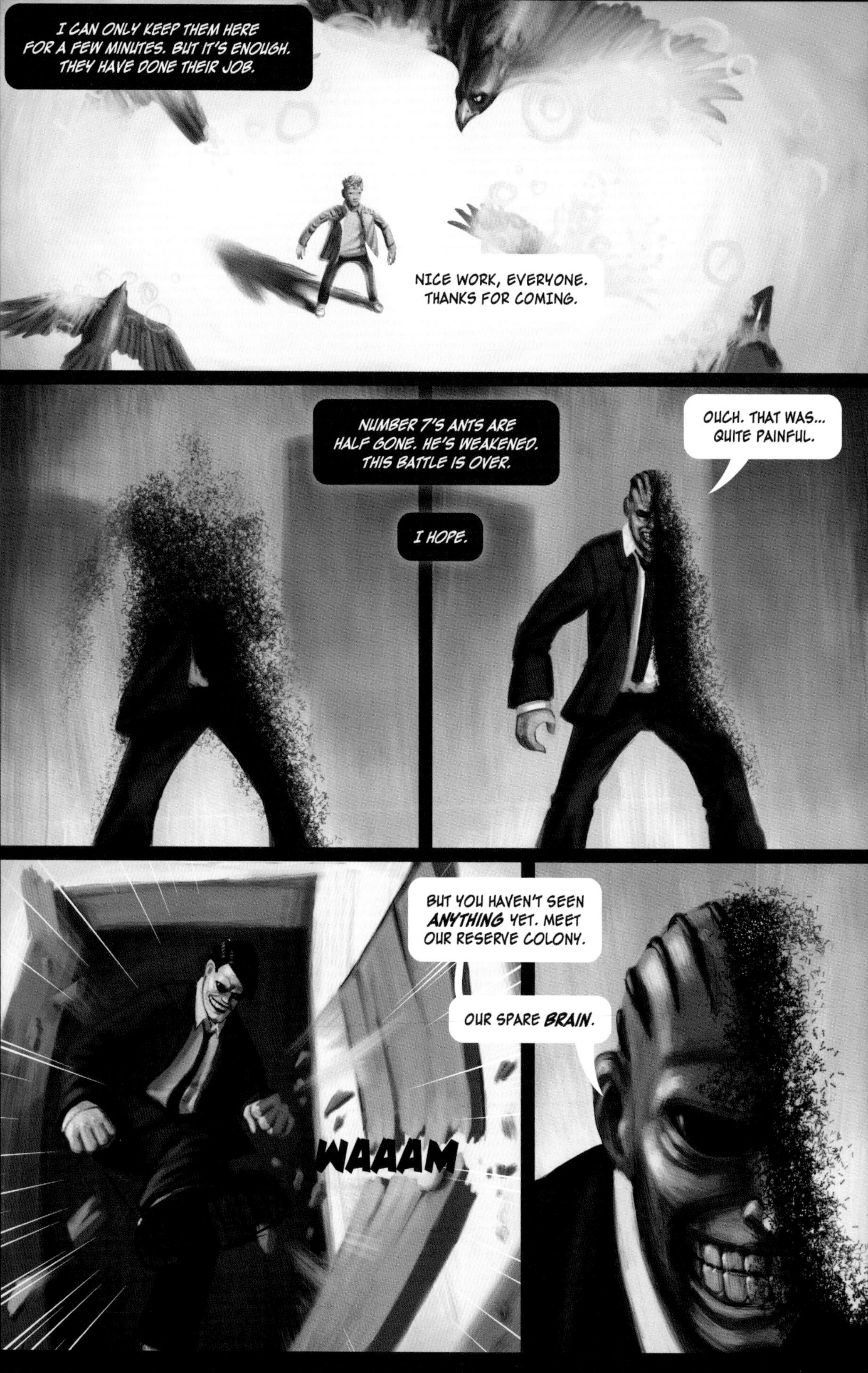

I CAN ONLY KEEP THEM HERE FOR A FEW MINUTES. BUT IT'S ENOUGH. THEY HAVE DONE THEIR JOB.
NICE WORK, EVERYONE. THANKS FOR COMING.
NUMBER 7'S ANTS ARE HALF GONE. HE'S WEAKENED. THIS BATTLE IS OVER.
I HOPE.
OUCH. THAT WAS... QUITE PAINFUL.
BUT YOU HAVEN'T SEEN ANYTHING YET. MEET OUR RESERVE COLONY.
OUR SPARE BRAIN.
WAAAM

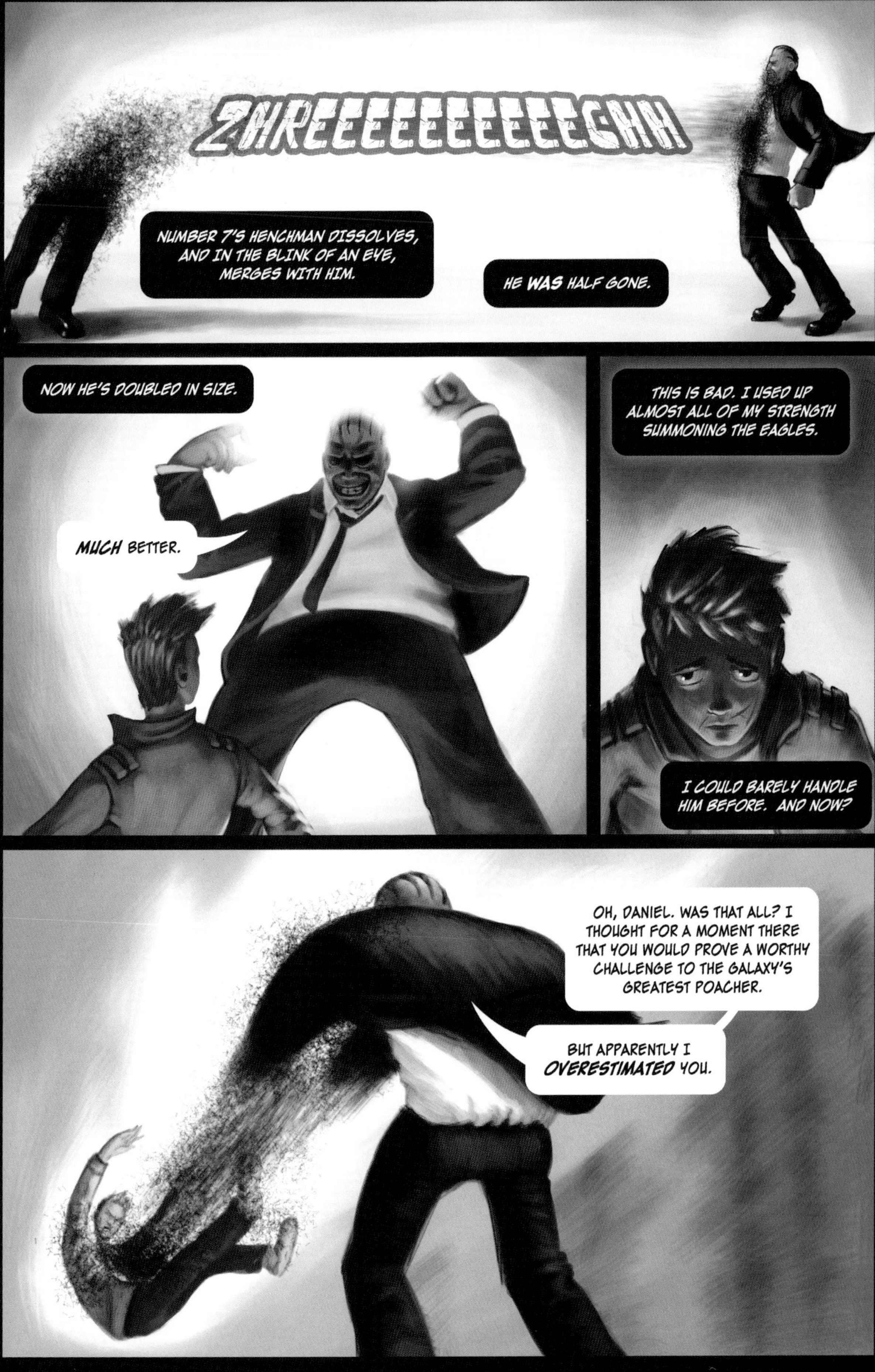

ZHREEEEEEEEEEEECHH
NUMBER 7'S HENCHMAN DISSOLVES, AND IN THE BLINK OF AN EYE, MERGES WITH HIM.
HE WAS HALF GONE.
NOW HE'S DOUBLED IN SIZE.
MUCH BETTER.
THIS IS BAD. I USED UP ALMOST ALL OF MY STRENGTH SUMMONING THE EAGLES.
I COULD BARELY HANDLE HIM BEFORE. AND NOW?
OH, DANIEL. WAS THAT ALL? I THOUGHT FOR A MOMENT THERE THAT YOU WOULD PROVE A WORTHY CHALLENGE TO THE GALAXY'S GREATEST POACHER.
BUT APPARENTLY I OVERESTIMATED YOU.

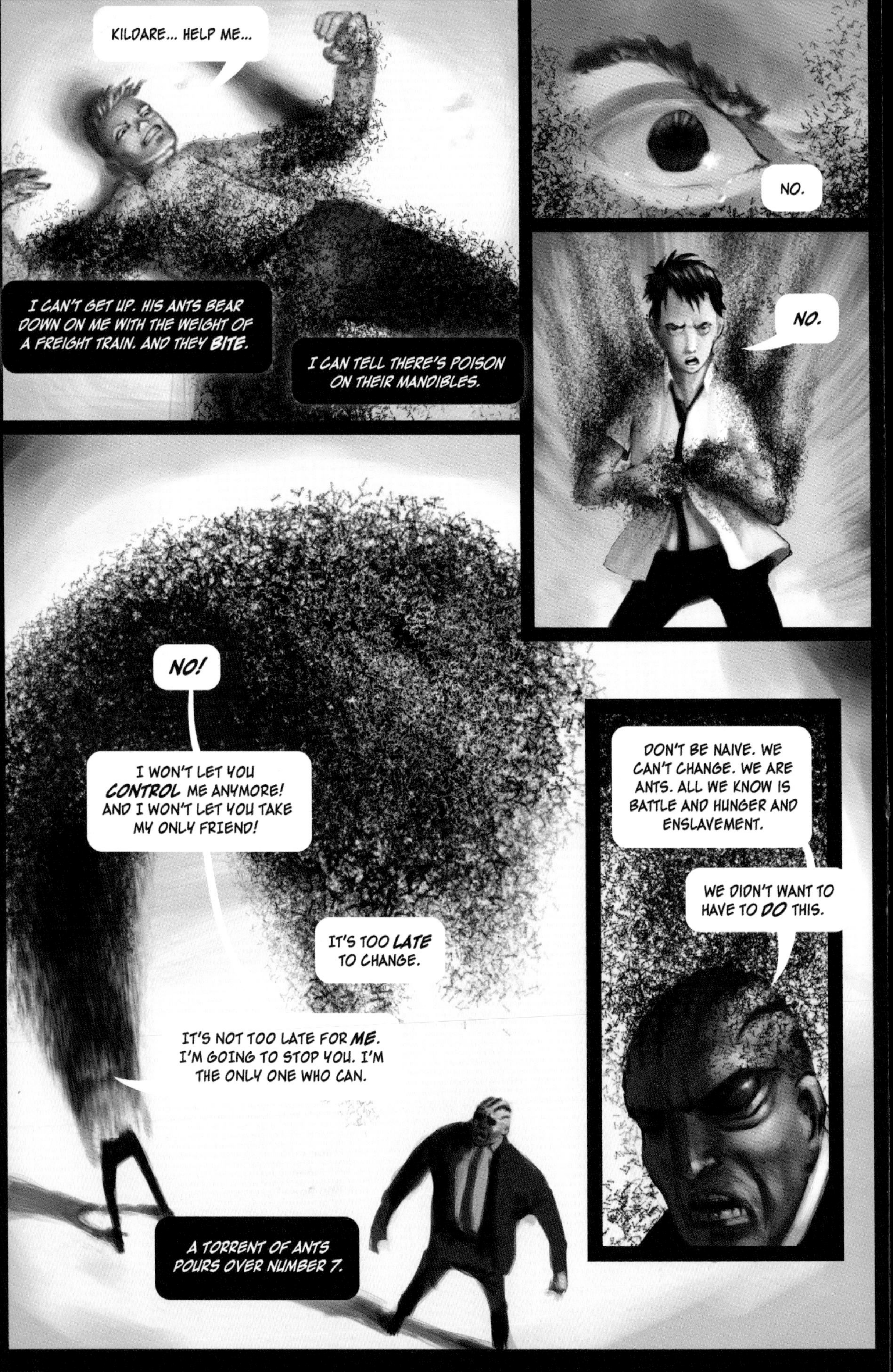
KILDARE... HELP ME...
I CAN'T GET UP. HIS ANTS BEAR DOWN ON ME WITH THE WEIGHT OF A FREIGHT TRAIN. AND THEY BITE.
I CAN TELL THERE'S POISON ON THEIR MANDIBLES.
NO.
NO.
NO!
I WON'T LET YOU CONTROL ME ANYMORE! AND I WON'T LET YOU TAKE MY ONLY FRIEND!
IT'S TOO LATE TO CHANGE.
IT'S NOT TOO LATE FOR ME. I'M GOING TO STOP YOU. I'M THE ONLY ONE WHO CAN.
A TORRENT OF ANTS POURS OVER NUMBER 7.
DON'T BE NAIVE. WE CAN'T CHANGE. WE ARE ANTS. ALL WE KNOW IS BATTLE AND HUNGER AND ENSLAVEMENT.
WE DIDN'T WANT TO HAVE TO DO THIS.

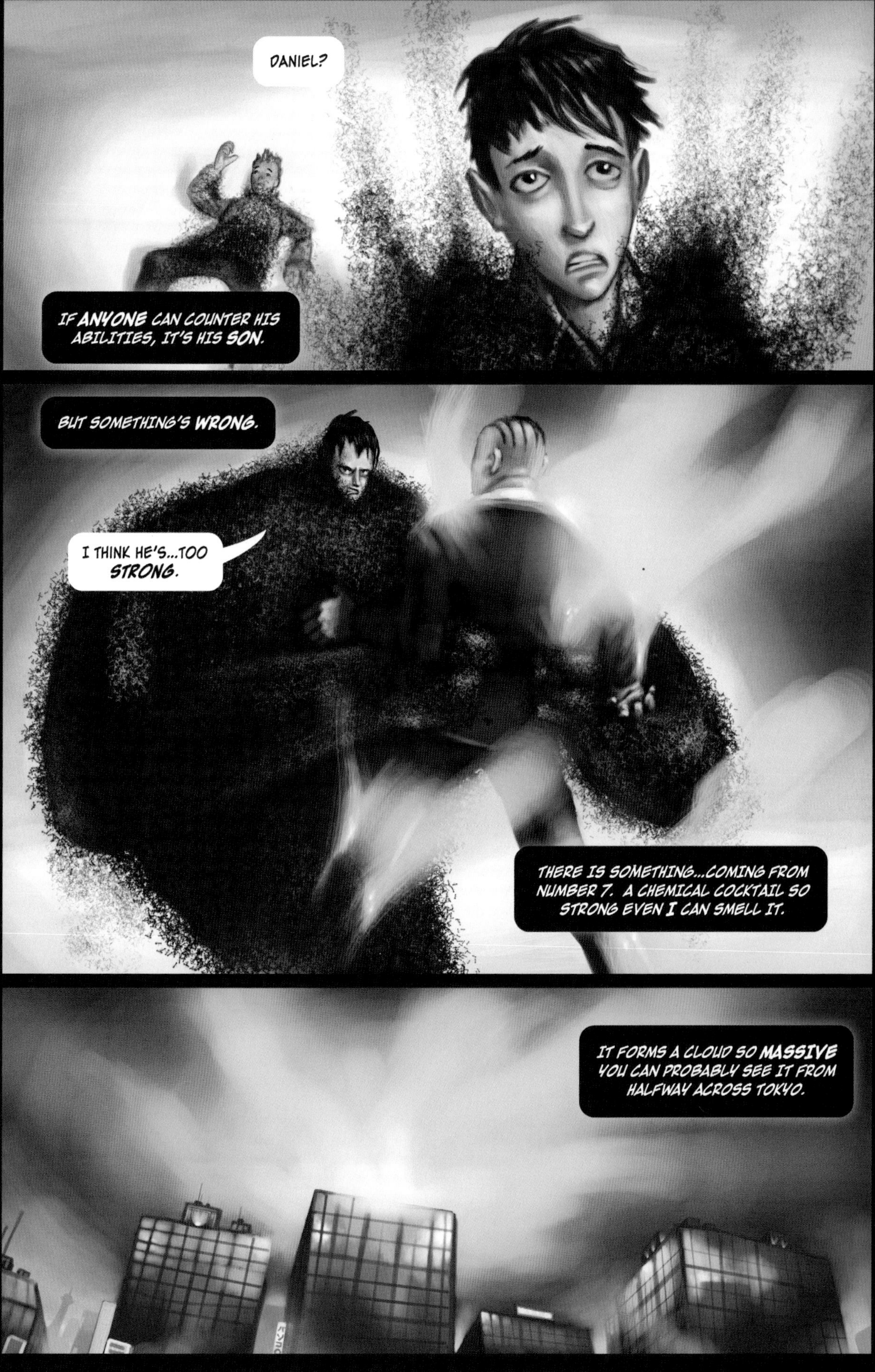
DANIEL?
IF ANYONE CAN COUNTER HIS ABILITIES, IT'S HIS SON.
BUT SOMETHING'S WRONG.
I THINK HE'S...TOO STRONG.
THERE IS SOMETHING...COMING FROM NUMBER 7. A CHEMICAL COCKTAIL SO STRONG EVEN I CAN SMELL IT.
IT FORMS A CLOUD SO MASSIVE YOU CAN PROBABLY SEE IT FROM HALFWAY ACROSS TOKYO.

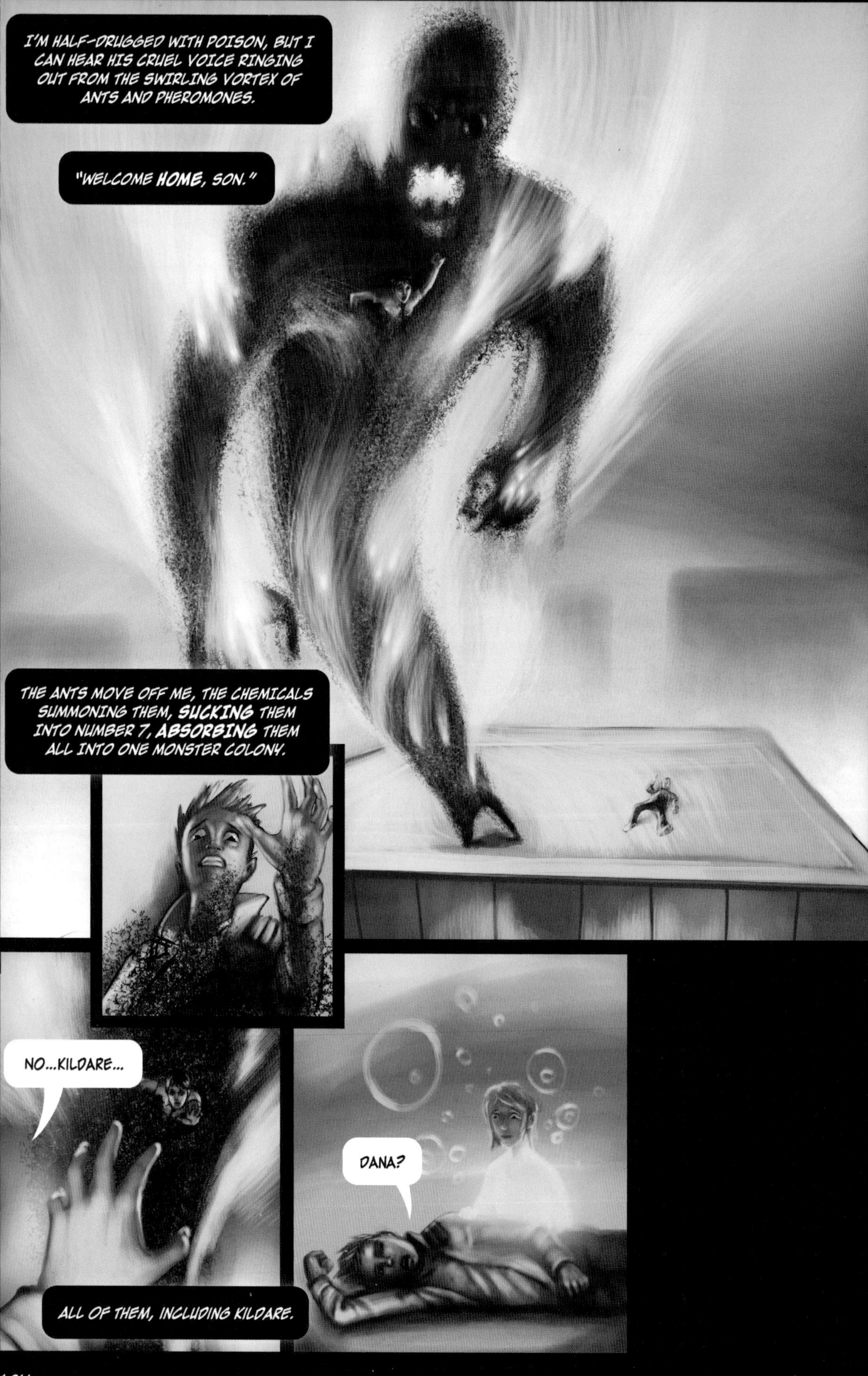
I'M HALF-DRUGGED WITH POISON, BUT I CAN HEAR HIS CRUEL VOICE RINGING OUT FROM THE SWIRLING VORTEX OF ANTS AND PHEROMONES.
"WELCOME HOME, SON."
THE ANTS MOVE OFF ME, THE CHEMICALS SUMMONING THEM, SUCKING THEM INTO NUMBER 7, ABSORBING THEM ALL INTO ONE MONSTER COLONY.
NO...KILDARE...
ALL OF THEM, INCLUDING KILDARE.
DANA?

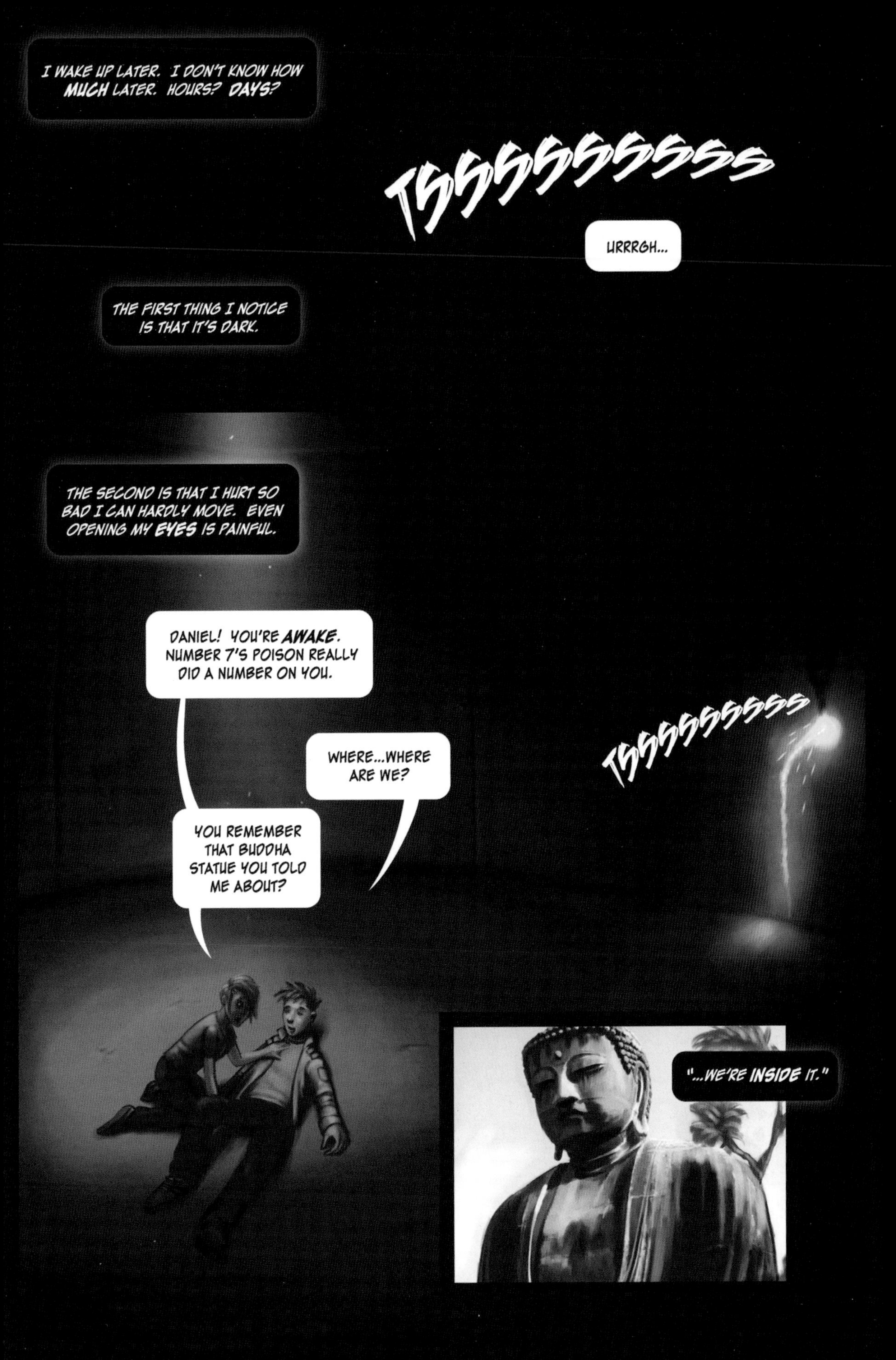
I WAKE UP LATER. I DON'T KNOW HOW MUCH LATER. HOURS? DAYS?
TSSSSSSSSS
URRRGH...
THE FIRST THING I NOTICE IS THAT IT'S DARK.
THE SECOND IS THAT I HURT SO BAD I CAN HARDLY MOVE. EVEN OPENING MY EYES IS PAINFUL.
DANIEL! YOU'RE AWAKE. NUMBER 7'S POISON REALLY DID A NUMBER ON YOU.
TSSSSSSSSS
WHERE...WHERE ARE WE?
YOU REMEMBER THAT BUDDHA STATUE YOU TOLD ME ABOUT?
"...WE'RE INSIDE IT."

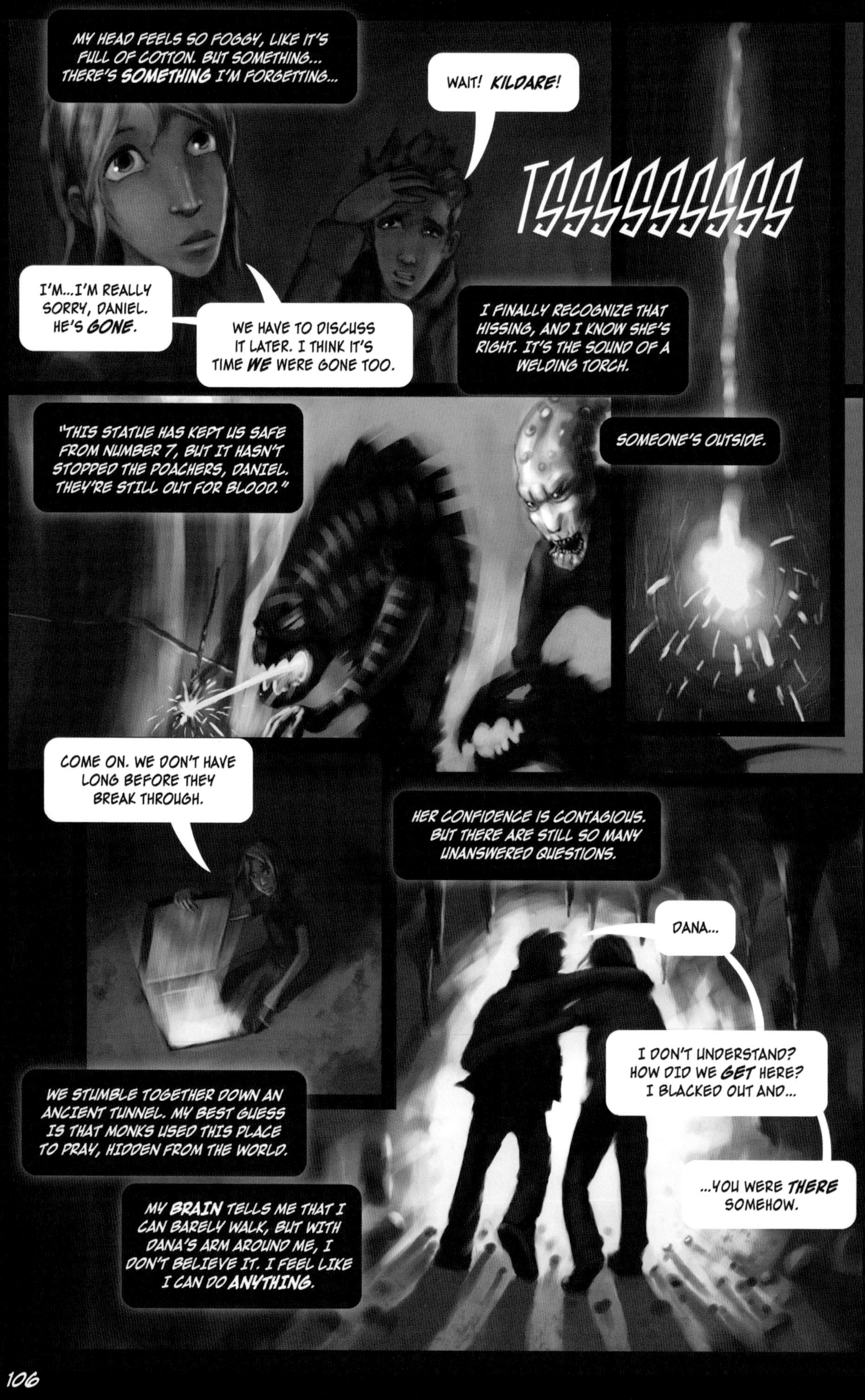
MY HEAD FEELS SO FOGGY, LIKE IT'S FULL OF COTTON. BUT SOMETHING... THERE'S SOMETHING I'M FORGETTING...
WAIT! KILDARE!
TSSSSSSSSS
I'M...I'M REALLY SORRY, DANIEL. HE'S GONE.
WE HAVE TO DISCUSS IT LATER. I THINK IT'S TIME WE WERE GONE TOO.
I FINALLY RECOGNIZE THAT HISSING, AND I KNOW SHE'S RIGHT. IT'S THE SOUND OF A WELDING TORCH.
"THIS STATUE HAS KEPT US SAFE FROM NUMBER 7, BUT IT HASN'T STOPPED THE POACHERS, DANIEL. THEY'RE STILL OUT FOR BLOOD."
SOMEONE'S OUTSIDE.
COME ON. WE DON'T HAVE LONG BEFORE THEY BREAK THROUGH.
HER CONFIDENCE IS CONTAGIOUS. BUT THERE ARE STILL SO MANY UNANSWERED QUESTIONS.
DANA...
I DON'T UNDERSTAND? HOW DID WE GET HERE? I BLACKED OUT AND...
...YOU WERE THERE SOMEHOW.
WE STUMBLE TOGETHER DOWN AN ANCIENT TUNNEL. MY BEST GUESS IS THAT MONKS USED THIS PLACE TO PRAY, HIDDEN FROM THE WORLD.
MY BRAIN TELLS ME THAT I CAN BARELY WALK, BUT WITH DANA'S ARM AROUND ME, I DON'T BELIEVE IT. I FEEL LIKE I CAN DO ANYTHING.

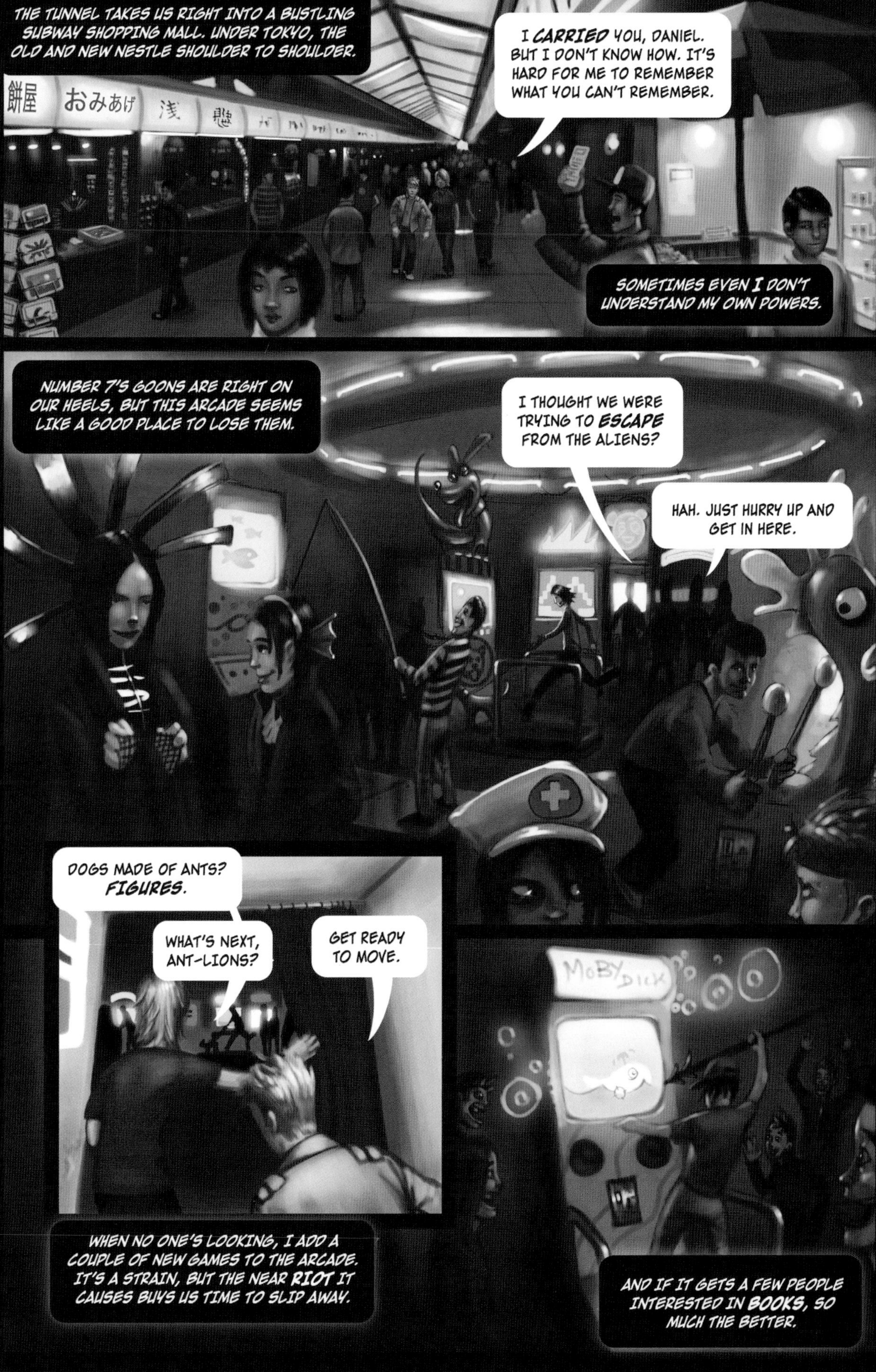
THE TUNNEL TAKES US RIGHT INTO A BUSTLING SUBWAY SHOPPING MALL. UNDER TOKYO, THE OLD AND NEW NESTLE SHOULDER TO SHOULDER.
餅屋
おみあげ
I CARRIED YOU, DANIEL. BUT I DON'T KNOW HOW. IT'S HARD FOR ME TO REMEMBER WHAT YOU CAN'T REMEMBER.
SOMETIMES EVEN I DON'T UNDERSTAND MY OWN POWERS.
NUMBER 7'S GOONS ARE RIGHT ON OUR HEELS, BUT THIS ARCADE SEEMS LIKE A GOOD PLACE TO LOSE THEM.
I THOUGHT WE WERE TRYING TO ESCAPE FROM THE ALIENS?
HAH. JUST HURRY UP AND GET IN HERE.
DOGS MADE OF ANTS? FIGURES.
WHAT'S NEXT, ANT-LIONS?
GET READY TO MOVE.
MOBY DICK
WHEN NO ONE'S LOOKING, I ADD A COUPLE OF NEW GAMES TO THE ARCADE. IT'S A STRAIN, BUT THE NEAR RIOT IT CAUSES BUYS US TIME TO SLIP AWAY.
AND IF IT GETS A FEW PEOPLE INTERESTED IN BOOKS, SO MUCH THE BETTER.

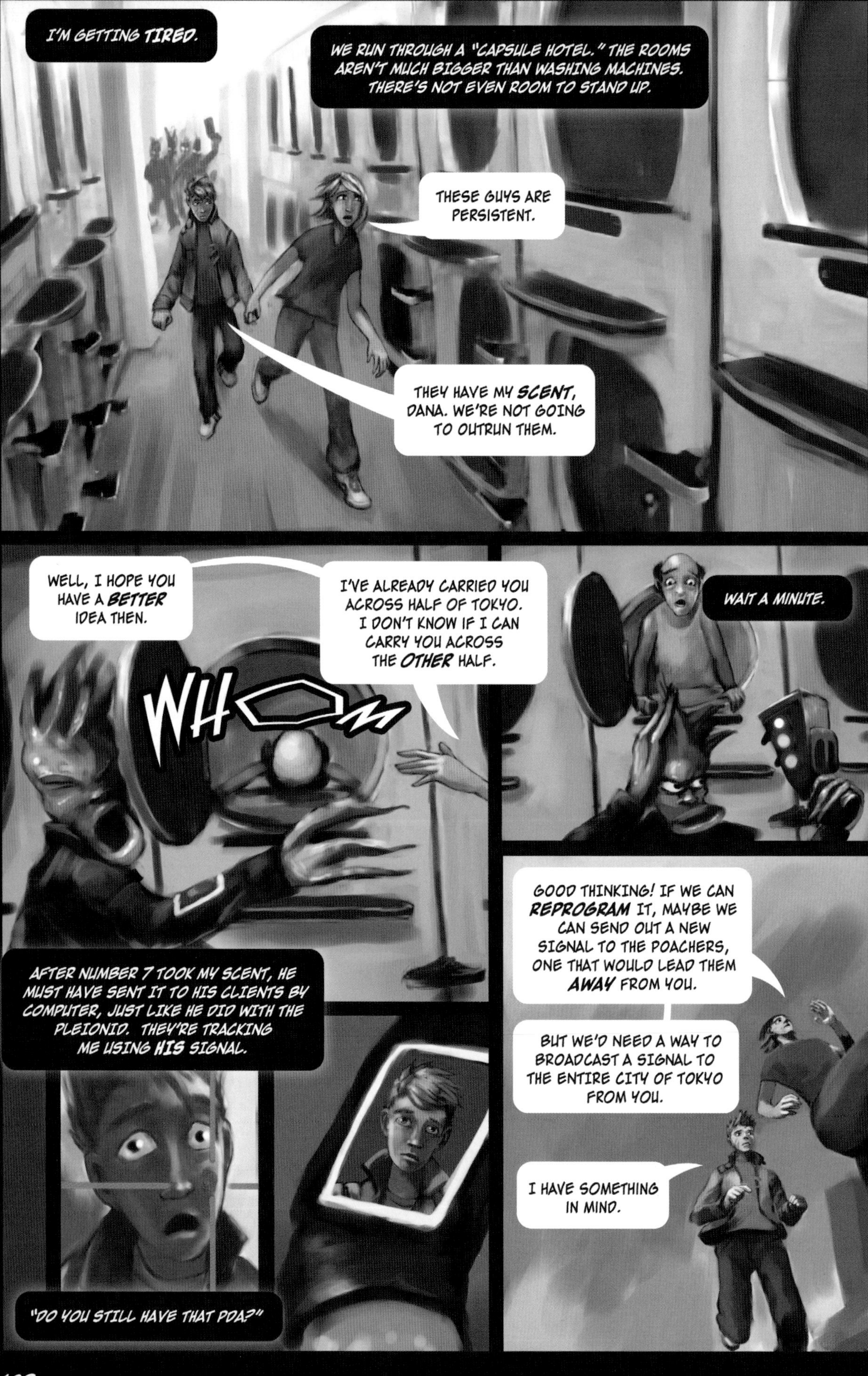
I'M GETTING **TIRED**.
WE RUN THROUGH A "CAPSULE HOTEL." THE ROOMS AREN'T MUCH BIGGER THAN WASHING MACHINES. THERE'S NOT EVEN ROOM TO STAND UP.
THESE GUYS ARE PERSISTENT.
THEY HAVE MY **SCENT**, DANA. WE'RE NOT GOING TO OUTRUN THEM.
WELL, I HOPE YOU HAVE A **BETTER** IDEA THEN.
I'VE ALREADY CARRIED YOU ACROSS HALF OF TOKYO. I DON'T KNOW IF I CAN CARRY YOU ACROSS THE **OTHER** HALF.
WHOOM
WAIT A MINUTE.
AFTER NUMBER 7 TOOK MY SCENT, HE MUST HAVE SENT IT TO HIS CLIENTS BY COMPUTER, JUST LIKE HE DID WITH THE PLEIONID. THEY'RE TRACKING ME USING **HIS** SIGNAL.
"DO YOU STILL HAVE THAT PDA?"
GOOD THINKING! IF WE CAN **REPROGRAM** IT, MAYBE WE CAN SEND OUT A NEW SIGNAL TO THE POACHERS, ONE THAT WOULD LEAD THEM **AWAY** FROM YOU.
BUT WE'D NEED A WAY TO BROADCAST A SIGNAL TO THE ENTIRE CITY OF TOKYO FROM YOU.
I HAVE SOMETHING IN MIND.

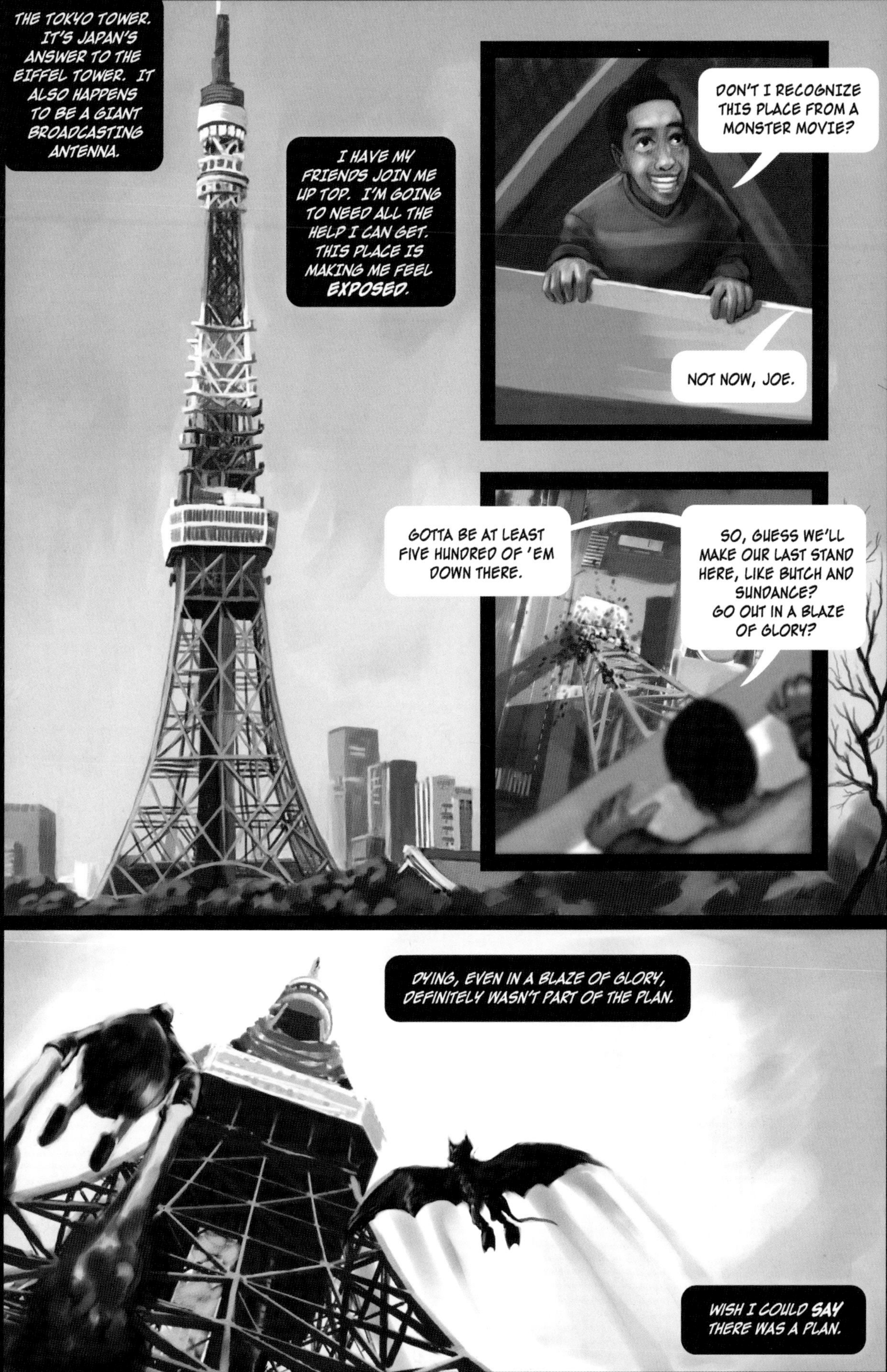
THE TOKYO TOWER. IT'S JAPAN'S ANSWER TO THE EIFFEL TOWER. IT ALSO HAPPENS TO BE A GIANT BROADCASTING ANTENNA.
I HAVE MY FRIENDS JOIN ME UP TOP. I'M GOING TO NEED ALL THE HELP I CAN GET. THIS PLACE IS MAKING ME FEEL EXPOSED.
DON'T I RECOGNIZE THIS PLACE FROM A MONSTER MOVIE?
NOT NOW, JOE.
GOTTA BE AT LEAST FIVE HUNDRED OF 'EM DOWN THERE.
SO, GUESS WE'LL MAKE OUR LAST STAND HERE, LIKE BUTCH AND SUNDANCE? GO OUT IN A BLAZE OF GLORY?
DYING, EVEN IN A BLAZE OF GLORY, DEFINITELY WASN'T PART OF THE PLAN.
WISH I COULD SAY THERE WAS A PLAN.

WILLY'S MY RESIDENT TECHNICAL EXPERT. THE GUY KNOWS EVERYTHING FROM CARS TO CAMPING TO COMPUTERS. BUT THE UNCERTAIN NOTE IN HIS VOICE IS NOT WHAT I WAS HOPING TO HEAR.
DANIEL, WE'VE GOT A PROBLEM. I CAN'T CRACK THE SECURITY ON THIS THING.
I JUST NEED TO TWIST TOGETHER A COUPLE OF WIRES AND ALL OF TOKYO WILL BE BLANKETED IN THIS SIGNAL.
BUT UNLESS WE CAN CHANGE THE DATA ON THE SURFACE OF THE CHIP ITSELF, THIS MIGHT AS WELL BE A GAME BOY FOR ALL THE GOOD IT'LL DO US.
bio match invalid: data locked.
DANIEL X
ALPARIAN
EVASION: N/A
ATTACK: MAXIMUM
WELL, I GUESS WE'LL HOLD THEM OFF WHILE YOU FIGURE OUT WHAT YOU'RE DOING. RIGHT, EMMA?
UGH. HOW DID I END UP ON THE BOTTOM?
MAKE CHANGES TO THE COMPUTER CHIP ITSELF? THERE'S ONLY ONE WAY I CAN THINK OF TO DO THAT.
DANA? CAN YOU -
SHHHHEEEEESSS
I'M READY.
DID I MENTION THAT DANA'S THE BEST THING SINCE SLICED BREAD?
JUST A BLINK, AND SHE BECOMES AN ELECTRICAL PULSE.

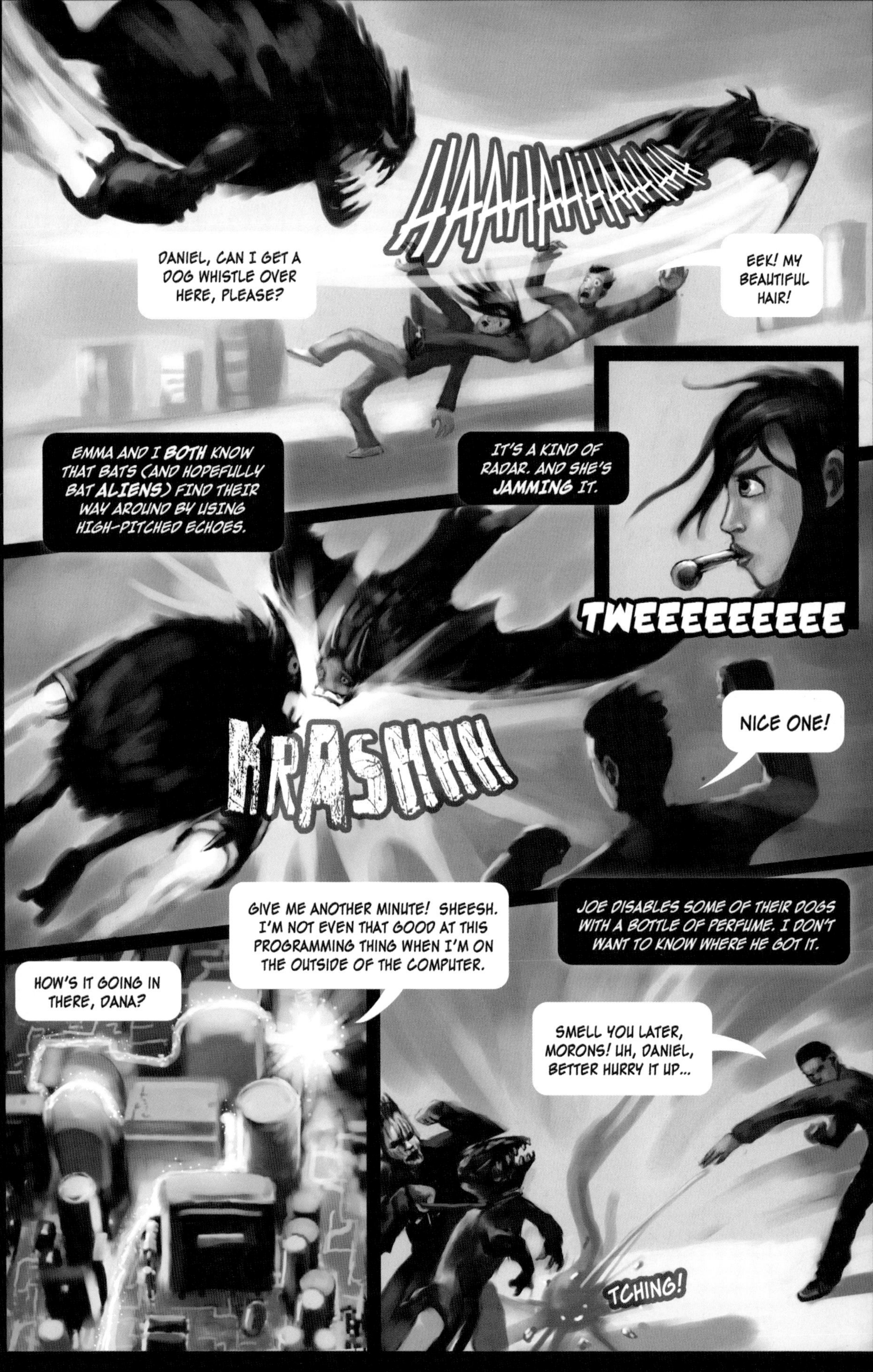
HAAAAHHAAAA
DANIEL, CAN I GET A DOG WHISTLE OVER HERE, PLEASE?
EEK! MY BEAUTIFUL HAIR!
EMMA AND I BOTH KNOW THAT BATS (AND HOPEFULLY BAT ALIENS) FIND THEIR WAY AROUND BY USING HIGH-PITCHED ECHOES.
IT'S A KIND OF RADAR. AND SHE'S JAMMING IT.
TWEEEEEEEEEE
KRASHHH
NICE ONE!
HOW'S IT GOING IN THERE, DANA?
GIVE ME ANOTHER MINUTE! SHEESH. I'M NOT EVEN THAT GOOD AT THIS PROGRAMMING THING WHEN I'M ON THE OUTSIDE OF THE COMPUTER.
JOE DISABLES SOME OF THEIR DOGS WITH A BOTTLE OF PERFUME. I DON'T WANT TO KNOW WHERE HE GOT IT.
SMELL YOU LATER, MORONS! UH, DANIEL, BETTER HURRY IT UP...
TCHING!

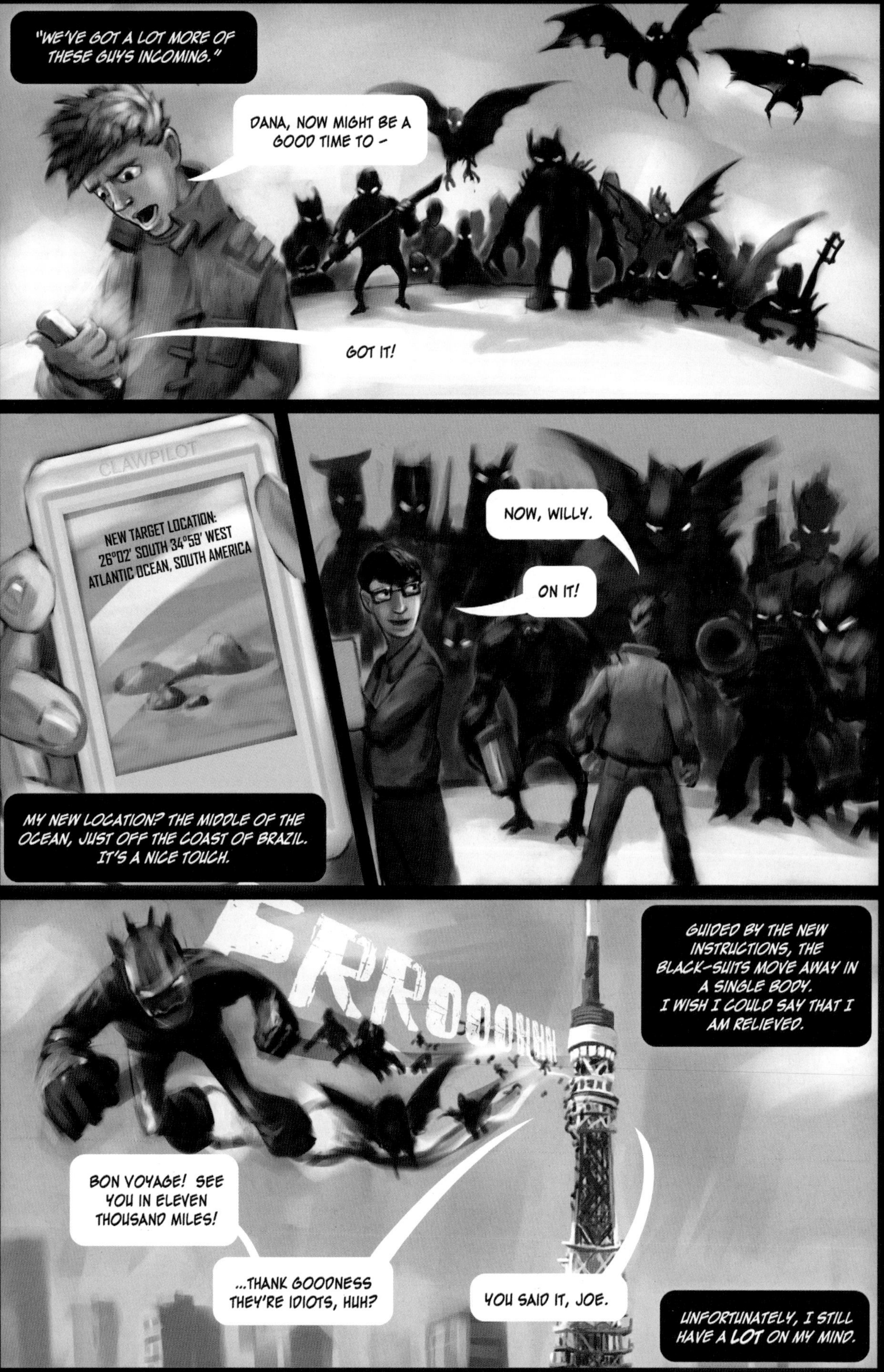
"WE'VE GOT A LOT MORE OF THESE GUYS INCOMING."
DANA, NOW MIGHT BE A GOOD TIME TO -
GOT IT!
CLAWPILOT
NEW TARGET LOCATION: 26°02' SOUTH 34°59' WEST ATLANTIC OCEAN, SOUTH AMERICA
MY NEW LOCATION? THE MIDDLE OF THE OCEAN, JUST OFF THE COAST OF BRAZIL. IT'S A NICE TOUCH.
NOW, WILLY.
ON IT!
GUIDED BY THE NEW INSTRUCTIONS, THE BLACK-SUITS MOVE AWAY IN A SINGLE BODY. I WISH I COULD SAY THAT I AM RELIEVED.
BON VOYAGE! SEE YOU IN ELEVEN THOUSAND MILES!
...THANK GOODNESS THEY'RE IDIOTS, HUH?
YOU SAID IT, JOE.
UNFORTUNATELY, I STILL HAVE A **LOT** ON MY MIND.

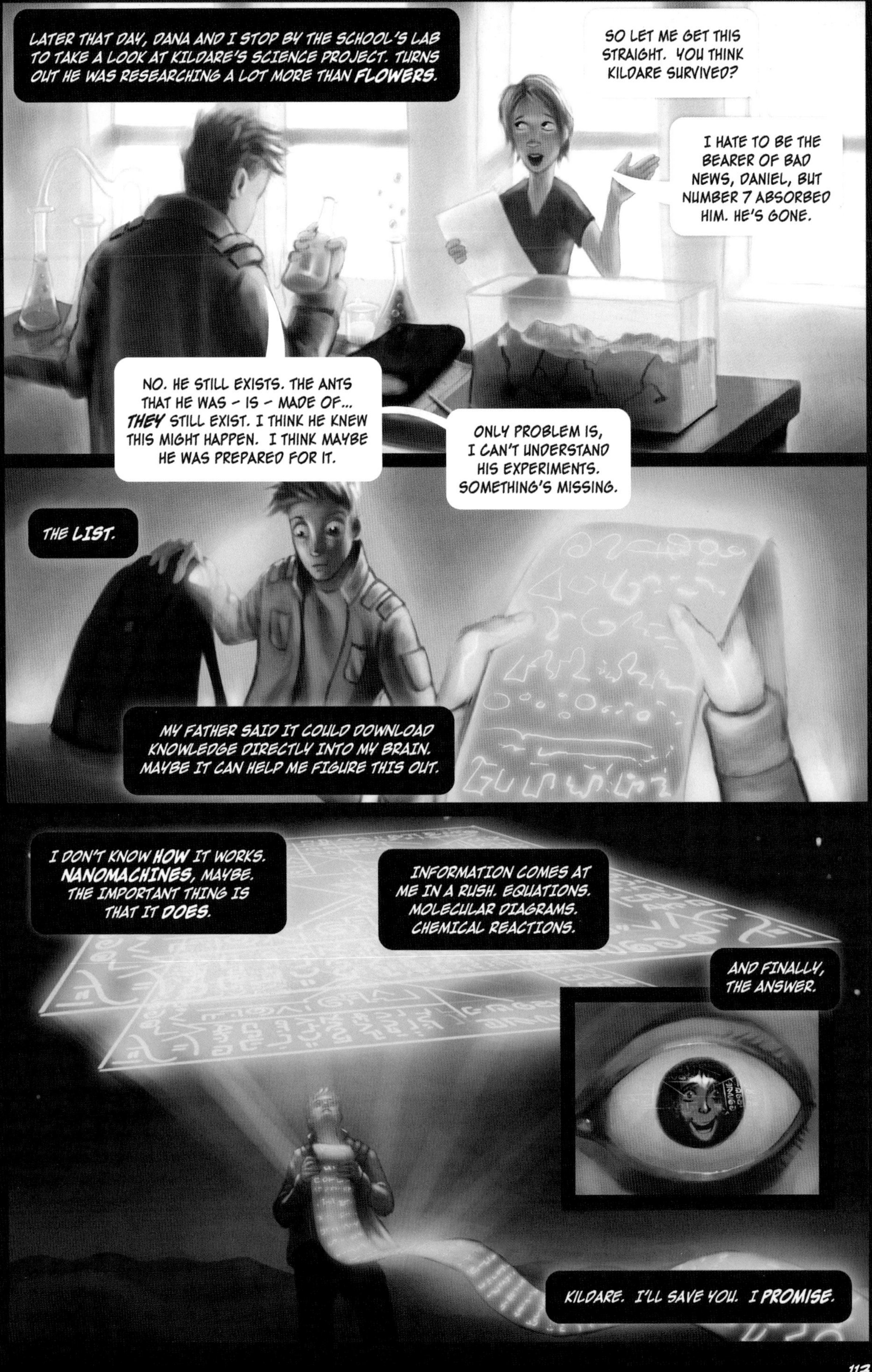
LATER THAT DAY, DANA AND I STOP BY THE SCHOOL'S LAB TO TAKE A LOOK AT KILDARE'S SCIENCE PROJECT. TURNS OUT HE WAS RESEARCHING A LOT MORE THAN FLOWERS.
SO LET ME GET THIS STRAIGHT. YOU THINK KILDARE SURVIVED?
I HATE TO BE THE BEARER OF BAD NEWS, DANIEL, BUT NUMBER 7 ABSORBED HIM. HE'S GONE.
NO. HE STILL EXISTS. THE ANTS THAT HE WAS - IS - MADE OF... THEY STILL EXIST. I THINK HE KNEW THIS MIGHT HAPPEN. I THINK MAYBE HE WAS PREPARED FOR IT.
ONLY PROBLEM IS, I CAN'T UNDERSTAND HIS EXPERIMENTS. SOMETHING'S MISSING.
THE LIST.
MY FATHER SAID IT COULD DOWNLOAD KNOWLEDGE DIRECTLY INTO MY BRAIN. MAYBE IT CAN HELP ME FIGURE THIS OUT.
I DON'T KNOW HOW IT WORKS. NANOMACHINES, MAYBE. THE IMPORTANT THING IS THAT IT DOES.
INFORMATION COMES AT ME IN A RUSH. EQUATIONS. MOLECULAR DIAGRAMS. CHEMICAL REACTIONS.
AND FINALLY, THE ANSWER.
KILDARE. I'LL SAVE YOU. I PROMISE.

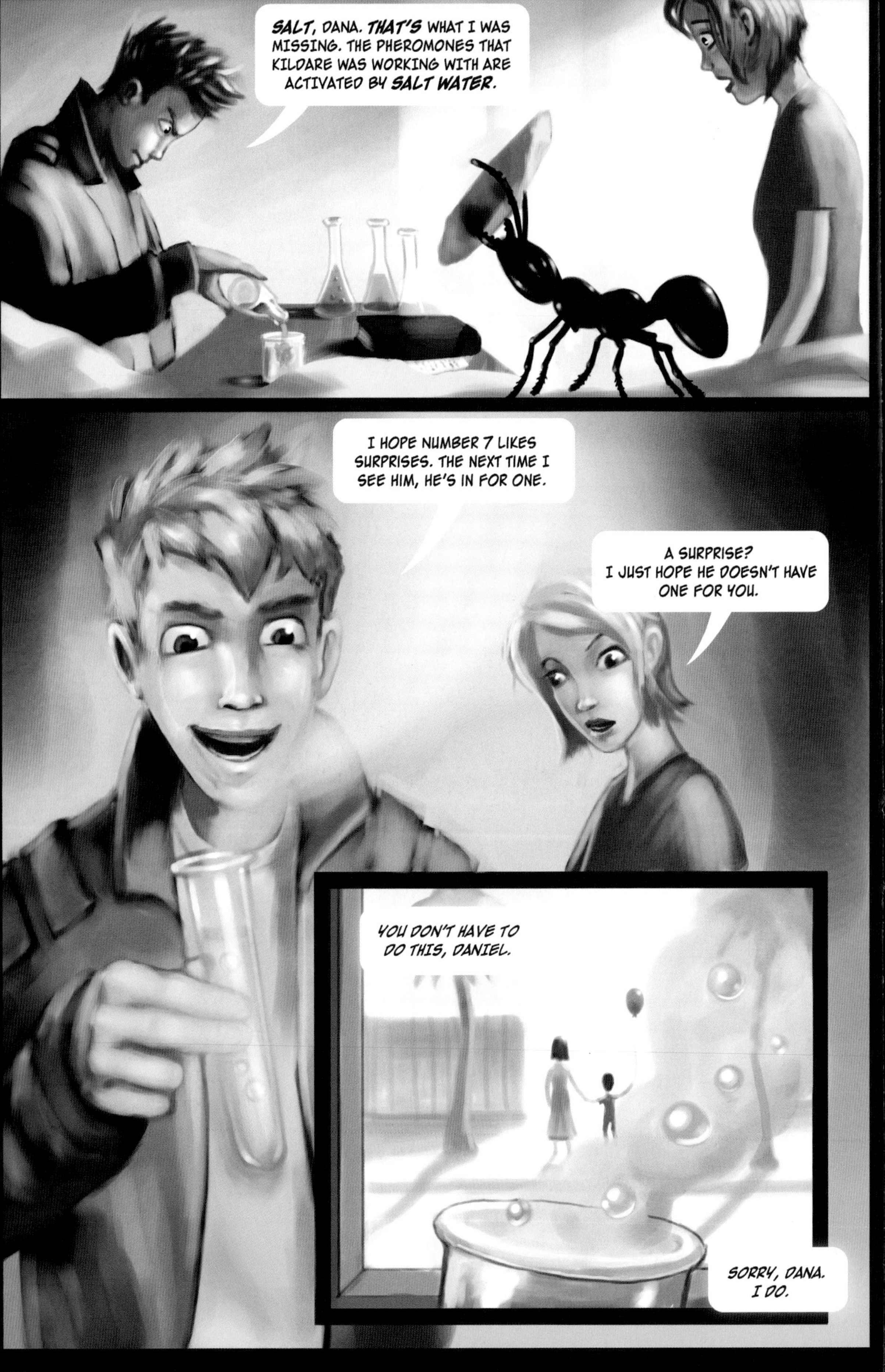
SALT, DANA. THAT'S WHAT I WAS MISSING. THE PHEROMONES THAT KILDARE WAS WORKING WITH ARE ACTIVATED BY SALT WATER.
I HOPE NUMBER 7 LIKES SURPRISES. THE NEXT TIME I SEE HIM, HE'S IN FOR ONE.
A SURPRISE? I JUST HOPE HE DOESN'T HAVE ONE FOR YOU.
YOU DON'T HAVE TO DO THIS, DANIEL.
SORRY, DANA. I DO.

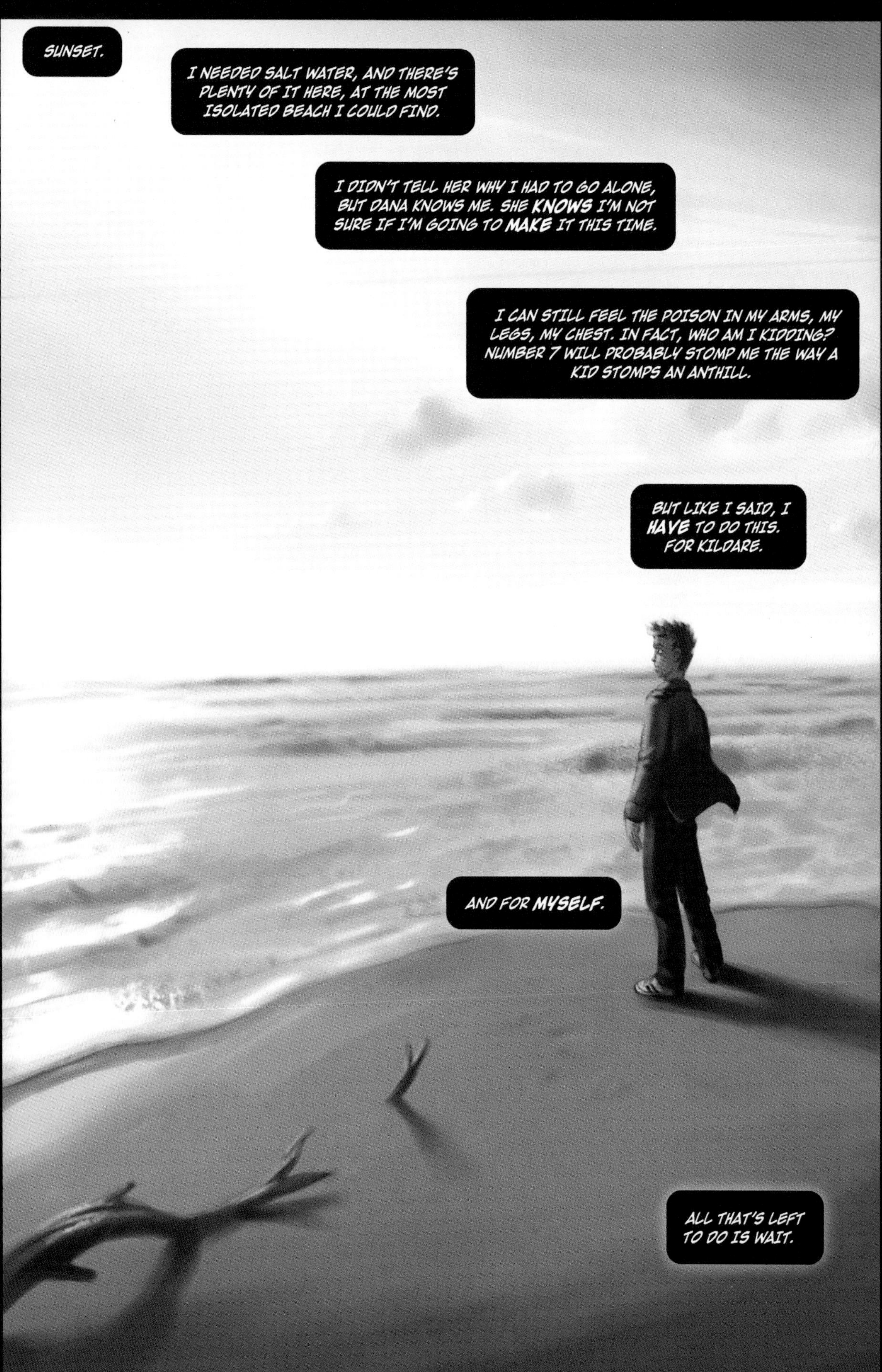
SUNSET.
I NEEDED SALT WATER, AND THERE'S PLENTY OF IT HERE, AT THE MOST ISOLATED BEACH I COULD FIND.
I DIDN'T TELL HER WHY I HAD TO GO ALONE, BUT DANA KNOWS ME. SHE KNOWS I'M NOT SURE IF I'M GOING TO MAKE IT THIS TIME.
I CAN STILL FEEL THE POISON IN MY ARMS, MY LEGS, MY CHEST. IN FACT, WHO AM I KIDDING? NUMBER 7 WILL PROBABLY STOMP ME THE WAY A KID STOMPS AN ANTHILL.
BUT LIKE I SAID, I HAVE TO DO THIS. FOR KILDARE.
AND FOR MYSELF.
ALL THAT'S LEFT TO DO IS WAIT.

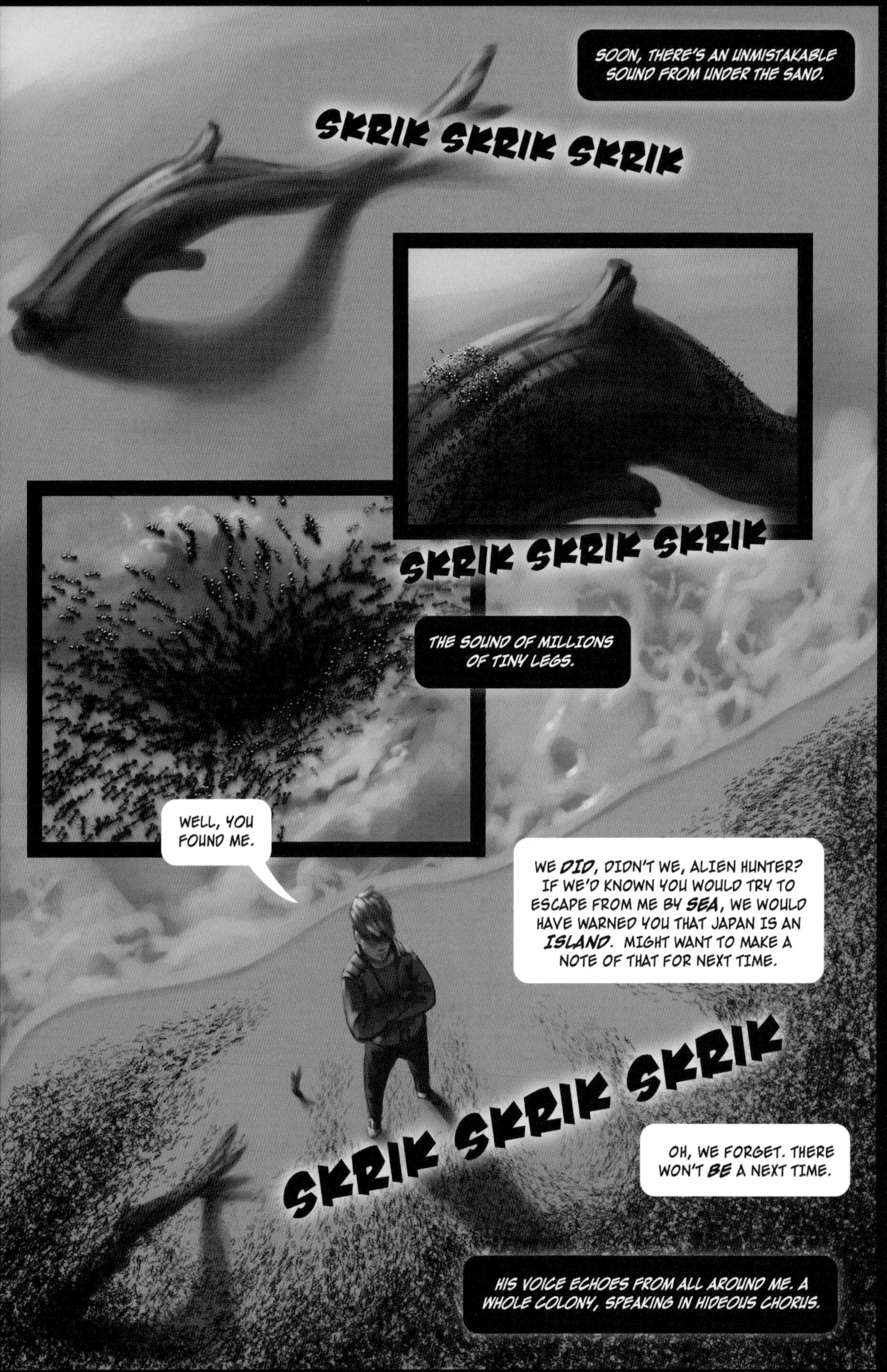
SOON, THERE'S AN UNMISTAKABLE SOUND FROM UNDER THE SAND.
SKRIK SKRIK SKRIK
SKRIK SKRIK SKRIK
THE SOUND OF MILLIONS OF TINY LEGS.
WELL, YOU FOUND ME.
WE DID, DIDN'T WE, ALIEN HUNTER? IF WE'D KNOWN YOU WOULD TRY TO ESCAPE FROM ME BY SEA, WE WOULD HAVE WARNED YOU THAT JAPAN IS AN ISLAND. MIGHT WANT TO MAKE A NOTE OF THAT FOR NEXT TIME.
SKRIK SKRIK SKRIK
OH, WE FORGET. THERE WON'T BE A NEXT TIME.
HIS VOICE ECHOES FROM ALL AROUND ME. A WHOLE COLONY, SPEAKING IN HIDEOUS CHORUS.

HIS HUMAN FORM MIGHT NOT BE HERE, BUT HIS PRESENCE SURROUNDS ME.
OF KILDARE, I SENSE NOTHING AT ALL.
AS HE SPEAKS, SOMETHING WRITHES TO LIFE IN THE WATER BEHIND ME.
YOU DID WELL GETTING RID OF OUR CLIENTS. BUT WE WERE ALWAYS GOING TO BE THE ONE TO CATCH YOU.
WHOOOOOSH
THE PLOT MAY HAVE CHANGED, BUT THE ENDING IS THE SAME.
WELL, THEY SAY WHAT GOES AROUND COMES AROUND. IT'S TIME FOR ME TO CALL IN A FAVOR.
POP
ROOOOAARR
THE FISH FROM THE TSUKIJI MARKET ARE GRATEFUL THAT I HELPED THEM GET BACK TO THE OCEAN, AND IT SHOWS.
SPLOOSH
I WIN THE FIRST ROUND. BUT I DON'T HAVE HIGH HOPES FOR THE SECOND.

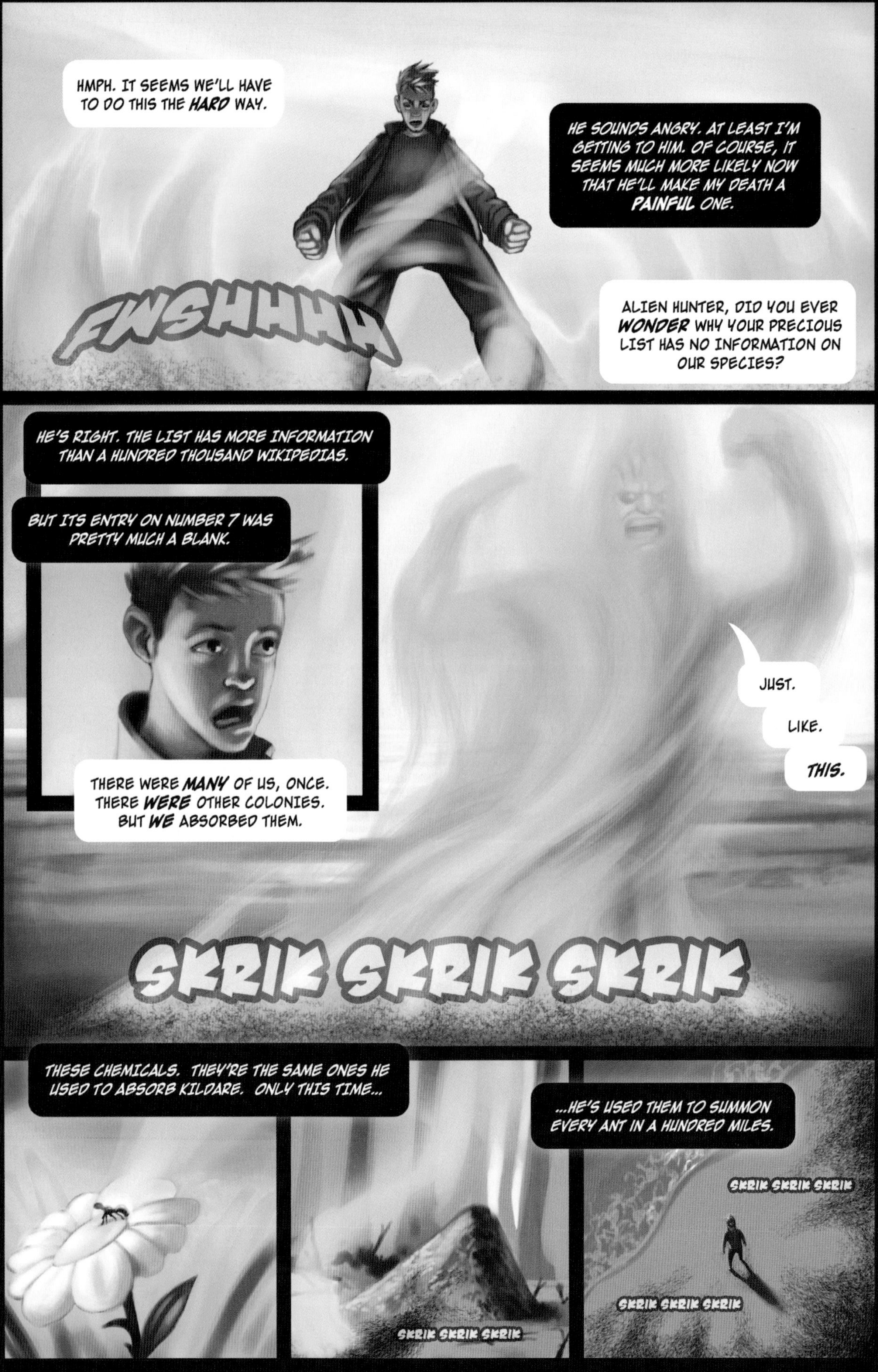
HMPH. IT SEEMS WE'LL HAVE TO DO THIS THE HARD WAY.
HE SOUNDS ANGRY. AT LEAST I'M GETTING TO HIM. OF COURSE, IT SEEMS MUCH MORE LIKELY NOW THAT HE'LL MAKE MY DEATH A PAINFUL ONE.
FWSHHHH
ALIEN HUNTER, DID YOU EVER WONDER WHY YOUR PRECIOUS LIST HAS NO INFORMATION ON OUR SPECIES?
HE'S RIGHT. THE LIST HAS MORE INFORMATION THAN A HUNDRED THOUSAND WIKIPEDIAS.
BUT ITS ENTRY ON NUMBER 7 WAS PRETTY MUCH A BLANK.
THERE WERE MANY OF US, ONCE. THERE WERE OTHER COLONIES. BUT WE ABSORBED THEM.
JUST.
LIKE.
THIS.
SKRIK SKRIK SKRIK
THESE CHEMICALS. THEY'RE THE SAME ONES HE USED TO ABSORB KILDARE. ONLY THIS TIME...
SKRIK SKRIK SKRIK
...HE'S USED THEM TO SUMMON EVERY ANT IN A HUNDRED MILES.
SKRIK SKRIK SKRIK
SKRIK SKRIK SKRIK

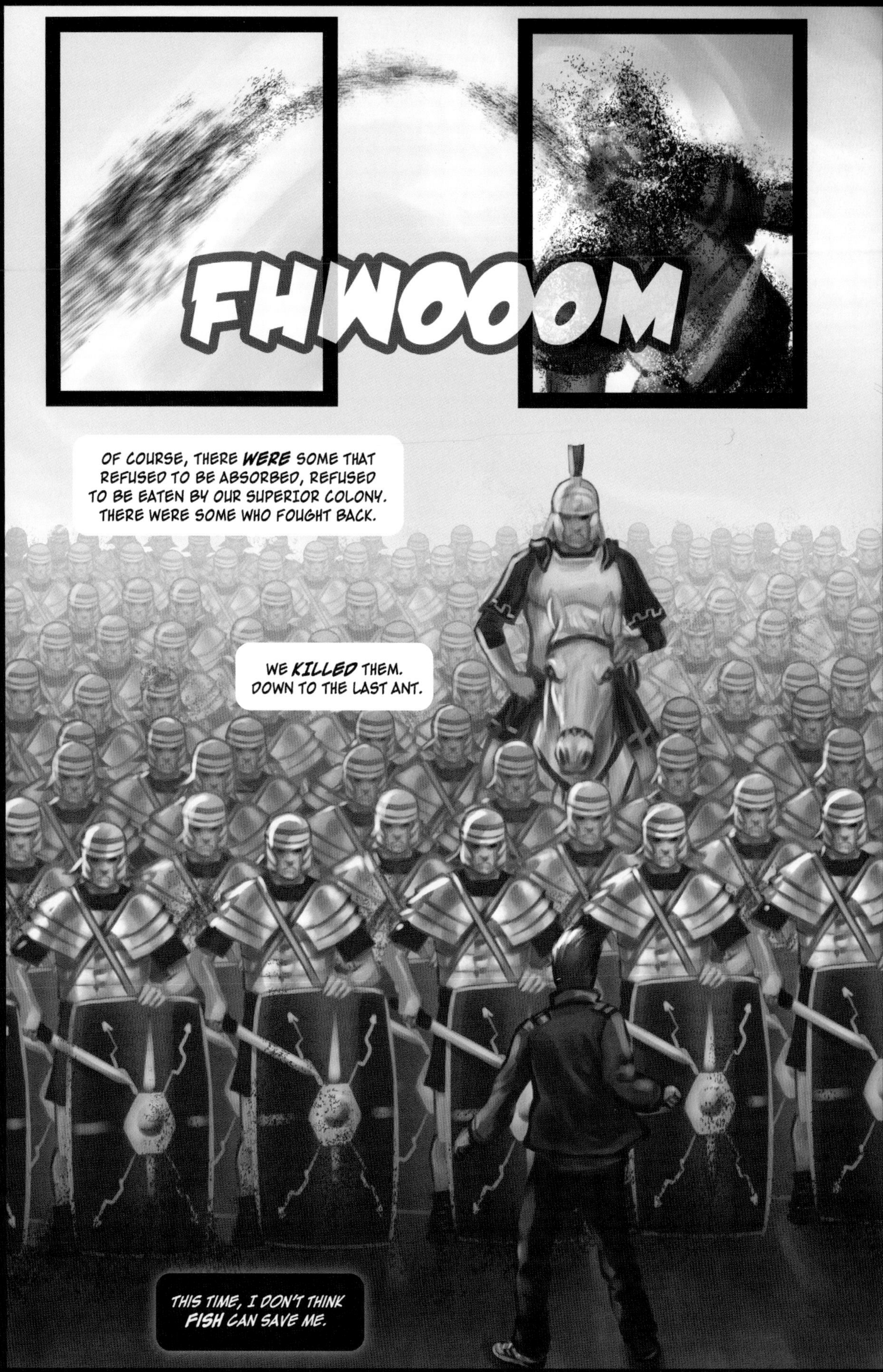
FHWOOOM
OF COURSE, THERE WERE SOME THAT REFUSED TO BE ABSORBED, REFUSED TO BE EATEN BY OUR SUPERIOR COLONY. THERE WERE SOME WHO FOUGHT BACK.
WE KILLED THEM. DOWN TO THE LAST ANT.
THIS TIME, I DON'T THINK FISH CAN SAVE ME.

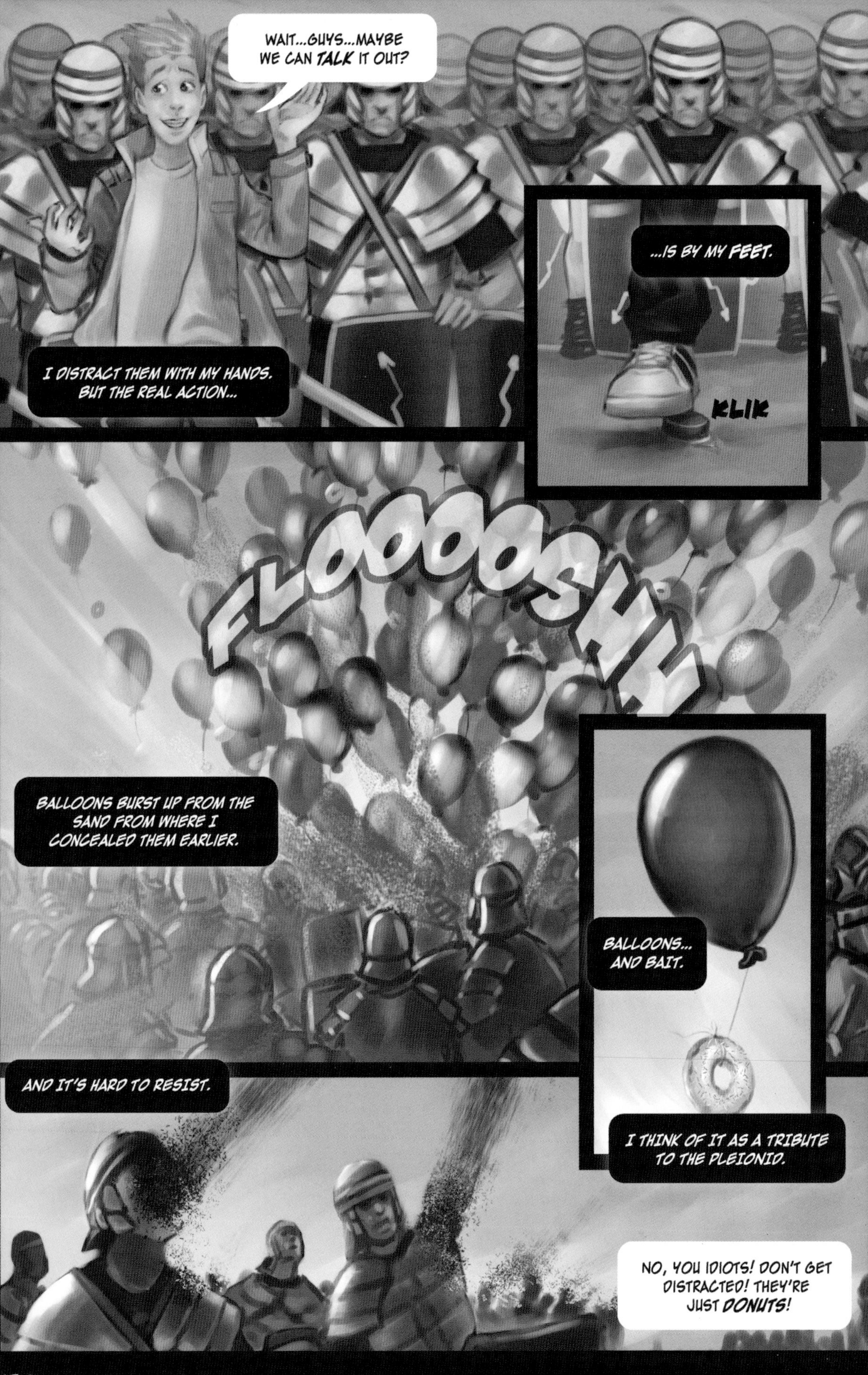
WAIT...GUYS...MAYBE WE CAN TALK IT OUT?
I DISTRACT THEM WITH MY HANDS. BUT THE REAL ACTION...
...IS BY MY FEET.
KLIK
FLOOOOSH!
BALLOONS BURST UP FROM THE SAND FROM WHERE I CONCEALED THEM EARLIER.
BALLOONS... AND BAIT.
AND IT'S HARD TO RESIST.
I THINK OF IT AS A TRIBUTE TO THE PLEIONID.
NO, YOU IDIOTS! DON'T GET DISTRACTED! THEY'RE JUST DONUTS!

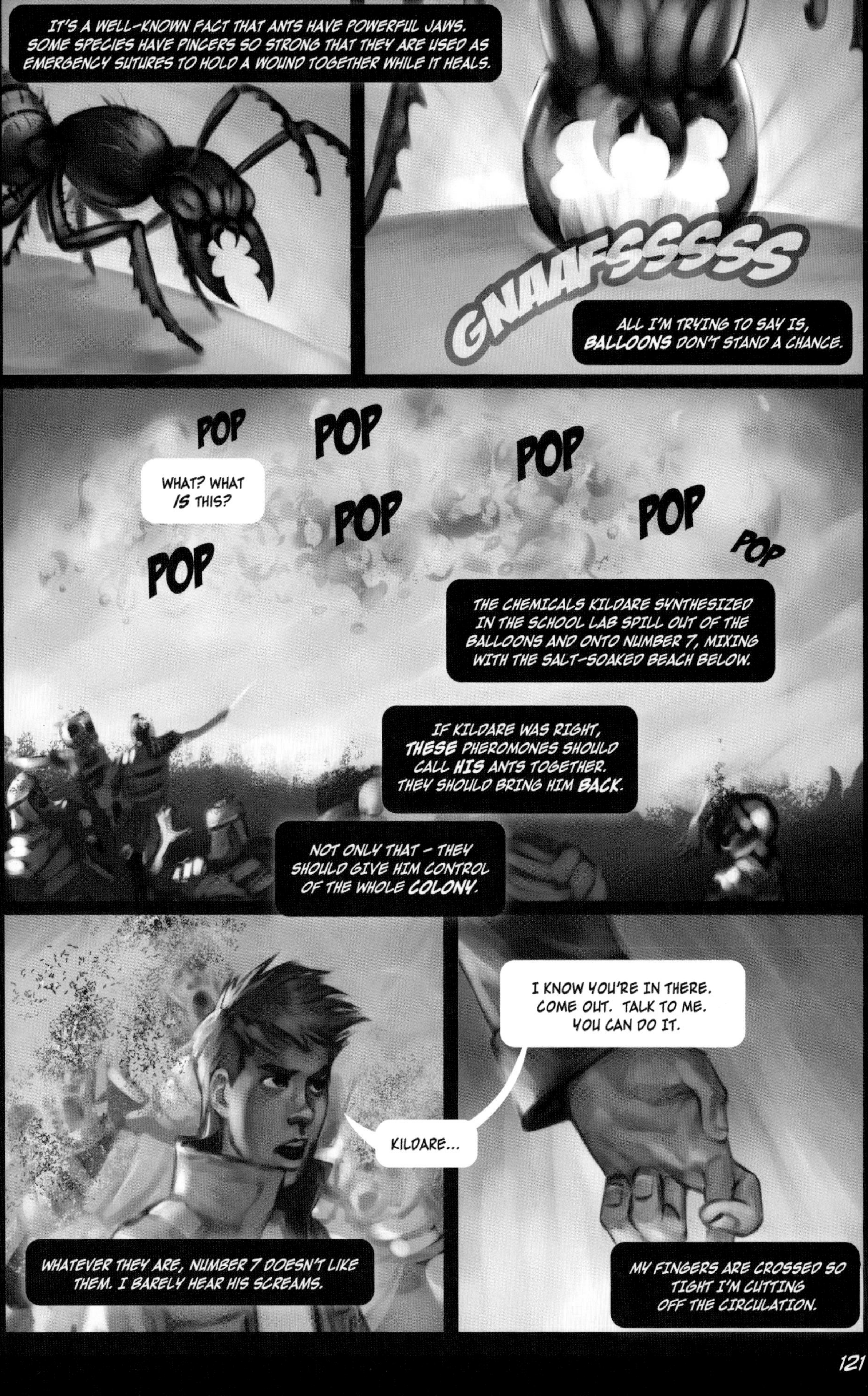
IT'S A WELL-KNOWN FACT THAT ANTS HAVE POWERFUL JAWS. SOME SPECIES HAVE PINCERS SO STRONG THAT THEY ARE USED AS EMERGENCY SUTURES TO HOLD A WOUND TOGETHER WHILE IT HEALS.
GNAAFSSSSS
ALL I'M TRYING TO SAY IS, BALLOONS DON'T STAND A CHANCE.
POP
POP
WHAT? WHAT IS THIS?
POP
POP
POP
POP
POP
THE CHEMICALS KILDARE SYNTHESIZED IN THE SCHOOL LAB SPILL OUT OF THE BALLOONS AND ONTO NUMBER 7, MIXING WITH THE SALT-SOAKED BEACH BELOW.
IF KILDARE WAS RIGHT, THESE PHEROMONES SHOULD CALL HIS ANTS TOGETHER. THEY SHOULD BRING HIM BACK.
NOT ONLY THAT - THEY SHOULD GIVE HIM CONTROL OF THE WHOLE COLONY.
KILDARE...
I KNOW YOU'RE IN THERE. COME OUT. TALK TO ME. YOU CAN DO IT.
WHATEVER THEY ARE, NUMBER 7 DOESN'T LIKE THEM. I BARELY HEAR HIS SCREAMS.
MY FINGERS ARE CROSSED SO TIGHT I'M CUTTING OFF THE CIRCULATION.

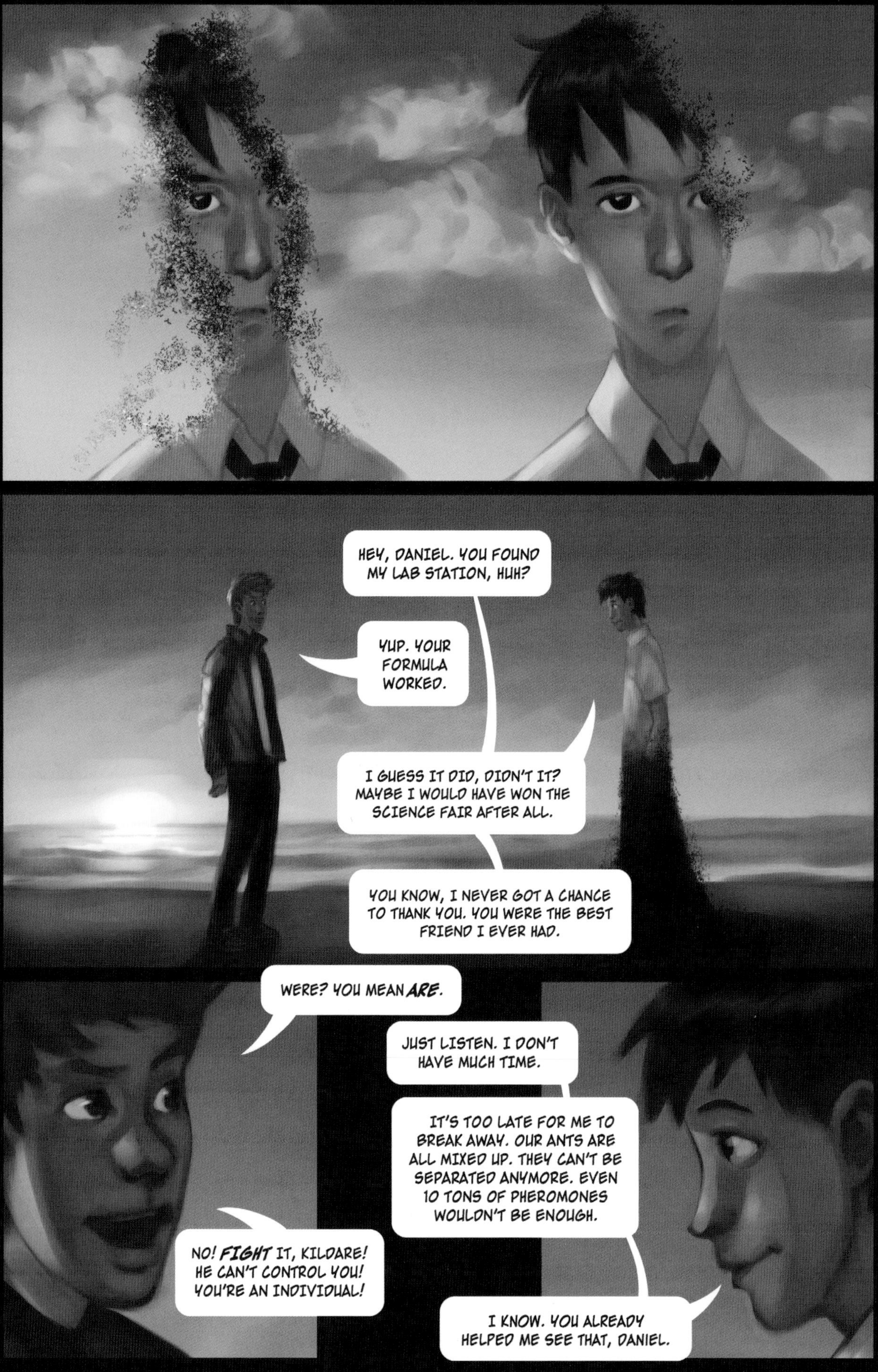
HEY, DANIEL. YOU FOUND MY LAB STATION, HUH?
YUP. YOUR FORMULA WORKED.
I GUESS IT DID, DIDN'T IT? MAYBE I WOULD HAVE WON THE SCIENCE FAIR AFTER ALL.
YOU KNOW, I NEVER GOT A CHANCE TO THANK YOU. YOU WERE THE BEST FRIEND I EVER HAD.
WERE? YOU MEAN **ARE**.
JUST LISTEN. I DON'T HAVE MUCH TIME.
IT'S TOO LATE FOR ME TO BREAK AWAY. OUR ANTS ARE ALL MIXED UP. THEY CAN'T BE SEPARATED ANYMORE. EVEN 10 TONS OF PHEROMONES WOULDN'T BE ENOUGH.
NO! **FIGHT** IT, KILDARE! HE CAN'T CONTROL YOU! YOU'RE AN INDIVIDUAL!
I KNOW. YOU ALREADY HELPED ME SEE THAT, DANIEL.

UNFORTUNATELY, KILDARE SEEMS TO BE RIGHT. THE CHEMICALS IN THE AIR **AREN'T** ENOUGH.

WITH A HORRIBLE SQUELCHING SOUND, NUMBER 7 PULLS HIMSELF BACK TOGETHER.

SO, SON...IT'S **INDEPENDENCE** YOU WANT? BEING A PART OF ME ISN'T GOOD ENOUGH FOR YOU?

WE WANTED YOU TO **JOIN** US. BUT WE SHOULD HAVE FOLLOWED OUR INSTINCTS FROM THE BEGINNING.

WE SHOULD HAVE **ANNIHILATED** YOU.

IT **IS** TIME TO END THIS, FATHER. BUT NOT THE WAY YOU'RE PLANNING. I'M SORRY.

I'M **SORRY.**

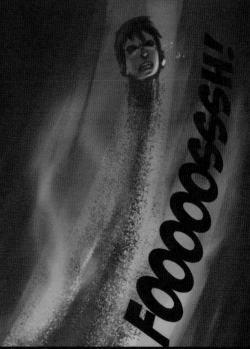

FOOOOOSSH!

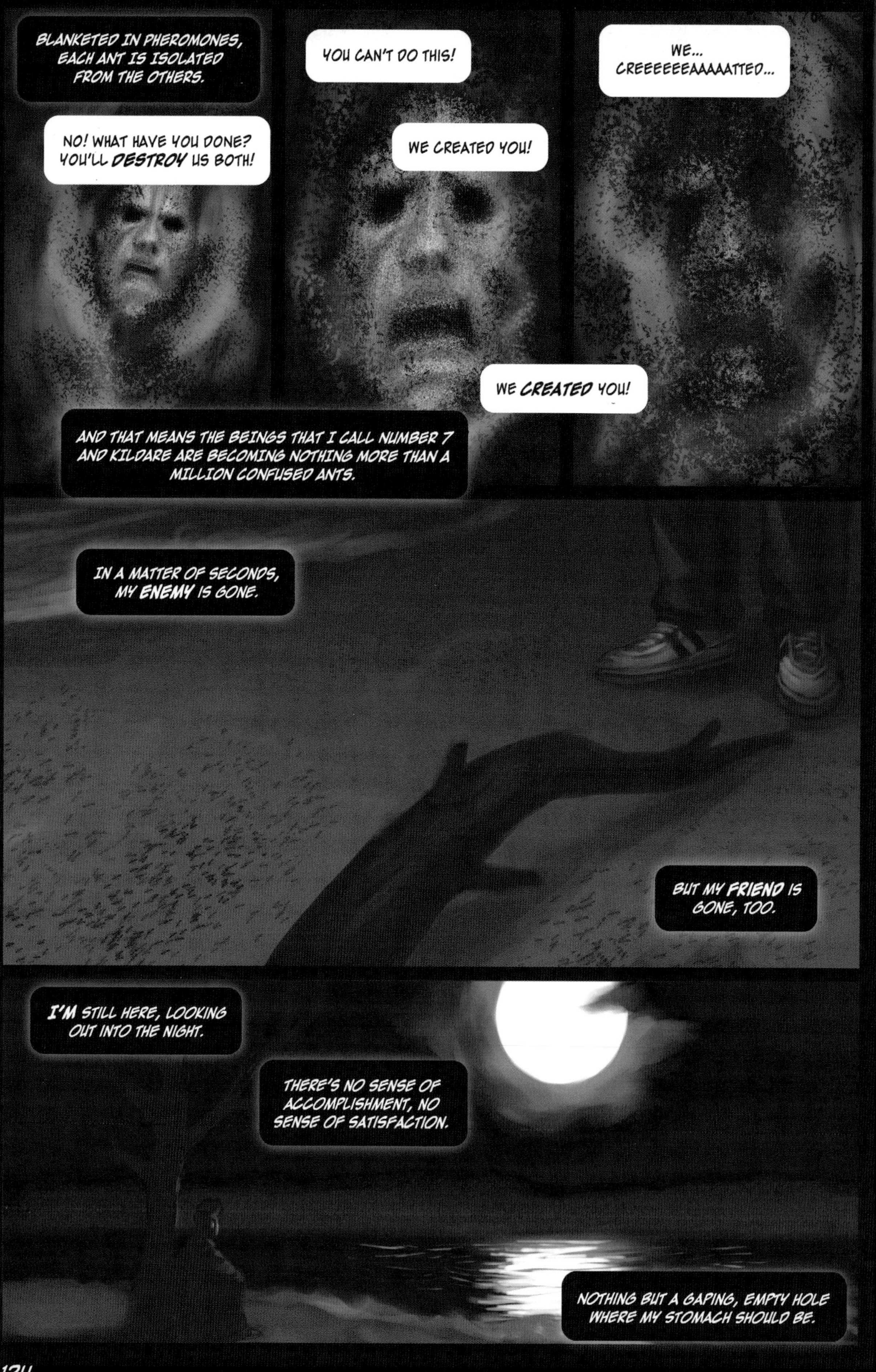
BLANKETED IN PHEROMONES, EACH ANT IS ISOLATED FROM THE OTHERS.
NO! WHAT HAVE YOU DONE? YOU'LL DESTROY US BOTH!
YOU CAN'T DO THIS!
WE CREATED YOU!
WE... CREEEEEEEAAAAATTED...
WE CREATED YOU!
AND THAT MEANS THE BEINGS THAT I CALL NUMBER 7 AND KILDARE ARE BECOMING NOTHING MORE THAN A MILLION CONFUSED ANTS.
IN A MATTER OF SECONDS, MY ENEMY IS GONE.
BUT MY FRIEND IS GONE, TOO.
I'M STILL HERE, LOOKING OUT INTO THE NIGHT.
THERE'S NO SENSE OF ACCOMPLISHMENT, NO SENSE OF SATISFACTION.
NOTHING BUT A GAPING, EMPTY HOLE WHERE MY STOMACH SHOULD BE.

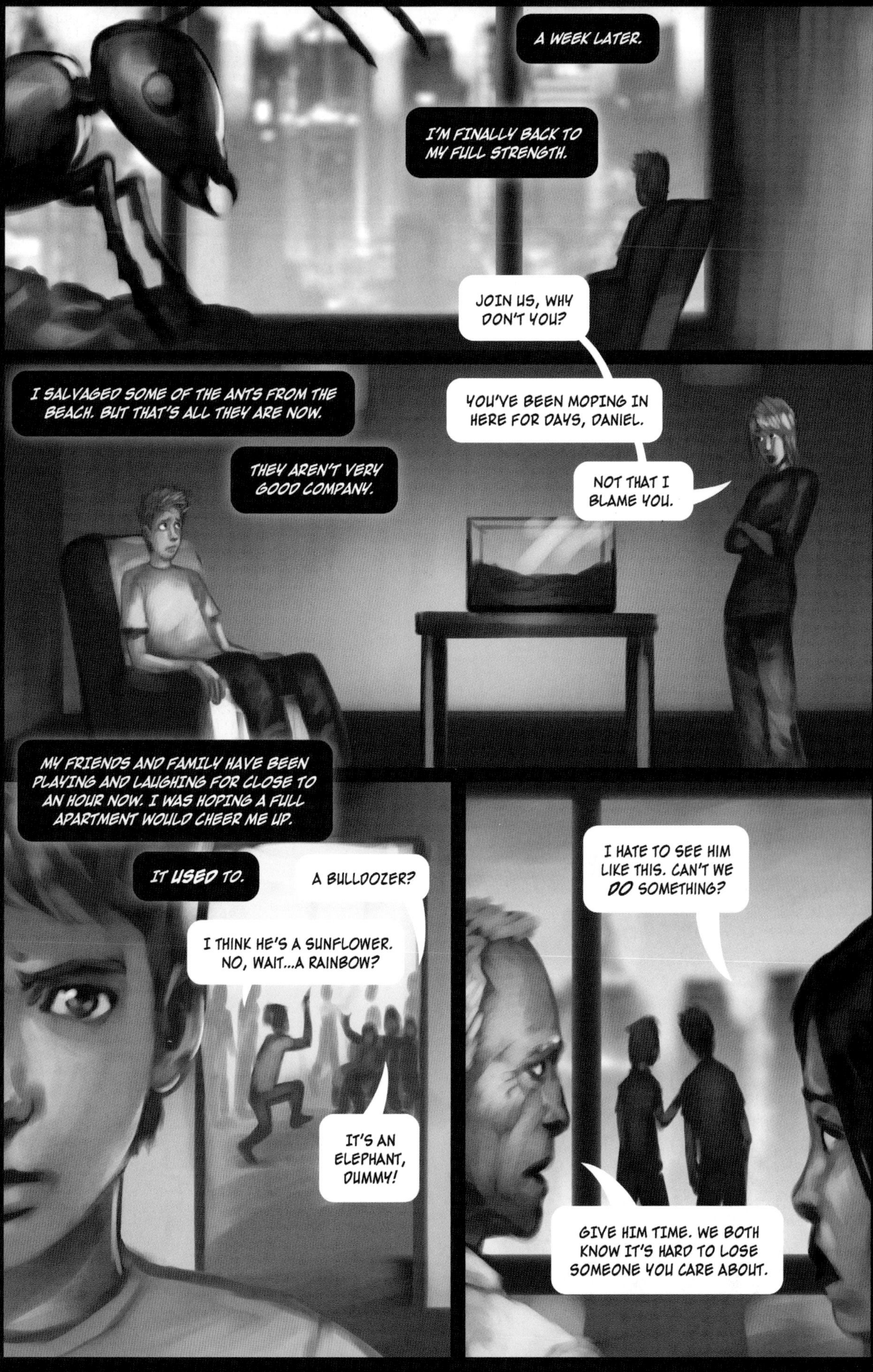
A WEEK LATER.
I'M FINALLY BACK TO MY FULL STRENGTH.
JOIN US, WHY DON'T YOU?
I SALVAGED SOME OF THE ANTS FROM THE BEACH. BUT THAT'S ALL THEY ARE NOW.
THEY AREN'T VERY GOOD COMPANY.
YOU'VE BEEN MOPING IN HERE FOR DAYS, DANIEL.
NOT THAT I BLAME YOU.
MY FRIENDS AND FAMILY HAVE BEEN PLAYING AND LAUGHING FOR CLOSE TO AN HOUR NOW. I WAS HOPING A FULL APARTMENT WOULD CHEER ME UP.
IT USED TO.
A BULLDOZER?
I THINK HE'S A SUNFLOWER. NO, WAIT...A RAINBOW?
IT'S AN ELEPHANT, DUMMY!
I HATE TO SEE HIM LIKE THIS. CAN'T WE DO SOMETHING?
GIVE HIM TIME. WE BOTH KNOW IT'S HARD TO LOSE SOMEONE YOU CARE ABOUT.

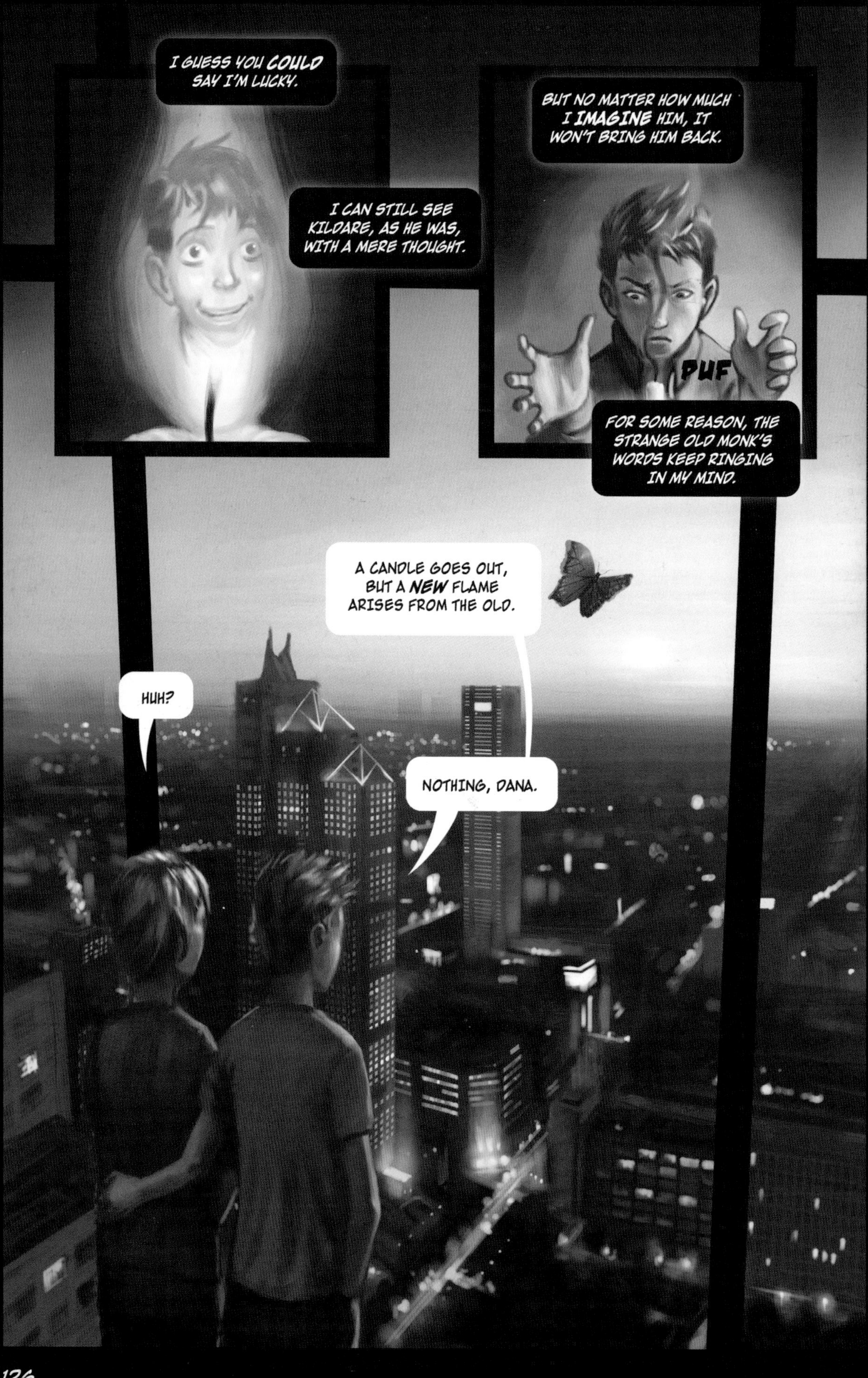
I GUESS YOU COULD SAY I'M LUCKY.
I CAN STILL SEE KILDARE, AS HE WAS, WITH A MERE THOUGHT.
BUT NO MATTER HOW MUCH I IMAGINE HIM, IT WON'T BRING HIM BACK.
PUF
FOR SOME REASON, THE STRANGE OLD MONK'S WORDS KEEP RINGING IN MY MIND.
A CANDLE GOES OUT, BUT A NEW FLAME ARISES FROM THE OLD.
HUH?
NOTHING, DANA.

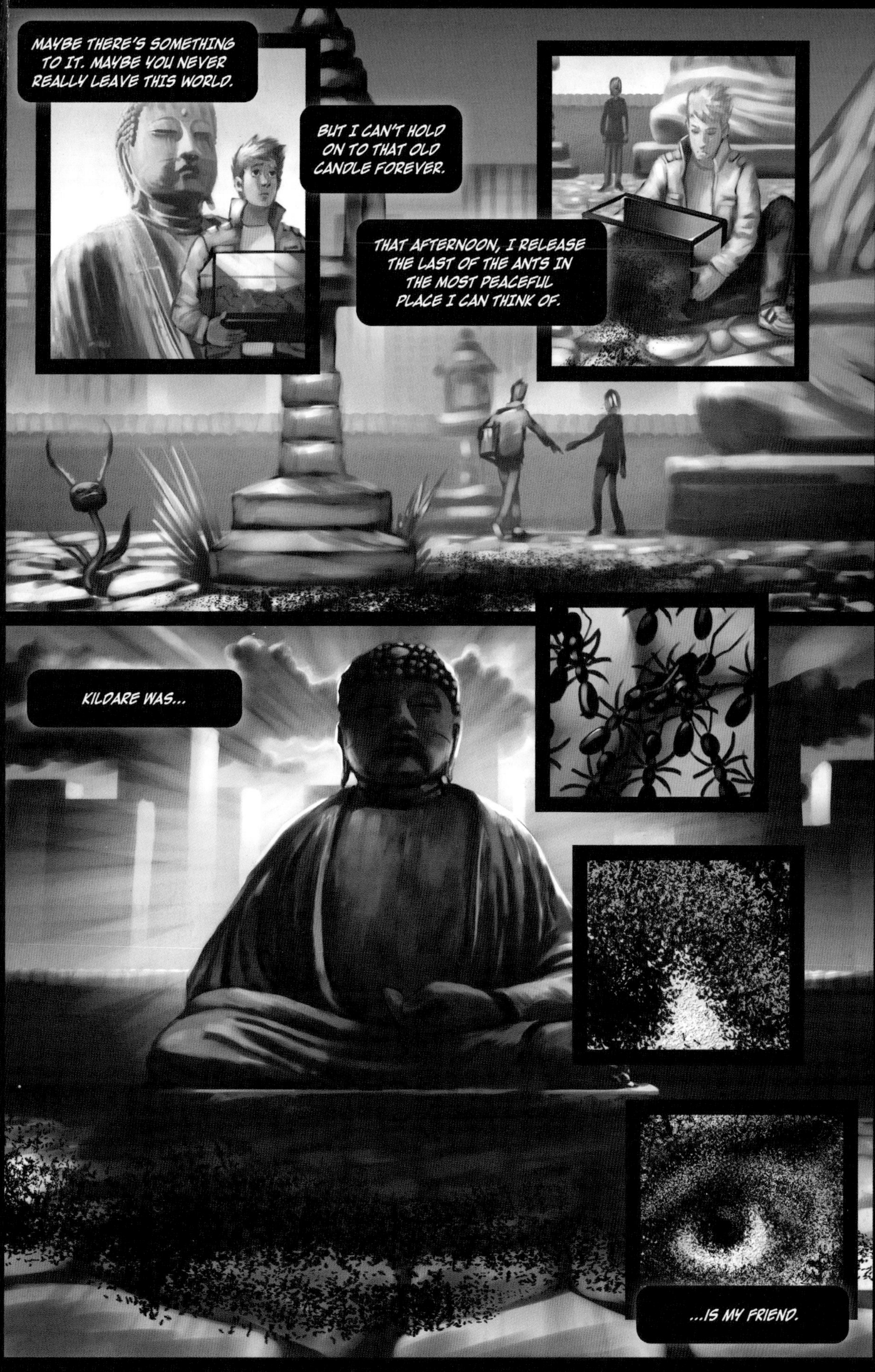
MAYBE THERE'S SOMETHING TO IT. MAYBE YOU NEVER REALLY LEAVE THIS WORLD.
BUT I CAN'T HOLD ON TO THAT OLD CANDLE FOREVER.
THAT AFTERNOON, I RELEASE THE LAST OF THE ANTS IN THE MOST PEACEFUL PLACE I CAN THINK OF.
KILDARE WAS...
...IS MY FRIEND.